# Everyday Life in the Aztec World

In *Everyday Life in the Aztec World*, Frances Berdan and Michael Smith offer a view into the lives of real people, doing very human things, in the unique cultural world of Aztec central Mexico. The first part focuses on people from an array of social classes – the emperor, a priest, a feather worker, a merchant, a farmer, and a slave – who interacted in the economic, social, and religious realms of the Aztec world. In the second part, the authors examine four important life events where the lives of these and others intersected: the birth and naming of a child, market day, a day at court, and a battle. Through the microscopic views of individual types of lives, and interweaving those lives into the broader Aztec world, Berdan and Smith recreate everyday life in the final years of the Aztec Empire.

Frances F. Berdan is Professor Emerita of Anthropology at California State University, San Bernardino. She is the author or co-author of fourteen books on aspects of Aztec culture, most recently *Aztec Archaeology and Ethnohistory*. Her four-volume co-authored *The Codex Mendoza* won the James R. Wiseman Book Award from the Archaeological Institute of America in 1992.

Michael E. Smith is Professor in the School of Human Evolution and Social Change at Arizona State University. Director of the ASU Teotihuacan Research Laboratory, he is the author of twelve books, including *At Home with the Aztecs: An Archaeologist Uncovers Their Daily Life*, which won the Best Popular Book award from the Society of American Archaeology in 2017.

# Everyday Life in the Aztec World

FRANCES F. BERDAN

*California State University, San Bernardino*

MICHAEL E. SMITH

*Arizona State University*

CAMBRIDGE
UNIVERSITY PRESS

# CAMBRIDGE
## UNIVERSITY PRESS

University Printing House, Cambridge CB2 8BS, United Kingdom

One Liberty Plaza, 20th Floor, New York, NY 10006, USA

477 Williamstown Road, Port Melbourne, VIC 3207, Australia

314–321, 3rd Floor, Plot 3, Splendor Forum, Jasola District Centre, New Delhi – 110025, India

79 Anson Road, #06–04/06, Singapore 079906

Cambridge University Press is part of the University of Cambridge.

It furthers the University's mission by disseminating knowledge in the pursuit of education, learning, and research at the highest international levels of excellence.

www.cambridge.org
Information on this title: www.cambridge.org/9780521516365
DOI: 10.1017/9781139031844

First published 2021

Printed in the United Kingdom by TJ Books Limited, Padstow Cornwall.

*A catalogue record for this publication is available from the British Library.*

*Library of Congress Cataloging-in-Publication Data*
NAMES: Berdan, Frances F., author. | Smith, Michael E., author.
TITLE: Everyday life in the Aztec world / Frances Berdan, California State University,
    San Bernadino; Michael E. Smith, Arizona State University.
DESCRIPTION: New York : Cambridge University Press, 2020. | Includes bibliographical
    references and index.
IDENTIFIERS: LCCN 2019052440 (print) | LCCN 2019052441 (ebook) |
    ISBN 9780521516365 (hardback) | ISBN 9780521736220 (paperback) |
    ISBN 9781139031844 (epub)
SUBJECTS: LCSH: Aztecs–Social life and customs–Juvenile literature. | Aztecs–History–
    Juvenile literature.
CLASSIFICATION: LCC F1219.76.S64 B47 2020  (print) | LCC F1219.76.S64 (ebook) |
    DDC 972–dc23
LC record available at https://lccn.loc.gov/2019052440
LC ebook record available at https://lccn.loc.gov/2019052441

ISBN 978-0-521-51636-5 Hardback
ISBN 978-0-521-73622-0 Paperback

# Contents

# Illustrations

## Maps

## Figures

# Preface

Many books have been written on the ancient Aztecs. Some are scholarly, some are specialized, some are general-interest. But the authors of this book, having contributed to that pile over many years, have decided on a somewhat different approach, as much as possible taking a look at these people as they saw themselves, and each other. In the pages that follow, we offer a selection of six lives and four events or circumstances as *entrées* into discussions of more general aspects of daily life in the Aztec world.

The first section of this book provides in-depth views into the lives of a selection of Aztec persons: an emperor, a priest, a featherworker, a professional merchant, a farmer, and a slave. We embed vignettes inside each chapter to provide a more intimate sense of what it was like to live in Aztec Mexico around 1500 CE. While these vignettes and their characters are fictional, everything about them – the people's names, activities, roles, relationships, even their thoughts and prayers – is based on what we know about Aztec culture. Our first "life" is a real historical figure, King Ahuitzotl, who ruled Tenochtitlan and the Aztec Empire from 1486 until his death in 1502. The other "lives" are representative, composite figures of particular occupations and social positions. Even Ahuitzotl, while a unique personality with his own considerable achievements, was typical in many ways of the rulers who preceded and succeeded him. For a taste of diversity, some vignettes are set within the city of Tenochtitlan, while others are set in other locales of the Aztec domain. In all, the vignettes provide backdrops for more general discussions of Aztec daily life based on current archaeological and ethnohistorical research.

While this perspective of dissecting individual lives is valuable, it tends to encapsulate and isolate these persons in their own little worlds. Yet all of these people interacted in the broader economic, social, political, and religious realms of the Aztec world. So the second section of the book is devoted to four specific and particularly important events through which these and other people intersect: the birth and naming of a child, a market day, a day at court, and a war. These microscopic views of individual types of lives, and the subsequent integration of them into the broader Aztec world, offer both depth and breadth to a view of everyday life in the late years of the Aztec Empire. Of course, every day new and exciting tidbits (and often more than tidbits) of information are unearthed and revealed – these turn our heads inside out and make us rethink things we thought we knew for sure. This book is built on what we know as of this moment.

Our hope is that you, the reader, leave with both a current understanding of Aztec culture and an intimate "sense" of its people – Aztec civilization was not just abstract social arrangements or economic exchanges or military conquests. It was real, live people doing very human things in their unique cultural world.

## ACKNOWLEDGMENTS

This book was written at the behest of Beatrice Rehl of Cambridge University Press. We owe a large debt of gratitude to her for her vision and her gentle prodding when we lagged. We are grateful to Jennifer Berdan Lozano for constructing expert maps and other images. Arizona State University anthropology majors Ciara Bernal, Molly Corr, and Leah Moyes helped process graphics. We also appreciate the kind advice of Emily Umberger and Karl Taube on individual images and artifacts. We are very fortunate to draw on the expertise of Pamela Effrein Sandstrom, who prepared the index. We are also grateful to Alan Sandstrom for contributing his keen eye and vast ethnographic experience. We thank our spouses, Cynthia Heath-Smith and Bob Berdan, for putting up with us during the writing and preparation periods.

# Pronunciation Guide

The Aztecs spoke Nahuatl (NA-watl), which means, in essence, clear and understandable speech. Other people around them, and in more distant regions of their imperial domain, spoke a wide array of other languages including Otomí, Matlatzinca, Mazahua, Tlapanec, Popoluca, Mixtec, Zapotec, Totonac, Huaxtec, Tepehua, and others.

The Nahuatl of pre-Hispanic Mesoamerica is called Classical Nahuatl by modern-day linguists. This language has survived to the present day, retaining its essential structure, speech patterns, and vocabulary; it has also adapted to nearly 500 years of linguistic, cultural, and historical change. Today, 1.5–2 million people still speak one or another dialect of this tenacious language; many of these speakers call their language Mexicano (Me-shee-KA-no). Sixteenth-century documents written in Nahuatl, along with present-day spoken versions of Nahuatl, provide us with clues to understanding the speech patterns of Classical Nahuatl. Here are some general rules to follow (several examples are personal names you will encounter in this book).

1. *Stress* or emphasis was always on the next-to-last syllable of a word, with very few exceptions.
2. *Vowels* were quite nuanced (with long and short variations), but they were essentially pronounced as follows:
   **a**  as in English c**a**lm: *Yaotl* (YA-otl): war, or enemy
   **e**  as in English g**e**t: *Tlexico* (tle-SHEE-Ko): Fire-Bee
   **i**  as in English b**ee**: *chilli* (CHEE-llee): chile
   **o**  as in English sl**o**w: *Tototontli* (to-to-TON-tli): Little Bird

   Note: In the colonial documents, **o** and **u** are often used interchangeably, and may actually represent an intermediate sound. So, for example, we see Tenochtitlan/Tenuchtitlan or calpolli/calpulli.

You will also encounter vowels attached to a preceding *hu-* or *qu-*:

**hua**   as in English **wa**sh: Cihuacoatl (See-wa-KO-atl): Woman-serpent, a
          goddess

**hue**   as in English **wai**ter: *huexolotl* (way-SHO-lotl): turkey

**hui**   as in English **wea**k: Ahuitzotl (a-WEE-tsotl)

**qua**   as in English **qua**ntity: *qualli* (KWA-llee): good

**que**   as in English **ke**nnel: Quetzalcoatl (Ke-tsal-KO-atl): Feathered-
          serpent, a god

**qui**   as in English **kee**p: *oquichtli* (o-KEECH-tli): man

3. For the most part, *consonants* resemble those in English or Spanish. The
   following are the others:

   **c**    before a, o/u, or a consonant = **k**: *cacahuatl* (ka-KA-watl): cacao bean

   **c**    before e or i = **s**: *cipactli* (see-PAC-tli): alligator

   **ll**   as in English fa**ll**, but held longer: *ollin* (O-lleen): movement

   **x**    as in English **sh**elf: *xochitl* (SHO-cheetl): flower

   **z**    as in English **s**ink: *mazatl* (MA-satl): deer

   **tz**   as in English ba**ts**: *centzon* (CEN-tson): plenty, lots

   **tl**   is one sound, a *t* followed by a soft *l*: *coyotl* (KO-yotl): coyote

Note: The Spaniards who met the Aztecs in the early sixteenth century had
particular difficulty with the -**tl** sound, especially at the ends of words. The
Spaniards were more at ease ending such words in -**te**, so *xitomatl* (shee-TO-
matl) entered Spanish as *tomate* (tomato), *tecolotl* (te-KO-lotl) became
*tecolote* (owl), and *zopilotl* (tso-PEE-lotl) became *zopilote* (vulture).

4. Nahuatl also had a *glottal stop*, like *uh-uh* in English. It was often missed in
   the early documents, but where it was recognized it was written as an *h*. So,
   for example, *ohtli* (road) is often seen as *otli*, and *ozomahtli* (monkey)
   usually appears as *ozomatli*.

5. Spelling rules in sixteenth-century Europe were rather fluid, and this is
   reflected in colonial Mexican documents. This is why the Mexica ruler
   Motecuhzoma (our preferred spelling) appeared variously as Moctezuma,
   Montezuma, Montecuzoma, Mohtecuzoma, and so on. Similarly, Texcoco,
   neighboring city of Tenochtitlan, was spelled at least sixteen different ways
   in the early Spanish documents (Johnson 2017: xiii).

# A Little Background

The year is Chicueye Tecpatl (Eight Flint Knife), or 1500 in the Christian calendar. The Aztec Empire has grown into the most power- ful force in central Mexico since its inception in 1430. During the intervening seventy years the military might and political prowess of three allied Basin of Mexico cities have extended their dominion from the Gulf coast to the Pacific coast, and as far south as the present-day border between Mexico and Guatemala. By the time of the Spanish arrival in 1519, the empire had expanded even further (Map 1). The three allied imperial capitals are Tenochtitlan, home of the Mexica; the Acolhua's primary city of Texcoco; and the Tepaneca city of Tlacopan (Map 2). Together, they have created the vastest empire ever seen in Mesoamerica. They have achieved this through military conquest and royal diplomacy, holding their vast domains through a combination of intimidation, fear, cajoling, outright military force, strategic trading, and promises of economic and social rewards.

The Aztecs were the last in a long series of great civilizations in the prehistory and history of Mesoamerica (a region stretching roughly between central Mexico and Central American countries adjacent to Mexico in the south and east). Among the best known of these are the Olmec (ca. 1200–600 BCE), Classic Maya (250–900 CE), Teotihuacan (150–700 CE), and the Toltecs of Tula (950–1150). These civilizations and cities were in ruins by the time the Aztecs arrived in central Mexico to make their own mark on history.

From around the eleventh to fourteenth centuries several separate but related groups, collectively called *Chichimeca*, migrated from the deserts of northern Mexico into the highland plateaus and valleys of central Mexico. The last of these to arrive were the people usually referred to as "Aztecs," who actually called themselves Mexica or

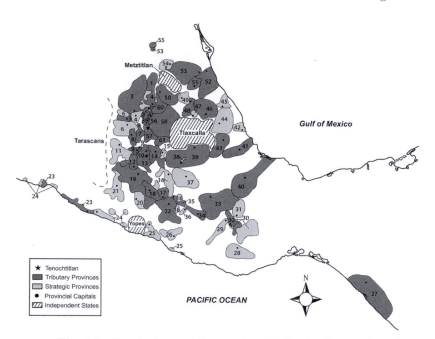

MAP 1. The Aztec Empire in 1519. Source: Jennifer Berdan Lozano, based on Berdan et al. (1996); reproduced with permission.

Culhua-Mexica. Other migrants included the Matlatzinca, who settled to the west of the Basin of Mexico; the Tlahuica, who settled just to the south; the Mexica's future enemies the Tlaxcallans, who settled to the east; and several groups such as the Chalca and Xochimilca, who preceded the Mexica into the Basin of Mexico. While all these groups spoke Nahuatl and shared a basic cultural core, they each fiercely defended their own separate identity and political autonomy. When we use the term "Aztec" here, we refer to the Nahuatl-speaking peoples of highland central Mexico during the Late Postclassic period (1350–1521 CE). Otherwise, we will focus on specific identified groups. Other peoples inhabited central Mexico during this period as well, notably the Otomí, who shared some of the Basin of Mexico with the Nahuatl-speaking groups.

In the year Two House (1325) the Mexica established themselves on a rather unpromising island in the midst of Lake Texcoco, a lake that dominated the highland Basin of Mexico (and now largely covered by Mexico City). Upon entering this basin, they encountered

MAP 2. The Basin of Mexico in 1519 with the three Triple Alliance capital cities. Source: Jennifer Berdan Lozano; reproduced with permission.

a scene left behind by the dissolution of Tula: a landscape divided into competing dynastic city-states, a rapidly growing population, and a flourishing economy based on intensive agriculture and lacustrine resources. They were not particularly welcomed, but they did become useful as mercenaries in the internecine wars among the Basin city-states. Gaining repute as stalwart and fierce warriors, they acquired resources and lands beyond their humble and rather impoverished island.

By the time a hundred years had passed the Mexica had orchestrated an alliance with two other prominent polities, Texcoco and Tlacopan, and had managed to gain political and military preeminence in the Basin. This was in 1430. From that date until their conquest by the Spaniards in 1521, the Mexica and their allies forged an empire of unprecedented scope in Mesoamerica. That empire stretched through ecologically diverse and resource-rich lands – from highland valleys to semi-tropical mountains to luxuriant lowland forests and coastal zones. Military and political control of these regions funneled resources and wealth into the bulging coffers of the Mexica and their allies. Food staples such as maize, beans, and chia arrived from highland and temperate lands; cacao and cotton were transported from the lowlands; massive amounts of clothing and ornate feathered warrior costumes were delivered from throughout the conquered provinces; and a wide diversity of goods and products such as exquisite feathers, gold, wild animal pelts, copper objects, turquoise masks, precious greenstone beads, wood and reed products, dyes, lime, and shells came from hither and thither about the imperial domain. Collectively, this wealth underwrote the exceptional lifestyles of the rulers and other elites, rewarded valiant warriors, financed future wars, and helped feed the burgeoning dominant populations in times of environmental stress or agricultural disaster.

THE YEAR 1500

In the year 1500, Tenochtitlan, the political and military capital of the empire, is a city of unprecedented size and grandeur. Its population approaches 200,000–250,000 people, its great temple dominates the urban landscape, its nearby market is the grandest and liveliest in the realm, and its island location attracts multitudes of travelers and traders, crowding the lake with canoes and the causeways with pedestrians. It is home to a vast array of people of different occupations, ethnicities, and stations in life. It is, in a word, cosmopolitan. But Tenochtitlan is not the only city in the region, although it is by far the largest and most powerful. The many other cities around the Basin of Mexico lakeshore are dwarfed by Tenochtitlan – the next largest are Texcoco at 25,000 and Huexotla at 23,000 (Smith 2008: 152). But most range from around 1,200 to 12,000 residents.

These concentrated urban populations are supported by intensive agricultural systems that produce large surpluses of staple foods (especially maize, beans, chia, and amaranth), vegetables (such as tomatoes, squashes, and chiles), and ornamentals (there were constant demands for flowers in rituals). The shallow, spring-fed lakes of the

Basin of Mexico allow farmers to build and cultivate *chinampas,* or artificially raised fields. Ranging from 2–4 meters wide and 20–40 meters long, they are built up in fairly regular fashion, resulting in an efficient network of canals. In this fashion, Tenochtitlan and the lakeshore cities have grown beyond their landed foundations. Despite the high altitude of the Basin of Mexico (around 7,000 feet above sea level), these plots provide high sustained productivity through multi-cropping, crop rotation, staggered seedbeds, and augmentation of natural fertilizers and water from adjacent canals (Berdan 2014: 80–81). Beyond the lakeshore and in other regions of the Aztec world, people draw on other agricultural techniques such as canal irrigation, terrace agriculture, household gardens, and check dams (Chapter 5) to make a living. People complement agricultural food supplies with domesticated dogs and turkeys (and their eggs), fish, wild animals (such as rabbit, deer, and waterfowl), and a plethora of wild plants for food and medicines.

Like every other economic enterprise in the Aztec world, agriculture is very labor intensive. There are no beasts of burden, iron or steel tools, or practical uses of wheels. Domestic economies dominate – while farmers toil in nearby fields and fishermen cast their nets in the lakes, their wives and daughters spin and weave cloth from maguey and cotton fibers. This industry should not be underestimated. All women learn to spin and weave, and clothing and cloth are universally needed. Cloths serve a multitude of purposes, from tortilla covers to ritual hangings to corpse wrappings. Decorated clothing serves as status symbols, gifts, and rewards; cloth is traded for other goods in the marketplaces; vast amounts of clothing are paid in tribute/taxes; and specific cotton cloths serve as money. The slave in Chapter 6 is undertaking a typical and important economic activity.

There is also a great deal of economic specialization in the Aztec world. Some specialists produce high-demand, commonplace objects such as pottery, reed mats, obsidian knives, and farming implements. Others manufacture high-status luxury goods. These include workers in gold and fine stones, in addition to the featherworkers highlighted in Chapter 3. And many people provide specialized services, from ambassadors, scribes and zookeepers to teachers, merchants (Chapter 4), midwives (Chapter 7), prostitutes, and porters. Many of these people work "at home," while others are employed in palaces by noble patrons or spend a great deal of time on the road (such as merchants and porters). Frequent and lively marketplaces (Chapter 8) bring together the producers of these many specializations, allowing individual people and households to diversify their diet, household goods, and social and ritual needs.

The world of the Mexica and their neighbors is divided into numerous *altepetl* ("water-hill"), or city-states, that normally contain a dominant city and adjacent rural areas. These are the essential building blocks for political life in pre-Spanish central Mexico. The Basin of Mexico contains from 30 to 50 *altepetl* – the entire landscape is divided up into these polities. To qualify as a city-state, a polity must have "a legitimate ruling dynasty, a sense (if not the actuality) of political autonomy, control over local lands and labor, a well-established founding legend, often with mythological underpinnings, and a patron deity complete with temple." Some also contain a dominant ethnic group, feature an economic specialization (such as feather-working or ceramics), and "may have enjoyed renown as extraordinary market or pilgrimage destinations" (Berdan 2014: 135–136). Each city-state is headed by a *tlatoani*, a ruler who commands the allegiance and loyalty of the *altepetl*'s residents who go to war on its behalf. While city-states vary considerably in size and influence, "a typical altepetl in the Basin of Mexico had a population of 10,000–15,000 and covered an area of 70–100 square km" (Smith 2008: 90) – so in 1500 the entire Basin of Mexico is crammed with these polities. It is a volatile environment, with wars set off by the barest social slight and alliances sought to strengthen political and social positions. There is constant posturing and jockeying through deft diplomacy, clever elite marriages, ostentatious feasting, threats of force, treacherous assassinations, and outright war.

*Altepetl* are divided into smaller segments, called *calpolli* or *tlaxila-calli*. These districts appear to have hierarchical internal structures, and unsurprisingly the ruler's *calpolli* was considered more important than the others (Johnson 2017; Lockhart 1992: 16–20). Each of these city sections boasts its own name, local leader, military school, patron deity, temple, and portion of city-state lands. Labor duties owed to the city-state are apportioned by *calpolli*. The merchants and featherworkers in this book live in particularly well-defined *calpolli*, and our warriors also go to war in line with their *calpolli* membership.

In Tenochtitlan and other city-state capitals, rulers and other nobles build sumptuous palaces, adorn themselves with exquisite clothing and jewelry, and command a multitude of slaves, servants, and even other nobles to serve them (Chapter 1). Their extraordinary lifestyle is supported by the vast majority of the population: commoners who work the land, fish the lakes, and manufacture everyday needs such as pottery, baskets, and stone tools. Birthright defines a person's place on the social ladder. Nonetheless, some people born as commoners can attain wealth and prestige through achievements in commerce and on the battlefield, and some born as nobles are becoming less and less "noble." The seemingly bald distinction between noble and commoner is becoming nuanced and complicated by persons in a fluid and dynamic middle range, especially professional merchants and luxury artisans.

Regardless of their occupation or social position, Aztec people experience similar life-cycle paths and are socialized into a strict set of cultural codes, social expectations, and behavioral etiquette. Virtues of obedience, moderation, and hard work are highly valued and instilled in children from an early age, from fathers to their sons and from mothers to their daughters. Formal schooling picks up where the parents leave off (probably around age fifteen). The culture's fundamental values continue to be reinforced into adulthood, when breaches of the society's norms are met with severe punishments in formal judicial institutions (Chapter 9).

Beyond the mundane, much of peoples' daily lives revolve around the world of the religious. People are exposed to the symbols and realities of Aztec religion at every turn. The Aztec religious world is populated with a grand assortment of gods and goddesses prevailing over just about every realm of nature and humanity. Myths and legends validate rulerships and *altepetl*; temples dominate the urban landscapes; sculptures, decorations, and even clothing depict the supernatural; and a trained hierarchy of priests (Chapter 2) performs daily and periodic ceremonies. Some of these ceremonies are amazingly theatrical and flamboyant, and may include sacrifices of human beings. This is the public arena, but individuals also frequently perform rituals in their own homes, whether as separate events or as part of larger public ceremonies (Berdan 2017).

The practice of human sacrifice among the Mexica and their neighbors is embedded in potent religious beliefs. One of these is the endless cycle of life and death, with death necessary for the continuation and rejuvenation of life. This is linked to the mythologically supported belief that the people have a debt to pay to the gods for their very existence, and they pay in their most precious commodity, human blood. In one important myth, Huitzilopochtli, a god of the sun and war and patron of the Mexica, battles his sister Coyolxauhqui (the moon) and brothers (the stars) for celestial primacy. This battle is reenacted daily at dawn – who can dispute that the sun fights off the forces of night (the moon and stars) every day? And how is Huitzilopochtli to gain the strength to prevail, to provide the world with heat and light? The Mexica inserted themselves into this essential battle, believing they are obligated to offer blood, notably human blood, to energize their patron god. They provide blood for this and other ritual necessities through autosacrifice as well as terminal human sacrifice. As the empire grows, human sacrifices increasingly come into the purview of rulers' political motives – some sacrificial ceremonies, while always performed ritually, are intentionally massive in order to intimidate friends and enemies alike.

By the year 1500, the Aztec Empire has held sway over central Mexico for only about seventy years – fewer than three generations. Some people have lived in this imperial world almost from beginning to end. During that short span, the small island city of Tenochtitlan has spread into its surrounding lake and grown into an enormous metropolis. The empire now fields impressive and well-equipped armies, expanding its political dominance into rich and exotic lands. Luxurious goods and ordinary foodstuffs flow into the palaces and marketplaces of Tenochtitlan and its neighboring cities. The magnificence of adornments and clothing dripping from rulers and nobles is unprecedented. People's everyday lives pivot around making a living, relating to one another, and maintaining good relations with the many deities that populate their supernatural world. In this environment, exuberant and flamboyant ceremonies punctuate a person's daily grind. Part of life is predictable, ordinary, and repetitive; part of life is so extremely different (especially with theatrical ceremonies) that the contrast must have jarred one's senses. Maybe that is the point.

This, then, is the setting in which the people highlighted in this book lived the mundane and spectacular moments of their lives. This is their world. It has a history. It has a landscape. It has hopes and dreams, tensions and conflicts. It has an intricate web of social and political relations. It has an ideological foundation. It has codes of conduct and rules of morality that guide each individual's life. Within this universe any person has occasion to see and perhaps interact with people of different languages, customs, styles of clothing, occupations, and social standing. We are fortunate to glimpse this colorful, vibrant world.

# A Note on Sources

The Aztec Empire came to an abrupt end with the Spanish conquest nearly 500 years ago. How do we reconstruct a way of life in some ways obliterated by a foreign conquest, and in other ways surviving but transformed? The Mexica city of Tenochtitlan was quickly overlain by the Spanish colonial City of Mexico; much of the native population was decimated by disease; and the trauma of conquest interrupted some native institutions and transfigured much of native culture. Still, many native languages and customs survived through the three centuries of colonial rule and up to the present day. We therefore have the luxury of studying, ethnographically, present-day descendants of the ancient Aztecs and other Mesoamerican peoples. Revealing tenacious customs, these studies shed a good deal of light on life in ancient times: modern native women weave on looms mirroring those of the Aztecs; men continue to cultivate the age-old crops of maize, beans, chia, chiles, and many others; men, women, and children undertake devoted and lengthy pilgrimages to honor artfully blended Christian and ancient gods (see Sandstrom 1991; Sandstrom and Sandstrom 2017). So there are some *ethnographic analogies* that we can draw on, keeping in mind the sometimes-dramatic effects of 500 years of intervening history. But this is only one of three primary keys to unlocking the ancient world of the Aztecs. Here we lean most heavily on two other major types of sources: *written documents* and *archaeological investigations*.

The Aztecs were literate. They had scribes. They had paper. They had books. They had enormous collections of books. These books were pictorial in presentation and their content ranged from histories and economic accounts to religious manuals and maps (see Chapter 2). Very few of these pre-Spanish pictorial codices remain from throughout Mesoamerica, and arguably only one that we may call "Aztec" (the *Matrícula de Tributos*). However, scores of pictorial documents, copied from or based on their pre-Columbian antecedents, were produced in the early colonial period. Among these, we rely most heavily on the *Codex Mendoza* (Berdan and Anawalt 1992), a seventy-one-folio pictorial codex with Spanish annotations and commentaries that documents Aztec military conquests, taxes or tributes paid by thirty-eight conquered provinces, and daily life from infancy to old age.

Some other colonial documents, such as the accounts written by the Dominican friar Diego Durán, derived from their authors' access to now-lost ancient pictorial codices. In a class by itself is the *Florentine Codex: General History of the Things of New Spain* compiled by Friar Bernardino de Sahagún. This Franciscan intellectual mastered the Nahuatl language and recorded an impressive compendium of Aztec cultural and historical knowledge; this information was communicated to him, about fifty years after the Spanish conquest, by native "informants" as text in Nahuatl and as visuals in hundreds of pictorial images.

Among the myriad other colonial documentary sources are accounts of the Spanish conquest itself by Hernando Cortés in his five letters to his king, and the "true" history of the conquest by one of his *conquistadores*, Bernal Díaz del Castillo. We also can draw on many secular writings, ranging from the mid- to late sixteenth-century *Relaciones geográficas* to the 1570s natural history of Francisco Hernández to historical chronicles written in Spanish by mestizos such as Fernando de Alva Ixtlilxochitl, a descendant of the rulers of Texcoco. In addition, many documents were composed in Nahuatl during the colonial period; these begin to appear as early as a decade after the Spanish conquest and range from poetry and chronicles to censuses, wills, and minutes of town council meetings. They encompass land disputes, inheritance, and even personal letters – all intriguing windows into lives played out on a daily basis. These are the major types of documentary sources, but it is a very rich and diverse corpus; a more detailed rendition of ethnohistoric sources can be found in Berdan (2014: 5–15).

We must, of course, look carefully at any written source – all too frequently they contain hidden (and not so hidden) biases of all sorts.

Some of these are overt, such as Spanish religious documents explicitly condemning native religious beliefs and practices. Others are more nuanced, reflecting perspective or attitude: Alva Ixtlilxochitl sees native history from his noble Texcocan viewpoint, the *conquistadores* perceive the exotic Aztec world through their familiar Spanish cultural lenses, and Hernando Cortés at the head of the Spanish contingent is clearly a self-promoter. Other matters sometimes peek through the pages: for instance, the *conquistador* Bernal Díaz del Castillo (1963: 238) apologizes for an incomplete report during the Spaniards' tense visit to Tenochtitlan ("I had other thoughts in my head at the time than that of telling a story. I was more concerned with my military duties"); the Spanish interpreter of the *Codex Mendoza* offers excuses for his rough and crude writing style since he was in a great hurry; and Hernando Cortés (1928: 89) gave up describing market commodities because of "their very number and the fact that I do not know their names." But we can be optimistic: these sorts of pitfalls and limitations permeate the documentary record, but careful and critical readings and interpretations have yielded (and continue to yield) a wealth of detailed information and nuanced understandings of the Aztec way of life on the eve of the Spanish conquest. As a general rule, the more that different types of unrelated sources corroborate one another, the more they can be believed. Furthermore, documents do not bear the total burden of this cultural reconstruction; this load is shared with archaeological findings.

Archaeological investigations complement the documentary record and constitute a particularly significant source of information on the ancient Aztecs. Archaeologists researching the Aztec civilization are relatively fortunate: the Aztecs built grandly and often with permanent materials; they produced massive amounts of pottery, stone tools, and other goods; and the elite were rather enamored of an extravagant lifestyle that required exquisite adornments of fine stones, metals, and other imperishables. In other words, there is a great deal for archaeologists to work with, since they focus on material remains. And these material remains and their histories often complement and have some advantages over historical documents. In the first place, archaeological remains do not suffer from the kinds of biases that are the bane of historical documents: "a commoner trash heap was not intended to impress or deceive, and the archaeologist will find it much as it was deposited in antiquity" (Berdan 2014: 20). In addition, archaeological investigations can reveal considerable time depth and changes over time. And furthermore, the material remains that are the "stuff" of archaeology often encompass areas of life largely neglected by the documents, especially the lives of commoners. For instance, based on archaeological remains, Michael Smith (2008: 172–173) has determined that the lives of Aztec commoners were similar in urban and rural settings; we could only guess this by reading the historical documents.

This is all well and good, but on the flip side, the archaeological record is still incomplete and uneven. Many objects produced by the Aztecs and their neighbors were perishable and fragile, and few of these have survived to be analyzed by modern scientists. These include huge quantities of paper (and the books made from paper); cloth, clothing, and sandals; reed baskets and seats; feathers and feathered objects; and so on. Some Aztec perishables that survived the conquest and the intervening 500 years include the seven (only seven!) pre-Spanish feathered objects held today in museums in Mexico and Europe; unfortunately, they resemble many other objects in museums by falling short in provenience information. So while they are technically interesting, they are historically wanting. Beyond material impermanence, archaeological explorations are sometimes impeded by settlement histories: it was common practice for colonial Spaniards to build their cities and towns on top of existing native cities and towns. Many native buildings were razed or ravaged as their stones were often pillaged for the new Spanish buildings. The placements of colonial and modern buildings all too frequently impede the possibility of tantalizing archaeological investigations. For instance, today Mexico's National Palace largely sits atop an inaccessible Motecuhzoma's palace. But there is cause for optimism: Aztec archaeology has never been so exciting and productive than in the past few decades. Among its shining stars is the continuing excavation of Tenochtitlan's Templo Mayor in downtown Mexico City; since 1978 numerous religious and civil buildings have been uncovered and more than 200 ritual caches have revealed thousands and thousands of artifacts. Analyses of these buildings and artifacts, along with archaeological investigations in other Aztec urban and rural settings, continue to change our views and refine our understanding of Aztec life. Our progress on these fronts is far from over.

For general modern-day syntheses of the Aztecs and their civilization, we refer you to Frances F. Berdan's *The Aztecs of Central Mexico: An
Imperial Society* (2nd ed., 2005) and *Aztec Archaeology and Ethnohistory*
(2014), Michael E. Smith's *The Aztecs* (3rd ed., 2012) and *At Home with
the Aztecs: An Archaeologist Uncovers Their Daily Life* (2016), Richard
Townsend's *The Aztecs* (2009), Davíd Carrasco's *Daily Life of the Aztecs*
(1998), Jacques Soustelle's *Daily Life of the Aztecs on the Eve of the Spanish
Conquest* (1970), Warwick Bray's *Everyday Life of the Aztecs* (1968),
Deborah L. Nichols and Enrique Rodríguez-Alegría's *The Oxford
Handbook of the Aztecs* (2017), and Manuel Aguilar-Moreno's *Handbook
of Life in the Aztec World* (2006).

# List of Fictional Characters

*(in order of appearance)*

| | |
|---|---|
| **Tzontemoc Tlacatecatl** | (Descending-Head Keeper-of-Men): Advisor to Ahuitzotl (r. 1486–1502) |
| **Malinalli** | (Grass): Commoner and a widow |
| **Ollin** | (Movement): Priest of Tezcatlipoca in Texcoco |
| **Tlexico** | (Fire-Bee): Assistant priest to Ollin |
| **Atapachtli** | (Water-Shell): Priest of Tlaloc in Texcoco |
| **Chimalchiuhqui** | (Shield-maker): Independent featherworker |
| **Centzon** | (Plenty, Accomplished): Palace featherworker |
| **Xochitl** | (Flower): Fifteen-year-old daughter of featherworker |
| **Quetzalhua** | (Feather-owner): Professional merchant (*pochtecatl*) |
| **Icnoyotl** | (Poor): Terrace farmer |
| **Ayotochton** | (Little Armadillo): Neighbor of Icnoyotl and a farmer |
| **Citlalin** | (Star): Icnoyotl's wife |
| **Xilotl** | (Tender maize): Female slave |
| **Ce Ocelotl** | (One Jaguar): Male slave and absent husband of Xilotl |
| **Quauhtli** | (Eagle): Potter |
| **Cihuacomitl** | (Woman-Pot): Wife of Quauhtli |
| **Tototontli** | (Little Bird): Daughter of Quauhtli and Cihuacomitl |
| **Chilpapalotl** | (Red Butterfly): A recently delivered mother |
| **Coyochimalli** | (Coyote Shield): Husband of Chilpapalotl and a warrior who goes to war |
| **Cuicatototl** | (Singing Bird): Midwife known for her soothing voice |
| **Yaotl** | (War): Newborn baby and later, at age seven |
| **Centzonxihuitl** | (Many Turquoises): Daughter of Chilpapalotl and Coyochimalli |
| **Huilotl** | (Mourning Dove): Basketmaker's daughter, fifteen years old |

**Cihuatlapalli**    (Woman-Colors): Pigment and copal seller in
                     Tlatelolco market
**Ce Mazatl**        (One Deer): Turquoise worker
**Xoxoacatl**        (Green Reed): Farmer, going to court
**Ozomaton**         (Little Monkey): Ce Mazatl's son and a turquoise
                     worker
**Tecolotl**         (Owl): Rank-and-file warrior from Texcoco and a
                     farmer

# Part I

## Lives

This section of the book is about people. People from another time and place. People long-gone. But people, nonetheless. Some are remembered today by their given names: famous emperors, warriors, or poets come to mind. Many more remain nameless. Yet in their time they were well-known by others – perhaps loved, perhaps despised; maybe admired, enjoyed, reviled, tolerated, or ignored by those around them.

For this viewing we have chosen an emperor, a priest, two featherworkers, a professional merchant, a farmer's family, and a slave. One, the emperor Ahuitzotl, is a pretty well-documented individual. The others we present as composite lives, reconstructed from a wide array of sources. We have given them names, purely of our own invention but consistent with the naming practices of the day. Likewise, the acts, musings, fears, and hopes with which we have endowed these fictional persons are in harmony with Aztec culture.

Let's take a look at these persons, whether their real names are known today or lost to history.

1

# The Emperor

*It was a privilege to be in his company at that moment. The entire city was cheering his return, and we could hear the drums and conch shells announcing his victory from the temple heights. Behind me, Ahuitzotl sat regally on his litter, the platform dripping with shimmering feathers and aromatic flowers, and carried by four stout men. Ahead of us trudged long lines of wailing and dejected war captives, for we had vanquished our rebellious foes to the northeast: the belligerent Huaxtecs. The celebration will go on for days with feasting, dancing, singing, gift-giving, visits from neighboring kings, and ultimately the sacrifice of these captives. With these extravagant celebrations, all the world will be reminded that Ahuitzotl is the all-powerful king and emperor.*

*This day is his, but once I see to the proper observances at the temple and palace, I will not turn down a good meal and a little leisure time in the temazcalli, the cleansing sweat bath. It will help clear my mind. It is an honor to serve my cousin Ahuitzotl as Tlacateccatl. I carry the same military title as he did under his brother Tizoc, and as Tizoc did under his brother Axayacatl. Perhaps I will continue this tradition and someday become lord of these rich lands. It is in the hands of fate and the gods.*

So mused Tzontemoc Tlacateccatl as the Mexica army triumphantly entered Tenochtitlan. He was Ahuitzotl's cousin and an extremely important man in the Mexica government, so important that his exalted title, Tlacateccatl, was attached to his name. He was of noble blood, scarred in wars abroad, and skilled in diplomacy. He served Ahuitzotl in the empire's capital city and in his ruler's military campaigns, but harbored his own ambitions. And he knew Mexica politics, and his ruler, very well. Nonetheless, his own ambitions will not be fulfilled.

## MEXICA RULER AND AZTEC EMPEROR: AN
## INDISPUTABLE PEDIGREE

Ahuitzotl was the eighth ruler (*tlatoani*) of Tenochtitlan, king of his
people the Mexica and emperor of vast regions beyond his home city
from 1486 until his death in 1502. He arrived in this enviable and
exalted position honestly, descending from the earliest rulers of
Tenochtitlan, most recently his grandfather the legendary ruler Motecuhzoma Ilhuicamina (r. 1440–1468) and his two brothers Axayacatl
(r. 1468–1481) and the ill-fated Tizoc (r. 1481–1486). Motecuhzoma
had died in 1468 without a suitable male heir. In a strategic political
marriage, his daughter Atotoztli had married Tezozomoc, son of
Motecuhzoma's uncle Itzcoatl, who had ruled Tenochtitlan earlier,
from 1426 until 1440. This union produced the three rulers, Axayacatl, Tizoc, and Ahuitzotl (Figure 1.1).

Ahuitzotl was intricately related to kings, queens, and high-ranking
nobles from other cities. By the time he acceded to the throne,
Ahuitzotl's royal forebears had provided him with a multitude of lordly
relatives situated in powerful positions in city-states in and around the
Basin of Mexico. Generations of aristocratic kinship ties were expanded
and complicated by the practice of polygyny whereby a noble man
acquired many (sometimes very many) wives also of noble blood. Much
as noble women from other city-states entered Ahuitzotl's palace as his
wives, his own sisters and half-sisters married into neighboring noble
lineages. It was a tangled web indeed, one that had been unfolding over
several prior rulerships. Ahuitzotl had numerous important cousins of
varying genealogical distance ruling in sometimes-allied, sometimes-
enemy city-states. Most notably, the second-most powerful king in the
realm, Nezahualpilli of Texcoco, was his cousin.

Ahuitzotl's bloodline was impeccable. But it was not sufficient by
itself to elevate him to the most powerful position in the land. He also
needed the support of the highest-ranking royal advisors, a rather
vaguely constituted (to us) noble council, and "the people." But he
especially needed affirmation by the two kings who were his primary
allies: his cousin Nezahualpilli of Texcoco and Totoquihuaztli of
Tlacopan (of unclear genealogical relation to Ahuitzotl).

As *tlatoani*, Ahuitzotl inherited long-standing traditions from his predecessors. His grandfathers, Itzcoatl and Motecuhzoma Ilhuicamina,

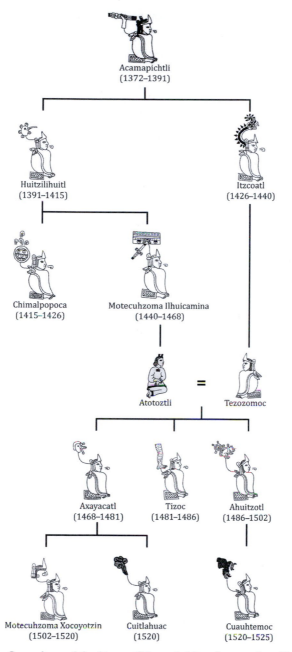

FIGURE 1.1. Genealogy of the kings of Tenochtitlan. Source: Jennifer Berdan Lozano; reproduced with permission. Based on Berdan (2014: 145).

had initiated the military expansion of Tenochtitlan. Itzcoatl had been at the forefront of the power shift that established Tenochtitlan as the primary military power in the Basin of Mexico. He had achieved this in collaboration with Nezahualcoyotl of neighboring Texcoco; the two had overthrown the most powerful Basin of Mexico city-state, Azcapotzalco, by 1430. Itzcoatl then extended that alliance to include Tlacopan to the east, the three city-states unifying as a Triple Alliance (see Map 2). Together, these three succeeded in subduing most of the city-states within the Basin of Mexico. Motecuhzoma Ilhuicamina completed those conquests and began Tenochtitlan's imperial expansion well beyond the Basin. Each successive ruler was expected to further these ambitions and continually expand the territorial boundaries of the imperial domain. They considered it their destiny.

In addition to military expectations, Ahuitzotl inherited weighty domestic responsibilities and ritual duties. His title was *tlatoani*, or "speaker," and he spoke often and eloquently. He was responsible for the safety and protection of his people and city, for motivating nobles and commoners in Mexica enterprises, and for punishing them when they fell short. He also took center stage in the grandest and most flamboyant religious celebrations, dancing in elegant attire and at times personally performing human sacrifices.

Ahuitzotl also inherited some significant problems from his immediate predecessors, especially his two rather ill-starred brothers Axayacatl and Tizoc. Their grandfathers' impressive reigns had been, reportedly, times of steady and irrepressible military expansion. However, some of that power, might, and respect had been diminished by Axayacatl and Tizoc, and the formidable reputation of the Mexica had been damaged under their reigns. Ahuitzotl's brothers had not lived up to the military expectations of their royal predecessors and had exposed the empire's vulnerabilities. Specifically, Axayacatl had suffered disastrous losses in a poorly conceived war against the powerful Tarascans to the west (see Chapter 10). Tizoc had only minimally extended the imperial domain, too often losing more warriors in battle than returning home with prisoners: in his military campaign against Metztitlan to obtain prisoners for his own coronation, he skulked back into Tenochtitlan with a meager forty captives, having lost 300 of Tenochtitlan's finest warriors (Durán 1994: 301). These failures (and non-expansion was considered a failure nearly as much as utter defeat) put considerable pressure on Ahuitzotl to excel in the military arena. Both of his immediate predecessors left Ahuitzotl with quite a bit of cleaning up to do to restore the prestige and power of the Mexica and their allies.

Still, Ahuitzotl benefited from existing, well-honed strategies for handling both positive and negative issues of office. Like the rulers before him, he had vast resources at his command, both human and material. He could amass enormous armies for distant conquests and extract massive quantities of tribute from his subjects. He glorified his city through majestic architecture and spectacular public rituals. He orchestrated political alliances through intimidation and the hosting of lavish feasts, collected strategic information through his association with merchants and merchants-as-spies, and rewarded loyal, valorous, and steadfast warriors. He took center stage in specified, intensely theatrical religious ceremonies. In short, he was a powerful presence at home and abroad. In all of this, Ahuitzotl placed his own personal stamp on coping with royal problems and furthering the goals of his city and empire. How did he do this, all the while staying within the bounds of his exalted office and the confines of his cultural expectations.

## THE PALACE AND ITS PEOPLE

Ahuitzotl lived in a grand, sumptuous palace located in the center of Tenochtitlan, at the hub of urban life. To the east the palace faced the ceremonial precinct dominated by the Huey Teocalli, or Templo Mayor, or Great Temple. Ahuitzotl, along with his periodic distinguished visitors, had premier views to the flamboyant ceremonies performed at the temple's twin sanctuaries. To the southeast bustled Tenochtitlan's marketplace where palace servants and artisans could easily acquire foods, materials, and manufactured goods for the palace's daily needs. The broad causeway to Tlacopan, linking Ahuitzotl's administrative center directly to his western subjects and lands beyond, ended close to the palace (Figure 1.2).

Ahuitzotl inherited the palace from his two immediate predecessors, and we do not know what, if any, modifications he personally made to the vast structure when he moved in. Nature had taken its shots at this building: a flood in 1449 necessitated rebuilding in the

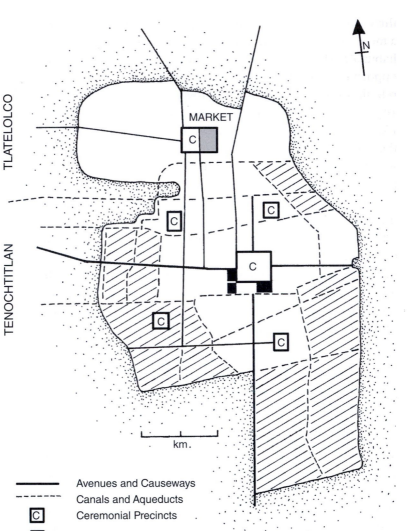

FIGURE 1.2. Plan of Tenochtitlan, showing the locations of the imperial palaces surrounding the sacred precinct. Source: Michael E. Smith.

early 1450s (Evans 2004: 21), and repairs were made to the palace by Axayacatl following a damaging earthquake in 1475. The disastrous flood of 1500, during Ahuitzotl's reign and at least partially due to his own pride and stubbornness, required a great deal of rebuilding throughout the city. Temples and houses were immersed in about half a meter of water and "The palace and the homes of the lords were not habitable" (Durán 1994: 372). Ahuitzotl saw this urban disaster as an opportunity to upgrade the city and his own palace: "the city was rebuilt with better, finer, and more splendid structures" (Durán 1994: 373). As expected, his palace was the first building to be rebuilt (Alvarado Tezozomoc 1975: 567), and he surely spared nothing in the refurbishing of his already ornate edifice. Although we have no specifics, it is likely that he selected finer stones, renewed fading wall paintings, and planted grander gardens.

If the Great Temple was the spiritual heart of the Aztec universe, the ruler's palace was its political nerve center. It was called *tecpancalli* ("lord's house") in Nahuatl. While we know precious little of the details of Ahuitzotl's palace, this vast structure would have followed the patterns of other better-known Aztec palaces. Comparable buildings provide us with some basics. Any *tecpancalli* worthy of its name sat on a walled, stone platform; the high stone walls were broken by a single main entry. The building would have looked immense and impenetrable from the outside, although while the Spaniards were besieged there in 1520, Mexica attackers demolished and breached the walls in several places (Díaz del Castillo 1963: 290, 292–293). Estimates of the size of Ahuitzotl's palace range from 11,439 to 34,200 square meters (Evans 2004: 20; Smith 2008: 117).

Only the finest materials and most masterful craftsmanship were used in the construction of royal palaces. The palace at nearby Ixtapalapa was constructed of "magnificent stone, cedar wood, and the wood of other sweet-smelling trees, with great rooms and courts" (Díaz del Castillo 1963: 215). Stone was the primary construction material, and López de Gómara (1966: 148), while never setting foot in Mexico, provides a long list including marble, jasper, and alabaster. Sahagún (1950–1982: book 11: 270–271) describes palaces as "smooth," "burnished," and "shining," a tribute to the high quality of stonework. Nonetheless, a substantial amount of wood must also have been used, since during that same siege of the Spaniards in Ahuitzotl's palace in 1520, parts of the palace were severely burned (Cortés 1928: 110). In addition to its extraordinary size, exceptional quality of materials, and construction care, the palace was readily identifiable as such by a string of decorative circles above the entry lintel. This was perhaps more symbol than decoration since it signaled

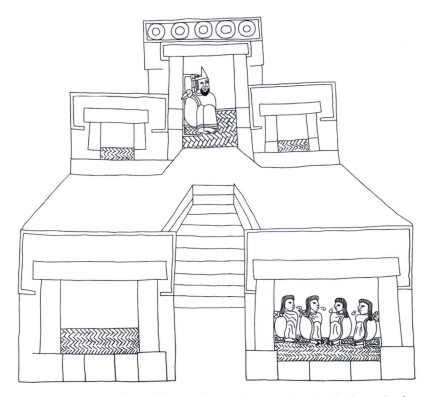

FIGURE 1.3. The palace of Motecuhzoma Xocoyotzin, who is shown in the top room. Reproduced from Berdan and Anawalt (1992: vol. 4: f. 69r).

the nobility of the structure (as seen in Figure 1.3). The discs may have been painted over stucco, but probably more often consisted of pumice cones about 10 centimeters wide by 30 centimeters long and "daubed with plaster and embedded, tenon fashion, into the wall surface" (Evans 1991: 71–72).

Entering the palace by climbing several steps onto the platform, the (usually intimidated) visitor walked onto a large open courtyard (*tecpanquiahuac*) surrounded by numerous roofed rooms dedicated to the administration of the ruler's city and empire (Figure 1.4). There was a courtroom for nobles and a separate one for commoners. The accumulated wealth of the empire was housed in extensive depositories, and consisted of tributes (including abundant foodstuffs) delivered from conquered subjects as well as palace-made goods. This

FIGURE 1.4. The Texcocan royal palace from the Mapa Quinatzin. Source: Boone (2000: 192). Reproduced with permission.

area also housed the overseers and accountants of these provisions and treasures, and palace-sponsored artisans were located here as well, or nearby. Courtrooms and chambers for warriors were standard fare. Nezahualcoyotl of Texcoco housed an extensive archive in his palace (Alva Ixtlilxochitl 1965: 179); a library or archive was probably a staple of royal palaces. The royal palace also accommodated the ruler's religious roles, providing rooms for idols, musical instruments, and ceremonial regalia. An armory full of weapons, armor, and shields was a necessity. Royal palaces were enriched by well-tended gardens, orchards, ponds, fountains, and other such pleasurable amenities (Díaz del Castillo 1963: 215; Evans 2004: 29).

For Ahuitzotl's palace in particular, some of the rooms were permanently set aside for the rulers of Texcoco and Tlacopan, this ruler's closest allies, and other rooms were always available for distinguished visiting dignitaries. Nezahualcoyotl of Texcoco repaid the favor, reserving rooms in his palace for the kings of Tenochtitlan and Tlacopan (Douglas 2010: 87). Ahuitzotl's successor, Motecuhzoma Xocoyotzin, maintained permanent quarters within his palace for the kings of neighboring Tenayuca, Chiconauhtla, and Colhuacan as well (Berdan and Anawalt 1992: vol. 3: f. 69r). We do not know if Ahuitzotl had done the same (see Figures 1.3 and 1.4).

At the opposite end of the palace entrance, through the central courtyard, the visitor's curious and anxious eye fell on an elevated throne or dais room, imbued with the ruler's symbolic and actual power. Here sat Ahuitzotl, facing his minions assembled in the court-yard for their daily work assignments, pleas for justice, or hopes for an audience. The courtyard would have been full of bureaucrats, judges, claimants, petitioners, leading merchants, hangers-on, and the king's personal guards. If an important lord was present to offer his obei-sance, he was accompanied by his own entourage of relatives, body-guards, servants, and possibly wives – all to a great number.

The royal palace served more than state and empire: on the domestic side, it contained a multitude of rooms to accommodate the ruler's personal life, including rooms for his many wives and children. In at least some cases, these rooms, while roughly square in shape, were arranged "with many patios and labyrinths" (Alva Ixtlilxochitl 1965: 179). One envisions a warren of private rooms dedicated to high-class royal living. Like other similar buildings, the domestic arm of Ahuitzotl's palace also would have enjoyed sweat baths, elegant and fragrant gardens, and housing for servants and slaves. Extensive cooking facilities would have served both domestic and state dining needs.

Little was spared in the matter of decoration. Wandering about the palace at nearby Ixtapalapa, the conquistador Bernal Díaz del Castillo (1963: 215) later mused that "Everything was shining with lime and decorated with different kinds of stonework and paintings which were a marvel to gaze on." While expensive stones were used throughout in palatial construction, in some cases, as with Nezahualcoyotl's palace, *tezontle*, a lightweight pumice, may have been used for walls, its crude-ness disguised with lime plaster and elegant painting (Evans 2004: 27).

Indeed, painting appears to have been a hallmark of the palatial scene. Red predominated, and not just solid red, but stripes and a diversity of intricate designs (Sahagún 1950–1982: book 11: 270; Alva Ixtlilxochitl 1965: 179). And mosaics. And abundant luxurious hanging textiles covering open spaces such as walls and doorways, or serving as awnings (Díaz del Castillo 1963: 215). And exquisite featherwork: one might envision the coyote shield (now located in Vienna, Austria; see Figure 3.6 below), of a design not seen in battle depictions, hanging on a palace wall. It appears that considerable thought, attention, and time were applied to palatial interior decoration; in Nezahualcoyotl's palace, every room (at least every important one) was decorated differently (Alva Ixtlilxochitl 1965: 174–178).

Furnishings and fixtures were sparse. The king sat on a woven seat, covered with a jaguar pelt. Woven reed mats would have been numerous and provided comfort (for everyone) while sleeping. Fires for heat and light were available throughout the palace, probably most often lit in large ceramic braziers (which would have needed frequent tending and replenishment) (Torquemada 1969: vol. 1: 167). Bunches of *ocotl* (resinous pine wood) hanging here and there would have provided additional light. While a prisoner of the Spaniards in Ahuitzotl's palace, Motecuhzoma reportedly sat on a small decorated stool for his many-dish meals, being served on a low table decorated to match the stool. He was shielded from being observed by a gold-worked wooden screen. Another decorated wooden screen was strategically placed between the king and a burning brazier, regulating his mealtime temperature (Díaz del Castillo 1963: 226). The only other furnishings would have been chests for storing personal possessions such as clothing and adornments. Almost every Aztec household had a storage chest made of reeds; a king undoubtedly would have had countless chests, only larger, more elaborately decorated, and made of finer and stronger materials such as finely polished woods.

This is the palace as structure, as administrative building and domestic house. But its unique form served very specific and important functions, turning the administrative building into a beehive of bustling routines and spirited intrigue, and the domestic rooms into an animated home (and also of spirited intrigue).

DAILY ROUND: AT HOME WITH THE ROYALS

As king and emperor, Ahuitzotl spent much of his time away from home, waging wars and returning with riches and glory. In this, he was perhaps much like King Richard the Lionheart of England. Still, his primary goals as king and emperor began at home: to consolidate power at home and impress any detractors, to restore the reputation of Aztec omniscience abroad diminished by his immediate predecessors, to expand his and Tenochtitlan's material wealth, and to assure his bloodline. Much daily life in the palace was directed toward these goals.

The king's palace was a showpiece, and as such it experienced a great deal of daily hubbub. We have already seen that the palace courtyard was the daily scene of innumerable persons milling about, awaiting audiences, assignments, or attention. The homage that these persons offered, on a daily basis, over and over again, reinforced and renewed the ruler's power over his subjects. Of course, some days were more eventful than others, whether by design or happenstance.

Ahuitzotl spent much of his homebound daily life planning and preparing. He had a steady stream of projects at home and abroad, for which he demanded laborers and warriors from throughout the Basin of Mexico and beyond. The rulers and their people responded with enthusiasm. He seemed to have had no difficulty commanding others, through his own decisiveness and the strategic seeking of advice. As a result, his construction projects were completed in record time, and he amassed enormous armies of conquest drawn from surrounding city-states. His charisma and amiable personality were keys to his success. One envisions him sitting in state on his palace dais, his four well-dressed advisors hovering, his minions awaiting his every command. Should he appoint one of his relatives to a newly vacated rulership in a nearby city-state? How should he respond to the recent insults by the people from the west who defied his "requests" for laborers? How can he pay for the upcoming feasts for his most loyal allies, having just depleted the treasury on a grand display of generosity to "the people"?

This was the administrative side of the palace. But the palace also had a domestic personality – it was the home of Ahuitzotl and his many wives and children. And these people all needed to eat, sleep, work, amuse themselves, and live in extreme comfort. As might be expected, the needs of these occupants were great and continual, and largely provided by servants and slaves. Every day saw the palace artisans diligently at work in the service of king, state, and gods. Every day gardeners bustled about the extensive palace grounds, planting, pruning, and manicuring the elaborate landscaping. Every day the palace experienced deliveries of maize and other foods, water, fire-wood, *ocotl* for torches, cotton for spinning and weaving, whatever the palace currently needed replenished. Within the palace, innumerable women leaned over *metates* and ground maize, cooked delicious meals, spun fine cotton into thread, and wove those threads into exquisite clothing. These activities went on all day long. Day after day.

Ahuitzotl's many wives were high-ranking noblewomen, mostly daughters and sisters of neighboring rulers. These wives provided Ahuit-zotl with twenty children (Anderson and Schroeder 1997: 154–157). One of his daughters married Ahuitzotl's successor, Motecuhzoma Xocoyotzin, bearing two children from that marriage. Ahuitzotl's first son, Cuauhtemoc, ruled Tenochtitlan during the dark days of the Spanish siege in 1521. Ahuitzotl had no difficulty assuring his bloodline and providing future leadership for his city, at least in the short run.

Life in the palace was not all hard work and stressful decisions. Drudgery was relieved by games and other diversions. They played *patolli* (rather like Pachisi) and the ballgame, betting heavily with golden adornments, precious stones, fine clothing, and cacao (Figure 1.5). They were entertained by singers, jesters, and gymnasts. They wandered the aromatic flower gardens and hunted nearby with blowguns and bows and arrows. On a larger scale, the rhythms of palace life were often interrupted by flamboyant ceremonies, by feasting of important visitors, or by war. The ruler had important roles in all of these, and required the support of his household, especially with feasts. Palatial eating was apparently always an event, with many delectable dishes – all manner of tamales, maize gruel with honey, chile sauces, squashes, turkey-in-a-pot, small *nopales* with fish eggs, roast quail, and more – served at every meal, topped off with a frothy chocolate drink and soothed with a tube of tobacco. The foods became even more delicious and creative at major ceremonial and political feasts, with the finest serving wares on display (Sahagún 1950–1982: book 8: 29–30, 37–40).

FIGURE 1.5. The game of *patolli* with wagered goods. Sahagún (1950–1982: book 8: fig. 63). Firenze, Biblioteca Medicea Laurenziana. All rights reserved. Further reproduction in any print or digital format is forbidden.

Everything that Ahuitzotl did was on a grand scale. Extravagance was the order of the day. He inherited the strict aristocratic policies codified by Motecuhzoma Ilhuicamina years before, but he imbued them with his own personal imprint. While seemingly burdened by custom and tradition, Ahuitzotl was something of an innovator: he was more egalitarian than other Aztec kings, and he was willing to incorporate new styles into the traditional symbolic regalia. Given his emphasis on success in warfare, and his resolve to reward achievements, it is not inconsistent to find that he promoted and installed achieved persons in his household and administration. This flew in the face of those elites who preferred (largely from self-interest) to maintain clear hierarchical distinctions between nobles-by-birth and the remainder of the population. Ahuitzotl's successor, Motecuhzoma Xocoyotzin, immediately purged Ahuitzotl's administrative appointees, disparaging their lowly status, and replaced those individuals with persons of his own choosing. One can only imagine this ruler's silent condemnation and abhorrence of Ahuitzotl's egalitarian policies in the years prior to his own election as *tlatoani* in 1502.

FIGURE 1.6. The ruler presents goods to the poor. Sahagún (1950–1982: book 8: fig. 92). Firenze, Biblioteca Medicea Laurenziana. All rights reserved. Further reproduction in any print or digital format is forbidden.

His egalitarian inclination was paired with a great generosity – he gave lavishly to his aristocratic visitors, to his valiant warriors, to his stonemasons and jewelers, to his merchants, to the poor widows and orphans of his city, to everyone (Figure 1.6). All received gifts at one time or another. He was also generous to himself. He donned the most exquisite clothing and adornments at ceremonies and feasts, went to war in high state, and adopted splendid regalia from distant Xoconochco reportedly captured and presented to him by his merchant-warriors. All this generosity and openness made him illustrious in appearance and beloved by his people. But it was immensely expensive. To balance the books, Ahuitzotl pursued an intensive military agenda that brought great wealth into his palace and city, and he never hesitated to call on neighboring cities to provide labor and materials for major construction projects.

## THE LIFE CYCLE OF AN EMPEROR

This was no ordinary man. He was king, emperor, supreme mortal, and godly delegate in his known world. Ahuitzotl's life's path, while played out within Aztec cultural conventions and expectations, was necessarily out of the ordinary. Where did his journey take him, from birth to death?

We do not know exactly when Ahuitzotl was born, and unfortunately the historical records only confound our uncertainties. First of all, there is some question about his age and experience at the time of his selection as *tlatoani*. The *Codex Mendoza* (Berdan and Anawalt 1992: vol. 3: f. 12v) states that Ahuitzotl held the title *Tlacateccatl*, a royal advisor and high-ranking military officer of his royal predecessor, Tizoc. Torquemada (1969: vol. 1: 186) acknowledges that Ahuitzotl carried the equally exalted title of *Tlacochcalcatl* at the time of his selection. Acquisition of both of these titles required the holder to be of noble blood and be experienced and proven in military exploits – more than a youth, therefore. However, both Durán (1994: 309–314) and Alvarado Tezozomoc (1975: 456) – related sources – insist that Ahuitzotl was very young, so young that there were serious questions about his suitability as the new ruler. It is worth noting that at the same time, throughout their histories, these two chroniclers emphasize the importance of the Mexica *tlatoani*'s second-in-command, the *Cihuacoatl* Tlacaelel, and make an elaborate point about the need for Tlacaelel to provide instruction and guidance to the young Ahuitzotl. Still, Durán indirectly contradicts himself elsewhere when he states that each new ruler came from the ranks of the prior ruler's four exalted advisors, all experienced and politically established men.

Assuming that Ahuitzotl was older than Durán and Alvarado Tezozomoc give him credit for, at the time of his election in 1486 he would be already tested in battle, experienced in diplomacy, and an eloquent speaker, all expected of any *tlatoani.* He had these minimum requirements for a city-state ruler, but also exhibited some important additional qualities. He was "by nature well disposed and virtuous," "powerful and generous," and "benevolent and affable." He was cheerful and popular, being inclined to lavish entertaining and generous gift-giving, essential components of diplomacy and political maneuvering (Berdan and Anawalt 1992: vol. 4: 30; Durán 1994: 341). He was also ambitious, heroic, fearless, and tenacious in war, a distinguished military leader likened by one modern author to Alexander the Great (Davies 1987: 80, 87). As his reign progressed, he also showed himself to be impetuous and stubborn, the latter quality perhaps leading to his ultimate downfall (Berdan 2014: 142–143).

Beyond his birth, Ahuitzotl's election and subsequent coronation were the first of his major rites of passage. They were set in motion by his brother Tizoc's premature and somewhat suspicious death, leading to a flurry of political and ceremonial obligations. These complex and extended events were laden with pomp and dripping with symbolism. Among the most significant of Aztec rituals, they established and validated the chosen ruler's transition from mere mortal to godly persona. We think that Ahuitzotl would agree with modern scholar Richard Townsend's (1987) sequence of events for his installation: separation and retreat, investiture and coronation, coronation war, and confirmation.

Ahuitzotl's election was in the hands of a variously reported collection of the allied rulers of Texcoco and Tlacopan, local nobles, priests, and many-leveled administrative officials. Through a series of carefully scripted sequences, Ahuitzotl was chosen, gathered up, brought to the royal palace, and seated on the royal throne. Summoned to the royal presence, many allied and subject lords offered Ahuitzotl their homage and loyalty. The elected ruler was not alone, as his four august advisors were chosen and entitled at this same time (Sahagún 1950–1982: book 8: 61). All of this happened, as was the custom, four days after the end of the prior ruler's funeral. News of the new ruler's election was immediately spread far and wide throughout the empire and beyond. Haste was important, as the hiatus between the death of one ruler and the election of his successor was considered a time of imperial weakness and instability, and an opportunity for rebellions by subject city-states (Berdan 2011).

Ahuitzotl (supposedly with his royal advisors) was carried to the city's central temple complex where he paid homage to the Mexica patron god, Huitzilopochtli. He was then sequestered for four days and nights in a nearby military headquarters (*Tlacocochcalcatl*), repeatedly visiting Huitzilopochtli's shrine where he offered his own blood, quails, and incense in pious obeisance. He also received dignified and sober speeches, using this time to reflect on the weightiness of his transformation from royal mortal to godly delegate. His four-day separation from everyday life, placing him in a sort of limbo, made this transformation all the more profound for both himself and for his subjects, as he was reborn with a godly aura.

Ahuitzotl now returned to his palace and throne (Durán 1994: 297, 314). There, the new Tenochtitlan king received a sacred bundle and uplifting lecture from the king of Texcoco, and the elaborate royal insignia and another motivating lecture from the king of Tlacopan. Imagine the visual transformation of the mortal man as the royal turquoise diadem was placed upon his head, and the septum of his nose perforated and a fine stone nose rod inserted. Imagine his hands and arms bright with bracelets and a glorious feathered adornment, his ears drooping with dangling pendants, his lip bedecked with an expensive labret, his legs arrayed with gold leg ornaments, and his royal feet wrapped in blue sandals. All of this was topped off with an exquisite cape of blue net design with precious stones attached, along with a matching loincloth (Alvarado Tezozomoc 1975: 460; Durán 1994: 313–314). Adorned in this traditional and elegant manner, Ahuitzotl was arranged on an eagle-jaguar seat and carried on the shoulders of high-ranking lords the short distance to the Great Temple where he was set in front of the statue of the Mexica titular god, Huitzilopochtli. There, following customary ritual, he made traditional, pious offerings: first his own blood from his ears, calves, and shinbone, then quail that he personally beheaded, then sacred incense. He repeated these solemn rituals at other temples, finally returning to his palace and throne (Durán 1994: 297, 314). There he received solemn homage and splendid gifts, all accompanied by lengthy and flowery speeches. Ahuitzotl then responded with a very mature and humble discourse of his own, accepting his new and onerous responsibilities to his present subjects and to the legacy of his royal predecessors.

The speeches presented in these situations, sounding much like motivational lectures, were expected, scripted, and carried great weight in the ceremonies. Indeed, speeches, exhortations, and admonitions were an integral part of Aztec moral life, up and down the social ladder. In every home, lengthy formulized speeches were delivered to young children, newlyweds, pregnant girls, even kings – anyone in need of little daily-life reminders and encouragements. The king operated on the grandest scale; he himself had been subject to endless exhortations on proper behavior as a child in his palace home and priestly school. On this occasion, the new ruler was exhorted by high-ranking dignitaries to be always vigilant, to be mother and father to his people, to be humble in the execution of his office, and to bring glory to his revered ancestors. In turn, the ruler lectured to his nobles and "the people," warning them of the dangers of drunkenness, thievery, and adultery, and encouraging their active involvement in warfare, religious observances, and working the land (Sahagún 1950– 1982: book 6: 47–85). Ahuitzotl's kingly responsibilities were embedded in these and other lectures directed to him by high-ranking nobles and priests. They reaffirmed his duties that included watching over and protecting the city, rewarding his valiant warriors, and generally caring for his people (especially orphans and widows). He also was admonished to revere the gods – he carried a supernatural aura and engaged in obligatory ceremonial activities. The speeches reminded him that he bore the onerous responsibility of maintaining social order, whether specifically with punishing wrongdoers or generally with upholding the social hierarchy explicitly formalized by his grandfather Motecuhzoma Ilhuicamina. In short, the exhortations, Ahuitzotl's acceptance speech, and a commoner representative's acknowledgment of the ruler's instructions laid out a sort of contract between the new ruler, his allies, and his subjects at all levels.

This was not all. Ahuitzotl's coronation war and confirmation were yet to come. But first he must conduct a military campaign to secure captives for sacrifice at his formal installation. Apparently, the king's official coronation was not contingent on great success in this military venture: Tizoc had returned home from his campaign in shame yet was still installed as ruler of Tenochtitlan, although this proved to be an ominous kickoff to his unproductive reign. Ahuitzotl, in contrast, brought honor and glory to the Mexica, returning with many prisoners, much loot, and promises of future tribute payments from seven vanquished city-states to the northwest (Durán 1994: 315–317).

Marching victoriously into his home city (and with much pomp and fanfare, for runners had alerted the city of the king's momentous victory), Ahuitzotl first paid reverence to the gods and then resumed his seat on the royal throne to confirm his rulership and to receive the worldly honors due him. These necessarily included lengthy but exquisitely crafted speeches by high-ranking personages from nearby cities and distant provinces – lectures much like those he already heard in his election and coronation ceremonies. Whether he gloried in the praise or impatiently dreamt of his awaiting sweat bath, he sat through the speeches, finally dismissing his guests, who were reminded that the king's royal confirmation was yet to come, set as always for the day Ce Cipactli (One Alligator, initial day of the ritual calendar). Invitations to the coronation were proffered, contingent on the invited guests' bringing with them "contributions" to defray the ceremony's vast expenses: wild game, fish, cacao, firewood, mats, cloth, feathers, weapons – whatever was available in the guests' home-lands (Durán 1994: 318).

The impending confirmation required elaborate preparations. The royal palace was profusely decorated with all manner of greenery. Luxury artisans were prodded to create the finest and most showy adornments in great abundance (Centzon the featherworker, who you will meet in Chapter 3, would have been exceedingly frustrated at this haste!). New reed mats and seats were woven and old ones repaired. Walls were replastered and repainted. The bustling city gleamed. Invitations first went to the high officials of the Aztec realm, and then to enemy lords, most of whom demurred. Two (from Cholula and Yopitzinco) sent representatives, but this minimal (more to the point, insulting) response was far less than Ahuitzotl expected, and he fumed. Still, the show must go on.

The confirmation ceremonies, as they unfolded, were flamboyant, highly scripted, deeply spiritual, and reverberated throughout the city. While they most closely impacted Ahuitzotl, his closest advisors and highest nobles, invitees, and priests, everyone felt the days' importance:

*I can feel it in the air, thought the widow Malinalli as she sat up in the night on her tattered reed sleeping mat. News of Ahuitzotl's impending coronation had rippled through the city, even to her humble dwelling toward the outskirts of the city. She had noticed the growing anticipation – people talking with greater urgency, canoes poled a little harder, a kind of eager nervousness. On the one hand, she welcomed the sense of security she felt with a potentially strong ruler in charge. That was Ahuitzotl's reputation already: strong and aggressive and generous. On the other hand, she worried (and hoped) that this new ruler would be good: the last ruler, Tizoc, had been a disaster. She reflected on her late husband, who had been killed in Tizoc's calamitous coronation campaign. It had been a shock at first, but she had adjusted to his death. She didn't like him very much anyway. Her daydreaming was interrupted by the distant sounds of conch shells and drums. The ceremony, and hopefully better days, had begun.*

The celebrations lasted four days and four nights. As Malinalli faintly heard, the festivities were announced by music, singing, and dancing, and followed by lavish feasting and extravagant gift-giving by the new ruler in recognition of his invited friends and foes. Gifts included costly clothing and beautifully crafted ornaments of gold and precious stones; the guests were also constantly showered with aromatic flowers, smoking tobacco, delectable foods, and abundant chocolate. While these gifts were certainly nice to receive, they were fraught with not-so-subtle messages of overarching wealth and power, meant to implant respect and instill fear. Some gifts, symbolically laden regalia of office and achievement, could be bestowed only by the ruler and stood as conspicuous reminders of the recipients' dependence on their new lord. The festivities were punctuated by the ritual sacrifice of the captive warriors obtained in Ahuitzotl's coronation war – perhaps as many as 1,000 men died on the temple altar that day to put the sacred stamp on Ahuitzotl's accession to the throne (Durán 1994: 323). His guests, departing shortly thereafter, left with a sense of awe and anxiety – in an especially symbolic move, the enemy envoys from Cholula and Yopitzinco carried weapons from Ahuitzotl to their own sovereigns, "sent as a reminder that war and enmity existed between them" (Durán 1994: 323). At the end of all of these ceremonies, from separation to confirmation, Ahuitzotl found himself religiously confirmed, militarily validated, and politically fortified. Tenochtitlan once again stood strong with an impressive new ruler.

Ahuitzotl's life as a ruler, between his coronation and his death, was part humdrum, part excitement, and was experienced variously at home and in military campaigns abroad. His reign was punctuated by ceremonies dedicating an expansion of Tenochtitlan's Great

Temple, numerous wars in distant lands, and a miserably failed
attempt at building an aqueduct to supplement the city's fresh water
supply. Natural disasters, common enough before and after his rule,
also bedeviled Ahuitzotl's time on the throne: a great hailstorm in
1490 after which many fish died, a grasshopper plague in 1491,
earthquakes in 1495 and 1499, a fierce snowstorm in 1498, and
drought and famine in 1502 (Berdan 2014: 54). The appearance of
a comet or meteor shower in 1489 and solar eclipses in 1490, 1492,
1493, and 1496 were ominous and heart-stopping events (Quiñones
Keber 1995). A disastrous flooding of Tenochtitlan in 1500 was essentially Ahuitzotl's own doing, as we shall see.

The dedication of Tenochtitlan's Great Temple took place barely a
year after Ahuitzotl had been installed as *tlatoani*. This massive construction project was initiated by his brother Tizoc, so one must
envision Ahuitzotl going through his election, coronation, and confirmation rituals in a temple-under-construction (Figure 1.7). The
temple's completion was cause for great celebration: an opportunity
to revere the gods, glorify the ruler, and provide diversion to the
mortals. In keeping with Aztec celebratory style, the dedication would
be extravagant and spectacular. To meet these criteria a great military
campaign was mounted to gain abundant prisoners for sacrifice.
Ahuitzotl personally commanded his own and allied forces far afield,
east to the lands of the fierce Huaxteca whose people had rebelled
against Aztec rule – again. He returned victorious (Malinalli would
have rejoiced) after considerable looting, decimation, and captures of
Huaxteca warriors, women, and children. The captive warriors, destined for ritual sacrifice, were augmented by prisoners taken by other
subject city-states and demanded by Ahuitzotl to be delivered to
Tenochtitlan for the temple dedication. And now they began to arrive,
in great splendid processions: the king of Texcoco with all of his
kingly subjects, likewise the king of Tlacopan and his. The invitations
to the enemy rulers of Tlaxcalla, Cholula, and Huexotzinco, and their
subsequent journey to Tenochtitlan, was a bit trickier. This required
considerable artifice, maneuvering, and secrecy. The enemy lords
were creatively disguised through garments and manner as they
arrived in Tenochtitlan and were ushered to Ahuitzotl's palace. There
they were concealed, along with many other enemy lords who soon
joined them. Although they were all housed in separate rooms, feted

FIGURE 1.7. The rulers Tizoc and Ahuitzotl, shown here on a dedication stone, were both associated with the expansion of the Great Temple. Source: Emily Umberger; reproduced with permission.

with great extravagance, and guarded by 200 warriors, this palatial setting nonetheless must have been a beehive of silent intrigue and aristocratic jockeying.

Aside from the overtly religious nature of the ceremony, Ahuitzotl had his own agenda: "to show Aztec grandeur and power to the enemies and guests and foreign people and fill them with bewilderment and fear" (Durán 1994: 336). As was his way, Ahuitzotl greeted his guests with great respect, lavish gifts, and delectable food. He paraded well-timed tribute deliveries so the wealth of his empire was not lost on his guests. He treated them with such extravagance that they "saw that the Aztecs were masters of the world" and "were filled with terror" (Durán 1994: 336). Feted and sated, Ahuitzotl's guests were then required to observe massive ritual sacrifices of long lines of captive warriors, some from their own lands. All of the people of Tenochtitlan and neighboring cities were ordered to attend the sacrificial ceremonies, to the extent that "the crowds swarmed through the city" (Durán 1994: 338). With lords composed and commoners agape, reportedly from 20,000 to 80,400 enemy warriors were sacrificed at that ceremony (very likely exaggerated) (Figure 1.8). Ahuitzotl himself, along with his allied kings, initiated the temple sacrifices. After the last captive was offered, Ahuitzotl once again presented splendid gifts to all of his guests; this was mainly for his benefit, to flaunt his wealth and power. He subsequently distributed more goods to all who had contributed to the ceremonies, and to old and poor people as well (Berdan 2014: 241; Durán 1994: 328–341). The gods were satisfied, the guests terrified, the citizens uplifted, and Ahuitzotl content in his extravagant show of power. Religious pageantry neatly coupled with political theater.

The intimidation intentionally promoted at the Great Temple dedication paved the way for Ahuitzotl's career of successful wars and political domination over vast areas (Figure 1.9). Indeed, he extended the bounds of the empire well beyond those of any other Aztec emperor (Map 1). His priorities clearly lay with military enterprises. He relished warfare and frequently served his troops as commander-in-chief in distant military campaigns. He was charismatic and gave inspirational speeches to his men to inflame them in battle. As a bonus he went to war resplendent in shimmering feather tunics, glittering gold adornments, and a headdress and shield of the finest flaring and flowing feathers – all bright red and blue and green (Sahagún 1950–1982: book 8: 33). He cut a striking and fearful figure, appearing on the field as the fearsome Xipe Totec, a god of agricultural renewal (Olko 2014: 109).

While generous at home and with his own people, this emperor was ruthless and relentless on the battlefield, depopulating whole communities (although typically sparing children). Still, he had a practical side, realizing that devastation also meant a lack of tribute revenues and that excessive looting left the inhabitants with little for Tenochtitlan's insatiable future economic demands. So, after one southern campaign left a region without tributaries, he arranged resettlements there from Basin of Mexico communities. And when his men became seriously out of control while sacking the city of Tehuantepec on the

FIGURE 1.8. Sacrificial offerings at the Great Temple dedication in 1487. *Codex Telleriano-Remensis* (Quiñones Keber 1995: 39r). Bibliothèque national de France, reprinted with permission.

FIGURE 1.9. Ahuitzotl's conquests. From Berdan and Anawalt (1992: vol. 4: f. 13r), reproduced with permission.

Pacific coast, he personally offered them compensation if they would cease their looting and destruction. They complied. He kept to his bargain.

Not all of Ahuitzotl's projects led him far afield. He was also concerned with the well-being of his home city, Tenochtitlan. And now, in 1499, the rapidly growing metropolis with its expansive *chinampas* required a second major source of fresh water beyond the "old" aqueduct from Chapultepec. Ahuitzotl saw the prolific springs of Acuecuexco to the south, at Coyoacan, as the perfect source of a new aqueduct. Tepiltzotzomatzin, the ruler of Coyoacan, saw things differently. He tried to convince Ahuitzotl that this was a bad idea, warning him of the catastrophic consequences of harnessing and unleashing these waters. It was also, of course, against his own self-interests for his home waters to be diverted elsewhere. For that bit of defiance, Ahuitzotl had him strangled (Anderson and Schroeder 1997: 215).

Ahuitzotl refused to listen to Tepiltzotzomatzin's advice and the channel was constructed by laborers from throughout the Basin of Mexico. Most likely constructed of stone and packed earth (Mundy 2015: 64), its inauguration in 1499 or 1500 was celebrated throughout Tenochtitlan with great ritual fanfare. The arrival of the fresh water was welcomed all along its channel by the playing of flutes, blowing of conch shells, offerings of incense and liquid rubber, singing, dancing, and sacrifices of children and quails. A human impersonator of the goddess Chalchiuhtlicue, sacred overseer of fresh waters, performed critical rituals and offered reverential words along the water's course. As the water reached Tenochtitlan, Ahuitzotl emerged from his palace to greet it, humbly offering flowers, tubes of tobacco, gold and stone jewels, and incense to the goddess. He personally decapitated quail, spoke ritually potent words, and may have served as the deity impersonator. While penitent, his ritual stance placed him in a position of control – control over mortals, over nature, and over the behavior of Chalchiuhtlicue herself (Mundy 2015: 67–69).

This was powerful stuff. But it was not enough, and as the project unfolded, it indeed turned out to be a bad idea. Despite skilled engineering and extensive religious intervention, within forty days the aqueduct soon proved inadequate to manage the enormous and persistent flow of water. Uncontrolled waters burst into Tenochtitlan and neighboring cities, inundating the landscape. The people tried to build a dike as a barrier; it failed against the great force of the water. Ahuitzotl consulted with his allied rulers, who recommended that the construction be dismantled and valuable offerings (including children, quail, stone idols, and jewels) made to Chalchiuhtlicue. The

waters responded and receded, reportedly responding to both practical and ritual solutions. But the city had suffered greatly – most of it
was still under water, and many of its residents had left the city and
settled elsewhere. Ahuitzotl again called on his allies and conquered
subjects – this time to provide materials and labor to restore the city.
Tenochtitlan was not just repaired and renovated, but rebuilt and
improved "with better, finer, and more splendid structures" (Durán
1994: 373). Meanwhile, Ahuitzotl made amends: he installed Tepiltzotzomatzin's son as new ruler of Coyoacan, made retribution to all
who had suffered, and paid for Tenochtitlan's renovation from his
own treasury (which, of course, was stocked from tributes paid by his
subjects). But the toll may have been larger than just buildings and
gardens, as Ahuitzotl died two years later. Although Diego Durán
(1994: 382) tells us that he succumbed to a debilitating illness he
suffered after a final military campaign on the southern Pacific coast,
his demise was possibly due to a head injury suffered during the flood
(Vela 2011: 60). If so, it was pride, stubbornness, and arrogance that
led to his final downfall.

And so passed the great Ahuitzotl. As *tlatoani*, he was nearly deified,
a godly delegate. Yet he was still mortal. In 1502 his imperial allies and
subjects deeply mourned his passing, as this larger-than-life ruler was
remembered as a generous and magisterial monarch. The supreme
lords of the land came to Tenochtitlan to offer him tributes and
remembrances, beginning with the rulers of Texcoco and Tlacopan
and followed by all the lords of the land. They arrived with slaves for
funerary sacrifices and luxuries for offerings, punctuating their visits
with lengthy and eloquent condolence speeches. There was "an enormous amount of gold jewelry, a variety of precious stones, a great pile
of feathers of many colors and worked in different fashions ... plates
and bowls, all of gold ... a great pile of mantles, exquisitely made in
different colors and designs" (Durán 1994: 385). The funerary
ceremonies followed customary royal rites: Ahuitzotl's corpse was
displayed at prearranged stations, regally adorned and religiously
consecrated, carried on a litter in a scripted procession, and deposited
at the base of Huitzilopochtli's shrine. He was cared for by priests,
honored by warriors, and remembered by kings, signifying his pivotal
roles as religious, military, and political leader of his people. Ahuitzotl
was then cremated, followed by a sacrifice of all the slaves the visiting

rulers had offered (numbering more than 200). Ahuitzotl's ashes and the bounty of riches offered for his memory were then buried together. These luxuries included his personal clothing and adornments, and possibly his personal slaves – Tizoc's had been slain for his funeral in 1486. As with earlier kings, Ahuitzotl's palatial chamber was cleaned out, making room for his successor.

## IN AND OUT OF TROUBLE

Growing up, Ahuitzotl had heard the story many times. It went like this: Iquehuacatzin was a son of an early Mexica *tlatoani*, Motecuhzoma Ilhuicamina. Iquehuacatzin did not inherit the throne from his father. Instead, that honor passed to Axayacatl, Motecuhzoma's grandson (and Ahuitzotl's brother). Iquehuacatzin was angry at losing what he considered his birthright, and in his rage appropriated the tribute of the rich city-state of Coayxtlahuacan (at least he was accused of this serious wrongdoing). For this, he was killed. This was not the only story recounting conflicts over power positions; Aztec and neighboring histories were rife with them.

Ahuitzotl came along at a time when there was a profusion of royal descendants. Rulers characteristically took many wives, and these wives produced many children. Several of Tenochtitlan's neighboring city-states were governed by Ahuitzol's royal relatives, and others resided in Tenochtitlan itself. His royal advisors were also his close relations. Any of these might claim rights, privileges, and titles, even the royal throne. One of Ahuitzotl's primary trouble spots was political competition. He coped with this through his overriding emphases on military expansion and exceeding generosity: he was successful and virtuous, powerful and popular. It would be difficult to dislodge him.

He was also his own worst enemy. His generosity and high living led to extravagant spending, a habit that had great potential to get him into economic difficulties. To compensate, his successful conquests filled and refilled his coffers with great wealth, and it was probably no accident that he targeted regions replete with precious and expensive goods such as tropical feathers, fine stones, shining gold, valuable jaguar skins, and the ever-desirable cacao. And he sometimes let pride and arrogance get the better of him. When his aqueduct failed and his people's homes were flooded and destroyed, he regained their affection by calling in workers from elsewhere to restore their homes and lives. It was a disaster, but they loved him. He was quite good at getting into trouble, and equally adept at getting out of it.

*I've lived through five kings, reflected Malinalli. The first Motecuhzoma was a legend, Axayacatl was a blur, and she only remembered Tizoc because her husband had died in his coronation war. But she recalled Ahuitzotl with affection. She had even received a gift of clothing from him after those incredible festivities at the Huey Teocalli. Now that was something! Ahuitzotl made everyone feel good, and strong, and secure. He was often away at war, but when he returned it was gifts, gifts, gifts; feasts, feasts, feasts; dancing, dancing, dancing. My how I love to dance, although I'm a bit too stiff to show well these days. And thinking of that, how hard it is now to bend down so low before this new Motecuhzoma – he seems so distant, and a bit frightening. I don't like him as much as Ahuitzotl. Ahh, the good old days – poctli, aiauitl, teiotl, mauiziotl: smoke, mist, fame, honor. Ahuitzotl's glory has not yet vanished, she thought.*

Malinalli seems to have forgotten Ahuitzotl's disastrous flood – a not uncommon case of selective memory. But her home had been rebuilt. To her, he was a good king not yet forgotten.

### RETROSPECT AND PROSPECT

When Hernando Cortés and his troops entered Tenochtitlan on November 8, 1519, they were ushered to Ahuitzotl's old palace. The Spanish captain was seated on the palace's dais by his host Motecuhzoma Xocoyotzin, symbolizing the respect the Aztec king held for his visitor. For his part, Motecuhzoma lived right around the corner in his own palace. Cortés and his band of conquistadores (and at least some of their allied Tlaxcallan warriors) continued to be housed in Ahuitzotl's palace while they were guests (and later kidnappers) of the Aztec ruler in 1519 and 1520; their accounts offer us some eyewitness descriptions of this "extremely strong" edifice. It was sufficiently spacious to "contain a native chieftain and some six hundred of his retinue" (Cortés 1928: 183), was built of stone and wood, and had more than one entrance. It featured the characteristic flat roof, large courtyard, a "richly worked" dais hung with cotton cloth, baths, and numerous "great halls" (Cortés 1928: 70, 74, 109, 112; Díaz del Castillo 1963: 218, 247). A sumptuous treasure was also stored there, which excited the Spaniards beyond measure (Tapia 1971: 579).

Regardless of Ahuitzotl's extensive refurbishing projects to his palace shortly before his death, his successor Motecuhzoma Xocoyotzin decided to build himself a new and grander palace. He chose a location to the southeast of the old palace, and directly east of the city's marketplace. A larger palace proclaimed the mightiness of Motecuhzoma and his political thrall, and this ruler was remarkable for undertaking grandiose projects to glorify himself and the image of his city. In addition to the usual amenities, this new palace housed a zoo and an aviary.

Ahuitzotl's magnificent palace was all but unrecognizable in 1554, when its Spanish colonial replacement was described by the Spaniard Cervantes de Salazar (1953: 40). He likened the building that had replaced the pre-Spanish palace to "another city." In his 1554 world, portions of the colonial building were used by diverse artisans and traders, from carpenters, blacksmiths, and locksmiths to bakers, candlemakers, and tailors. The greater portion of the building and its upper floors were occupied by the Royal Audiencia; most of the building's interior space had been transformed to conduct the intricate and unrelenting legal business of the colony. Today the space is occupied by the National Lottery. Ahuitzotl would have been truly perplexed, and would not have recognized his old coveted and comfortable seat of power.

## 2

## The Priest

*Ollin has just arrived in the temple storerooms to begin his planning for the big Toxcatl ceremony to be held in a few months. There are still two smaller monthly ceremonies to organize between now and then, but Toxcatl has long been the major public ceremony in the city of Texcoco. As the head priest of the cult of the high god Tezcatlipoca, Ollin wants to make sure this ceremony will be a memorable one. The Texcocan kings have been cozying up to their cousins in Tenochtitlan lately. Rumor has it that the Mexica king has asked his colleague in Texcoco to elevate the Mexica god Huitzilopochtli to a place on the main temple of Texcoco! At first Ollin couldn't believe that anyone would even suggest demoting Tezcatlipoca as one of the two temples on top of the main pyramid. But now it looks like this may actually happen, in spite of his lobbying of the kings and nobles.*

*Ollin is pleased to see Tlexico arrive, out of breath and carrying a big bag filled with the documents, ink, and paper of a scribe. Tlexico is a rising young apprentice priest with a bright future. Of course, he has to go out before dawn every morning to draw blood from his ear and make offerings of blood-spattered paper and incense in a secluded place. But, to his credit, Tlexico always manages to arrive for work on time, with his gear. He now pulls out some long, folded sheets of bark-cloth paper covered with glyphs. These list the supplies they used during the Toxcatl ceremony last year. Ollin suggests they multiply everything by two, to make a real splash this year. More incense to burn, in more censers, and more wood for the fires. More costumes for special ceremonies. More food for feasting, and more flags and musical instruments for the processions. And, of course, more sacrificial victims, both animals and humans.*

*Tlexico wonders if Ollin is not being excessive. We always put on a good show, he thinks, and it might be hard to double the scale of the five-day celebration. They go to inspect the storerooms. They seem full, but Ollin asks Tlexico to have a new apprentice priest take an inventory. It will require the king's permission, however, to get more sacrificial victims. Can they be sure to find extra people for all of the processions and offerings that fill the streets and temples for five days?*

*The elderly head priest for Tlaloc, Atapachtli, overhears them and wanders over. "Why do you people have to make such a show for every ceremony?" he asks. "The great Tlaloc has been worshipped for centuries, by a few priests and by the farmers. Tlaloc is the most important god, the one who brings the rain, yet he does not need throngs of musicians and dancers, and piles of fancy food, just so he will keep his pact with the people." Ollin and Tlexico are sick of Atapachtli's complaints. As the old Tlaloc priest hobbles away, Ollin muses, "If Tlaloc is so hugely important, why does he have only three priests in the city? We have more than ten for Tezcatlipoca." Tlexico nods his agreement, but then articulates the thing most worrying them both: "Yes, but how can Huitzilo-pochtli, a minor patron god of the Mexica people, think of muscling out our patron, here on the high temple of Texcoco?"*

*"That is why we need a Toxcatl ceremony that is elaborate and memorable: to hold up the honor of the top god. We need to do everything we can to make Tezcatlipoca – and his priesthood – look rich and powerful."*

Much as they tried, the strategy of the high priest and his apprentice was not successful. By the time Hernando Cortés arrived in central Mexico, the two temples atop the Texcoco main pyramid were dedicated to Tlaloc and Huitzilopochtli, and Tezcatlipoca was worshipped at a lesser temple elsewhere in the city.

## PRIESTS, DEITIES, AND TEMPLES

Priests were among the most powerful and feared groups in the Aztec world. But as seen in this vignette, they were by no means a unified group. Aztec religion was polytheistic, with its multitude of deities presiding over virtually everything in the celestial, terrestrial, and under worlds. Every god and goddess boasted their own temple, daily rites, prescheduled public ceremonies, retinue of priests (and sometimes priestesses), and lay support. Like Aztec society itself, deities and their servants were arranged hierarchically. Some deities – such as Quetzalcoatl, Tlaloc, Tezcatlipoca and the many fertility and mother goddesses known various as Coatlicue, Toci, and Tonantzin – were more important and omnipresent than others. Some rose to local importance as patrons of specific city-states, as Huitzilopochtli did for Tenochtitlan. The temples and priests of these deities also enjoyed particular prestige, distinction, and religious centrality, in line with the importance of their deities.

There were many types of priests in Aztec society, serving this vast variety of gods, cults, and temples. Most priests were specialized in

FIGURE 2.1. Priests traveling with the god Huitzilopochtli on the migration from Aztlan. *Codex Boturini* (Tira de la Peregrinación 1944); reproduced from Wikipedia Commons.

their dedication to specific gods; Ollin headed the Tezcatlipoca cult in Texcoco and Atapachtli was dedicated to Tlaloc. Others were in charge of specific ceremonies, while still other priests taught in the schools or supervised the books and records of the temples. Within each group of priests associated with a cult or temple, individuals formed a hierarchy. Most priests were called *tlamacazqui* ("giver of things" or "offering priest"). The highest priests, like Ollin, were called either *Quetzalcoatl* (named after the feathered serpent god, the patron deity of priests and learning), or *tlenamacac* ("fire seller" or "fire priest"). Lowest in the hierarchy were the novice priests like Tlexico; their title was *tlamacazton* ("little priest"). In Tenochtitlan, the supreme priests were called *Quetzalcoatl totec tlamacazqui* and *Quetzal-coatl tlaloc tlamacazqui*, the first associated with the temple and cult of Huitzilopochtli and the second serving Tlaloc. This hierarchy is a little murky (to us), since Tenochtitlan also had a priest called *Mexicatl Teohuatzin* who "was like the ruler of the [lesser] keepers of the gods indeed everywhere" (Sahagún 1950–1982: book 2: 206). Perhaps, as Richard Townsend (2009: 205) suggests, this priest was a ritual overseer and head of the *calmecac* school in Tenochtitlan.

Priests were important in Aztec society going back to the early migrations from Aztlan. Each group that trekked through the desert before finding a home in central Mexico was led by one or more priests, who carried an image of their patron god and other sacred items in a bundle on their back (Figure 2.1). Once these groups settled in central Mexico, kings asserted their power and built up dynasties and cities. Still, the priesthood as a group remained influential because it controlled the public ceremonies and temples in each city. Education of the elite, including future rulers, was also in the hands of priests. Importantly, politics and religion were viewed as a unified whole rather than as separate dimensions of life. As an example, the god Tezcatlipoca was associated with earthly royalty: god and king shared a common title (*Telpochtli*); lengthy Tezcatlipoca prayers were dedicated to rulers in "rites of kingship"; and the faces of deceased kings were covered with the mask depicting that god (Baquedano 2014). Intertwined in such ways, rulers depended on priests as much as priests depended on rulers.

Archaeologists have excavated temple-pyramids at many Aztec cities. In the major political capitals of the Early Aztec period (1100–1300 CE), such as Tenayuca and Teopanzolco, priests and architects designed a new style of temple: a single pyramid with two parallel stairways leading to twin temples at the top (Figure 2.2). After a century or two, however, the older Mesoamerican style of a single

FIGURE 2.2. A twin temple pyramid at Teopanzolco in Cuernavaca. Source: Michael E. Smith.

temple room reached by a single stairway regained popularity, and this became the dominant temple form in Aztec cities. When the Mexica founded Tenochtitlan in the year 1325, they resurrected the archaic twin-temple style. Soon this style spread to other major capitals, including Tlatelolco and Texcoco. At Tenochtitlan, one temple was dedicated to Tlaloc – the ancient Mesoamerican rain god – and one to Huitzilopochtli – the patron war god of the recently arrived Mexica people (Figure 2.3). To get a sense of size, the great temple of Tenochtitlan, at the end of its final building stage, rose 45 meters high and measured at its base 84.47 meters from north to south, and 77.24 meters from east to west (López Austin and López Luján 2017: 605, 617).

Unfortunately, archaeologists can rarely reconstruct the patron gods of most excavated Aztec temples, apart from those at Tenochtitlan, Texcoco, and Tlatelolco. While some writers assign Tlaloc and Huitzilopochtli to the Early Aztec twin temples, the latter god is unlikely, since these temples were built before the Mexicas arrived with their patron god to found Tenochtitlan. Similarly, we have little information about which gods were worshipped at most single-temple pyramids. However, there are occasional clues: at Calixtlahuaca, for example, archaeologists excavated offerings of ceramic vessels in the form of Tlaloc at one temple, so it is likely that the ancient rain god was worshipped there.

But there is one kind of Aztec pyramid whose patron god is known – the distinctive circular temple (Figure 2.4). Written sources confirm that the wind god Ehecatl – an avatar of Quetzalcoatl – presided over circular temples. Myths say Ehecatl preferred temples without sharp corners so that the wind could pass easily around the structure. Offerings of sculptures of Ehecatl at several of these round temples, throughout central Mexico, confirm the written accounts.

Temples were located in the center of cities and comprised the most prominent buildings in any city's ceremonial precinct. Indeed, the Great Temple of Tenochtitlan formed the *axis mundi* not only of the Mexica's capital city itself but of their entire known world, natural and supernatural. In these ceremonial districts, temples were accompanied by other religious structures; Tenochtitlan's precinct included not only several temples but also a *calmecac*, eagle (and probably jaguar) warrior chambers, a ballcourt, a *tzompantli* (skull rack), and

FIGURE 2.3. The sacred precinct of Tenochtitlan, with the Great Temple in the center. The left shrine was dedicated to Tlaloc and the right shrine to Huitzilopochtli. Source: Michael E. Smith, based on Sahagún (1905–1907: vol. 6: 39).

FIGURE 2.4. A circular temple dedicated to Quetzalcoatl at the city of Calixtlahuaca. Source: Michael E. Smith.

numerous shrines and buried offerings. This was downtown Tenochtitlan, and it was presided over by the priesthood.

The largest and most important temples would have required a team of priests. *Tlenamacac* like Ollin presided at ceremonies and offerings at the temples, *tlamacazqui* represented the god during processions and public ceremonies, and *tlamacazton* like Tlexico kept the temple clean and repaired and maintained the sacred fires. Priests were also needed as teachers and scribes at the schools found in the central precincts and in most neighborhoods, being entrusted with the education of noble boys and with the training and punishing of priestly novices. They also went to war on behalf of their ruler, some gaining renown and rewards, and priests provided supernatural validation on military expeditions by forming the army's front ranks (Chapter 10). And they were the intellectuals: they were literate (books were stored in temples) and engaged in astronomical observations (Berdan and Anawalt 1992: vol. 3: f. 63r).

There are a few scattered references to female priests, *cihuatlamacazque* ("female givers of things"), but scholars know next to nothing about them or their roles. Girls who were dedicated to the priesthood, or who entered that vocation of their own will, usually spent only a

FIGURE 2.5. Female curer in front of a platform decorated with skull and bones. Reproduced from *Códice Tudela* (1980: f. 50r).

short time as priestesses in the temples, spending much of that time producing elaborate cloth for the deities' images. With proper offerings and permissions, they were allowed to leave, marry, and start conventional families (Sahagún 1950–1982: book 2: 246). On the other hand, we know that female ritual specialists, such as curers and diviners, plied their trades in most communities (Figure 2.5). These women are usually not labeled "priestesses." It is likely that they worked independently, having little to do with the priests and temples of the state religion. They either worked out of their own homes or visited their patients at their homes. Their craft focused on issues of importance to families and households: health, fertility, and divination.

## LIFE IN THE TEMPLE AND SCHOOL

Priests lived in a *calmecac*. This was a large building with two main functions: a residence for priests and a school for sons of the nobility (plus the most talented or promising commoner children). The *calmecac* was where future leaders were trained, and running the school was an important duty for the priests in each city and town. Apparently girls attended their own *calmecac* (Alberti Manzanarez 1994). In the largest cities there were several *calmecac* tied to specific temples – it appears that the type of training in each such school was tailored to the orbits and demands of the deities of their associated temples. In general, learning focused on a wide range of subjects. In the words of Fray Diego Durán (1971: 293), priests at the *calmecac* taught

all the arts: military, religious, mechanical, and astrological, which gave them knowledge of the stars. For this they possessed large, beautiful books, painted in hieroglyphics, dealing with all these arts [and these books] were used for teaching.

Books were essential to the boys' education. They typically took the form of screen-folds (opening up accordion-style) or individual sheets of paper. They were not bound in the current sense of a book. We normally call them pictorial codices, and the Aztecs had four main types of these. Historical accounts traced the history of peoples and dynasties, recording topics from migrations to conquests and exalting the achievements of kings. Economic records kept track of people and taxes/tributes. Maps were used, at the very least, for planning wars far afield (Sahagún 1950–1982: book 8: ill. 76). The type of book most heavily used at the *calmecac* and the temple, however, were ritual books, used to keep track of the calendars, gods, and ceremonies. Priests were the most fully literate in their use of the ritual almanacs and other religious accounts. In the largely pictorial writing system of the Aztecs, only the key concepts, people, objects, and events were recorded. The writers and readers (mainly priests, scribes, or historians) would fill in the details with their personal knowledge. Most nobles were probably literate to some degree, whereas it is unlikely that many commoners would have understood the content of most Aztec books.

Beyond learning to read, students at the *calmecac* also received military training, learned about the heavenly bodies, performed myths and practiced rituals, and gained other advanced knowledge needed by nobles or specialized functionaries. Students were also taught proper behavior and comportment, including such virtues as self-control, discipline, obedience, and moderation in all things.

Most Aztec temples had an adjacent complex of storerooms and workrooms (where Ollin and Tlexico were talking in the vignette above), and one of the important temples in each city was located adjacent to the *calmecac*. Unfortunately, none of these compounds adjacent to a temple has been excavated by archaeologists, although one has been uncovered that was associated with the temple of Ehecatl-Quetzalcoatl in Tenochtitlan's great temple precinct (López Austin and López Luján 2017: 611). Having the temple, its workrooms, and the *calmecac* grouped together helped the priests, since they had to split their time between ceremonies, administration of the temple, and teaching and administrative duties at the *calmecac*. There were likely workers – in addition to the apprentices – who helped with many tasks.

How did the temple and *calmecac* support a large staff and obtain all the materials needed for offerings? In some cases the temple organization maintained estates that were farmed for the benefit of the priests, but usually they were supported by the king, using some of his tax and tribute income. They also were sustained by offerings, gifts, and alms from their temples' worshipers, "and even the ability to steal from the general public on certain ceremonial occasions" (Berdan 2014: 235). Gifts from the general populace to deities and priests were based on the idea of reciprocity – the anticipation of some return, such as a good harvest or commercial success, from offerings made (Berdan 2007: 258; López Austin and López Luján 2017).

In terms of ceremonies alone, Aztec priests had a wide range of duties and activities. Each month they supervised a series of events at the monthly ceremony that lasted several days. These included sacrifices and offerings at the temple, processions and dances in the streets, and sometimes going door-to-door to burn incense for individual families. Many state events – from funerals and royal accessions to temple dedications and triumphal returns of victorious armies – required priests to organize people and ceremonies. Priests also had regular temple and community responsibilities, such as incensing the temple's idol at sunrise, midday, sunset, and midnight, and blowing conch shells and playing flutes at midnight (Durán 1971: 119). They also spent a good deal of time performing their own private rituals, often bloodletting, carried out alone and in secret.

DAILY ROUND

The allocation of responsibilities and duties in the priestly world was based on age, gender, experience, rank, and inclination. While all boys were taught the arts of war as well as more erudite skills, some were found to be more proficient in one arena than in the other. So, Diego Durán (1971: 112–113) tells us that some boys were sent to war to become warriors while others remained at temple and *calmecac* to pursue more strictly religious matters.

In the *calmecac*, the first ones to rise – long before dawn – were the novices like Tlexico. On most mornings, they gathered up their "auto-sacrifice" kit and headed out to find a quiet and secluded place to worship the gods. "Autosacrifice" is the term we give to the ritual letting of one's own blood as a form of worship. The most important items in a novice's kit were several maguey thorns, often still attached to long strands of fiber from the maguey leaves. These thorns pierced the flesh – of the earlobe, the thigh, the tongue, or other fleshy and sensitive areas – so that blood would flow. This practice was embedded in Aztec mythology: the gods themselves had offered their own blood to create and help humanity. In one of these myths, human beings were created by Quetzalcoatl when he let his own blood into a pile of powder from ground-up bones of a former race of people.

The novice would let his blood flow, either into a bowl or directly onto a piece of bark paper or maguey leaf. Later, the paper or maguey leaf would be burned as an offering to the gods. The final item in a novice's autosacrifice kit was a small bundle of straw that was used to store the bloody maguey thorns. These items were probably carried in a small basket or bag. When a novice returned from his daily blood offering, his regular temple duties began. He would sweep to keep the temple area clean, make sure the fires in the large braziers were kept alive all day, and serve at the beck and call of the senior priests. Someone – like Tlexico – had to help keep the temple's supplies in order, make sure students were attending the *calmecac*, and carry out countless other small duties.

The regular priests spent most of their "down time" – the time when there were no ceremonies going on – in the storerooms and workrooms of the temple and at the *calmecac*. There was less down time than one might expect. Aside from their endless rounds of daily offerings, prayers, penance, playing drums, and marking time with the blowing of conch shells and playing of flutes, more experienced priests also spent time observing the heavens (Figure 2.6) and advising rulers. This was a world where politics and religion were tightly

FIGURE 2.6. Priest observing the heavens. Reproduced from Berdan and Anawalt (1992: vol. 4: f. 63r), with permission.

interwoven, where priests could be warriors and rulers could perform religious sacrifices.

Priests also helped plan and supervise construction work on the temples. In line with ancient Mesoamerican practices, the Aztecs enlarged their temples regularly. Each new ruler "made a statement" by improving the temples of his predecessors, and key state and religious commemorations often required a rebuilt temple. The work required that the old chamber walls and roof on top of the pyramid be torn down, and then a new outer "layer" of stone was added to the outside of the pyramid, with nice cut stones as a veneer on the exterior, laid over a fill of construction rubble, trash, and soil. A new stairway had to be installed, and, finally, the sacred chamber on top was rebuilt. With more than twenty temples in the city of Texcoco, it must have seemed that there was always some construction going on. Indeed, some of the priests may have served more as architects and general contractors than as teachers or ritual masters.

As if this were not enough, priests were also charged with the all-important calendrical cycle of ceremonies. The priests were masters of tracking and recording time, and in this, as in their other duties, they were precise, meticulous, and knowledgeable. The Aztecs and their neighbors ordered their lives around two intertwined calendars: a 365-day agricultural calendar (*xiuhpohualli*) composed of eighteen months of twenty days each (with a five-day dangerous period at the end), and a 260-day ritual calendar (*tonalpohualli*) made up of twenty day names multiplied by the numbers 1–13. Readers of this latter horoscope-style calendar named a baby, divined a person's fate, or even advised whether or not a ruler should go to war (see Chapter 7). López Austin and López Luján (2017: 612–613) suggest that this ritual calendar operated primarily in more private spheres of life, while the 365-day calendar ordered the world of public ceremonies and state religion.

In this public world, each month featured its own patron deity, specially tailored ceremonies, and retinue of responsible priests. Several days of each twenty-day month were taken up with the appropriate monthly ceremonies. The Spanish chroniclers wrote extended descriptions of these complex affairs, each of which involved activities at the temples, in the plaza, around town, and even in the homes of all or most of the people. Each priest would be busy all day during these extended celebrations. He might alternate between supervising a ceremonial dance in the plaza (getting the musicians set up, making sure all participants had on the correct clothing, helping different groups of dancers get their start into the mix, and handling any problems that come up); helping get the dishes, food, incense, and seating plan organized for a big feast of the nobles; sending out the novices with incense to make sure they are able to visit every house in the neighborhood; and organizing the participants in a sacrifice (whether a human sacrifice or an offering of animals) at the temple.

Scholars today have no idea whether Aztec priests like Ollin were bothered by the fact that most people would have feared them. There was probably a basic wariness around someone who controlled mysterious and powerful forces. Possibly the fact that priests did not wash their hair – which was thick and matted with dried blood from bloodletting – didn't increase their appeal (people in Aztec society generally valued and practiced cleanliness). But even more to the point, one of the many duties of some priests was to perform human sacrifices which occurred at most temples on predictable schedules. Most victims were members of specific categories, particularly enemy soldiers captured in battle and a special class of victims called "bathed slaves" who were purchased at the market to be sacrificed (see Chapters 4 and 10).

LIFE CYCLE

Infants, boys and girls, could be dedicated to the priesthood by their parents. The *Codex Mendoza* (Berdan and Anawalt 1992: vol. 4: f. 57r) tells us that the parents of an infant took their child to the *calmecac* for that dedication, carrying with them gifts of clothing and food for the priests. This took place twenty days after the child's birth. These parental vows apparently could be changed later on – at age fifteen, or perhaps earlier, it could be determined that a boy would enter either the *calmecac* or the *telpochcalli*, the local military school. A girl could enter temple service when "she was a maiden," and apparently she had some choice in the matter (Sahagún 1950–1982: book 2: 246). In the meantime, the children were raised by their parents in expected skills, attitudes, morals, and perhaps a specialized trade. If they failed to learn competently and properly, severe punishments were meted out – a preamble to the harsh discipline they would endure when (and if) they entered the priestly school.

It appears that not all children were dedicated to the priesthood according to the same criteria. Those dedicated to Huitzilopochtli came from specific residential districts, while those sent to serve Tezcatlipoca were offered by their parents, especially if the children were ill (Olivier 2003: 183). Perhaps other temple institutions had their own specific criteria as well.

Even if a child was vowed to a priestly life, there was no guarantee that he or she would in fact enter that service. A girl would go "purely of her own will," and if she did, it was only a brief moment in her life on her road to marriage, raising a family, and managing a household (Sahagún 1950–1982: book 2: 246). Our information on priestesses is limited, but it is possible that they were dedicated to the service of goddesses: we do know that offering priestesses served the goddess Xilonen and participated in this goddess's hallmark ceremony during the month of Huey Tecuilhuitl (Sahagún 1950–1982: book 2: 104).

Boys entering the *calmecac* tended to have longer priestly careers than girls. It has already been mentioned that the education and duties of boys in the *calmecac* were determined by age, experience, rank, and inclination. Social class also played a part: while apparently boys from any social rank could be dedicated to a priestly life, "the sons of monarchs and great men were always more highly respected and carefully attended" (Durán 1971: 112).

From the moment the boys entered the school, they were called "offering priests," but as novices they basically did as they were told: mostly menial duties such as sweeping, carrying wood, cutting maguey spines, and dissolving black coloring used by the priests to smear on their bodies. As the boy gained experience he was charged with carrying fir branches and guarding the nighttime fires. Both neophyte and more experienced boys blew the shell trumpets, an important duty that marked time and inaugurated special events. They were also taught proper comportment, obedience, and moderation. Much of this was instilled in them through rather harsh living conditions: "They were not permitted to sleep comfortably and also ate poorly," with the idea that they would become strong through deprivation (Durán 1971: 112).

Also, if boys committed themselves to the priesthood they allowed their hair to grow very long and covered their bodies (hair included) with a black soot. Durán (1971: 114) offers detailed descriptions of these bodily adornments: some wore braids, he says, and some adorned their braids with white ribbons. If the priests performed sacrifices, the tangled, matted hair also became spattered with blood, as observed by the conquistador Bernal Díaz del Castillo in Cempoala (1963: 123–124). A priest could cut his hair only in old age upon retirement.

Not all boys found the priesthood to their liking. In the perform-ance of their duties, some boys were found to be negligent, and their behavior rebellious and incorrigible (Figure 2.7). Perhaps they were discovered having "excessive relations" with a woman (Berdan and Anawalt 1992: vol. 3: ff. 61v–63r). Punishments were severe in these cases, mirroring the kinds of punishments dealt children by their own fathers: multiple piercings with maguey spines or pine needles.

This was a complex realm of life, populated with numerous gods and goddesses, and even more temples dedicated to those deities. All of this required a specialized retinue of priests trained and dedicated to these godly needs. So the exact education and duties attached to

FIGURE 2.7. Novice priest being punished. Reproduced from Berdan and Anawalt (1992: vol. 4: f. 62r), with permission.

individual temples and *calmecac* would have required some "on the job training," tailoring priestly behaviors to the realms and demands of each specific deity. All priests, even if on the same rung of the priestly ladder, engaged in specifically designed and targeted religious activities. There was not only hierarchy, but also specialization in the priestly world.

Within this varied religious world, a neophyte might climb the priestly hierarchy, taking advantage of opportunities along two parallel routes. The route an individual took as he moved through his priestly life cycle was based primarily on his inclination (say, warfare or singing or deity image care), and his success depended largely on hard work, dedication, and luck.

It was essentially a two-track system. One track led to a career as a priest-warrior who not only would accompany troops on the march (see Chapter 10), but could also gain renown and rewards in their own right by capturing enemy warriors in battle (Figure 2.8). These rewards included "honorable titles and heraldic arms and devices" (Berdan and Anawalt 1992: vol. 3: f. 64v), similar to those granted to

FIGURE 2.8. Priests gaining rewards as warriors by capturing an enemy soldier. Reproduced from Berdan and Anawalt (1992: vol. 4: f. 65r), with permission.

secular warriors who exhibited extraordinary bravery on the battle-field. These priests were still "offering priests," but were graded and honored in ceremonies according to the number of captives they had taken (Sahagún 1950–1982: book 2: 79).

A second track for the neophyte involved a more stationary life in a temple: first as an offering priest, then fire priest, then perhaps an even higher position. As he climbed this hierarchy, he was given more and more responsibility over more and more important arenas in caring for the deities, temples, and ceremonies. Durán (1971: 114) suggests that the aspiring youth rose to a "higher institution" with different teachers, suggesting two different levels of schools and cur-ricula. In one likely scenario, the aspiring priest moves from carrying firewood, decorative boughs, and maguey spines to playing drums and singing, to tending to godly images in their sanctuaries. With increased experience, he may regularly incense the godly idols, assemble and account for the vast stores of ceremonial paraphernalia, attend to the writing and reading of books, organize and announce a major public ceremony, oversee temple construction or repairs, teach in his *calmecac*, and even advise his ruler. He also becomes more and more central in the observance of ceremonies by fasting, feasting, dancing, singing, censing, and perhaps even performing human sacrifices.

People who successfully climbed the priestly hierarchy endured considerable hardships and deprivations, but also reaped considerable rewards. The priest-warrior, with enemy captures, gained public renown and symbolic regalia as proof of his achievements on behalf of the state and the gods. The temple priest likewise enjoyed special perquisites: the opportunity to be center stage on defined ritual occasions (if he liked that sort of thing), the ability to influence the next generation of nobles (some of them to become priests themselves) through control over education, the capacity to potentially sway rulers in their political decisions, and the several occasions on which he could adorn himself with the elaborate and exquisite adornments of the gods themselves, including fine clothing and gold (Baquedano 2014).

## IN AND OUT OF TROUBLE

*The ceremony of Toxcatl is fast approaching; it will begin in just a week (five days). The main sacrificial victim – an unblemished youth captured in battle over a year ago – seems ready. In accordance with tradition, he has been treated to a life of luxury for the past year. He seems to have accepted his fate, although who knows for sure whether sacrificial victims really believed in their mission? The king approved their plan to expand the scope of the celebrations this year, and the food and other paraphernalia are just about ready. But the expanded ceremony will require an additional four sacrificial victims, and Ollin does not have them at hand. The slave markets have been almost bare over the past few months. This could be a real disaster. It could undo all the careful preparations the Texcoco priests have been making in order to hold on to their traditional high god at the main temple.*

*We can always run over to the Azcapotzalco market to buy the needed slaves to sacrifice, Ollin thinks. But there was not enough time in one week to prepare the victims. Each victim had specific pre-sacrifice activities to carry out, and it was now too late to begin the sequence of preparation. On the one hand, this meant that the full required set of actions could not be carried out, potentially limiting the efficacy or success of the sacrifice. Ollin was not too bothered by that; they could do some quick substitute rites and no one would ever know. He was sure the gods would be fine with that. But, on the other hand, the victims needed time to learn their parts in the scripted ritual. What if one of the victims forgot his lines, or did not walk in the correct choreographed manner? Everyone – including the king and all the nobles – would be watching. Everything had to be perfect.*

*Just then, one of the novices came running up to Ollin, out of breath. "Tlexico has just arrived at the edge of town with four sacrificial victims from Huexotla! He will wait till darkness to bring them down to the temple. They are trained victims, ready to go, not some batch of random slaves from the market! Some kind of gift from the head priest in Huexotla." Well, thought Ollin, Tlexico has saved my skin again! I knew he was related somehow to the chief priest of the Ehecatl temple in Huexotla. That evening, after dark, Tlexico arrived with his trophies. "These four guys were part of a big group already training for a sacrifice in Huexotla. Unlike us, their king did not allow an expanded ceremony this year. They actually had too many victims!" It turns out that Tlexico was a cousin of the Huexotla priest, and he had heard about the extra victims by chance through a family member. He had gone running off to Huexotla, six kilometers' distant, before he had a chance to tell Ollin what he was doing.*

*If Ollin and Tlexico were lucky, the kings of Texcoco and Huexotla (a vassal state under the king of Texcoco) would never hear about this "loan" of sacrificial victims. The priests liked to keep their affairs private, since meddling by palace bureaucrats could cause all sorts of problems. But now Ollin really owed a big favor to the priests in Huexotla. Even if it was a small city, with a weak king and small temples, the people of Huexotla were proud and often resented their Texcocan neighbors. Before heading off to catch a little sleep, Ollin said one more thing to Tlexico: "As soon as the festivities of Toxcatl are done, remind me to start thinking about how we are going to pay back our colleagues in Huexotla. And, thank you for your initiative today! You have a bright future ahead of you."*

Fate and some quick thinking saved Ollin that day. But other worries haunted him daily. His was not a stress-free job. With so many important deities and temples, priests were always competing with one another and vying for the ear of their ruler for resources and the most prestigious boons and theatrical moments. Resources for proper temple and idol appearances, flamboyant ceremonial enactments, and just daily sustenance needed to be constantly renewed. For these, the priests depended on the largesse of their ruler and the commitment and generosity of their worshippers, both potentially serendipitous. And priests, while they served the gods, were nonetheless human. With extremely high expectations for perfection, the possibility of errors, with their dire consequences, always hung over them.

## RETROSPECT AND PROSPECT

When the Mexica established their city of Tenochtitlan in 1325, towns and cities throughout central Mexico featured tall and impressive temples as their supreme motif. A colorful array of gods and goddesses, impressive temples, varied priestly assemblages, and a schedule of flamboyant ceremonies was well entrenched. The Mexica arrived with their own religious beliefs, ritual behaviors, and retinue of priests, meshing these with the vibrant and diverse religious world they encountered. In this eclectic and syncretic environment, the Mexica celebrated the apex of their greatest temple, their *axis mundi*, with their own patron war god Huitzilopochtli and the long-standing Mesoamerican rain god Tlaloc, recognizing war and agricultural fertility as central to their way of life.

Less than two decades after Ollin's successful Toxcatl ceremony, priests within the Aztec thrall were faced with unimaginable trauma – the arrival of people from across the sea who did not share their religious beliefs and practices. But even more, these strangers began almost immediately to disrespect their godly idols and disrupt their ceremonies, even before they had conquered them. On more than one occasion, the priests watched in horror, fear, sorrow, and anger as the Spaniards toppled their gods from their sacred sanctuaries atop lofty pyramids, and replaced them with another, totally alien, statue.

The priests were among the first casualties of the Spanish conquest. Of all the native occupational groups, the priests appear to have disappeared the most rapidly and completely, although some may have survived in the colonial world, conceptually transformed as *tlamatinime*, or "wise men," a category of people understood in the Spanish world view (Lee 2017). Most other occupations still appear in the colonial world: merchants continued to trade merchandise, potters made pots, women wove cloth, masons built buildings, porters carried loads, and featherworkers continued to make feathered masterpieces, albeit with Christian motifs. Even the local aristocracy retained many rights and resources, at least for a time. But not the priests – they were quickly replaced by a new priesthood, although that act did not erase many native beliefs and practices (see the Epilogue).

# 3

## The Featherworker

*The day dawned clear, calm, and cool. Chimalchiuhqui thought about his plans for the day. It will be a good opportunity to continue work on the shields he had underway, as he had hoped. He had suffered delays in obtaining the best feathers from his merchant supplier, Quetzalhua. And now, he could not pay Quetzalhua until he sold his shields in the market. And he could not make his shields without the right feathers. He was tired of this same problem, over and over again. Why had he not accepted the offer to work in Ahuitzotl's palace?*

*At the same time, Centzon was fidgeting. He was behind schedule, and that was unacceptable. He was relieved that the day promised to be sunny and the air still; he should be able to make good progress. The feast of Huitzilopochtli was just a few days away, and he was responsible for the god's feathered array. And it needed to be perfect. To work fast but carefully at the same time. Didn't Ahuitzotl understand? Why had he ever agreed to work in the palace?*

These two accomplished featherworkers plied their exacting craft in the sister cities of Tlatelolco and Tenochtitlan. They both fashioned elegant feathered attire and adornments for exalted purposes, and they both relied on the same traditions and used the same technologies and procedures. Yet they worked in different settings, and those settings prompted important differences in their lives and their creations.

### LUXURIES OR NECESSITIES?

Objects fashioned of feathers included elaborate textiles (especially cloaks, tunics, and decorative hangings), warrior costumes, back

FIGURE 3.1. High-ranking nobles with feathered devices. Reproduced from
Berdan and Anawalt (1992: vol. 4: f. 67r), with permission.

devices, headdresses, banners, fans, shields, and other miscellaneous
adornments (Figure 3.1). Professional featherworkers fashioned this
glamorous feathered finery for gods, rulers, nobles, priests, and warriors, bedecking them all in exquisite, shimmering arrays. They were
the artisans who made the religious processions glimmer as the participants strode and danced along the streets. Their creations provided warriors an edge on the battlefield as they confronted their
enemies in astounding, sometimes frightful feathered devices. They
supplied rulers with their elegant array, and the rulers' high-born
guests with exquisite presents worthy of their station in life. They
worked with materials that exuded radiance, luminosity, and movement (Ségota 2015). In short, fancy, shimmering featherwork ended
up in the hands and houses of the aristocracy, decorated the sanctuaries and idols of the many deities, and announced the achievements
of courageous warriors. In such intimidating settings and on such
august gods and mortals, these objects were laden with social, political
and religious significance. They unambiguously proclaimed power
and wealth in Aztec society and throughout Mesoamerica.

Featherworkers needed to develop and maintain profitable relations with their consumers, the elite of the Aztec world. Unlike most
primary producers and many artisans, the featherworkers rarely used

FIGURE 3.2. Macuil ocelotl, a featherworker god. Sahagún (1950–1982: book 9: fig. 71). Firenze, Biblioteca Medicea Laurenziana. All rights reserved. Further reproduction in any print or digital format is forbidden.

their own creations; they were almost all distributed to persons other than themselves. The seven major featherworker deities were decked out with feather adornments and feathered clothing (Figure 3.2). It was said all these deities were arrayed with long green quetzal feathers, and that two of them (the goddesses Xiuhtlati and Xilo) wore tunics covered with many different colored feathers. These goddesses also carried feathered fans, bore feathered headdresses, and wore sandals "sprinkled with divers precious feathers" (Sahagún 1950–1982: book 9: 85). But this was about the extent of the use of feathered works by the featherworkers themselves.

On the other hand, there was an extensive and continuous demand for exquisite featherwork by the Aztec aristocracy. Much of the high demand for featherwork was a response to the demographics and the politics of the Late Postclassic Mesoamerican world. The population of central Mexico was at an all-time high, the numbers of nobles were increasing at an increasing rate, and these nobles were extremely competitive. In part they fought on the open battlefield, but they also fought with image and finery to impress their allies and intimidate their enemies. Dressing well, bedecked with expensive and shimmering featherwork, was a necessity for ambitious and competitive nobles. Their exquisite adornments may look like luxuries, and today we surely view them as such. Yet any self-respecting Aztec noble, man or woman (and deity for that matter), considered them necessities and could not live and thrive without them. Flamboyance was the order of the day, and dazzling displays translated into political power. The only way to compete successfully in this contentious and often violent field was to look the part.

Much demand for feathered objects responded to more or less regularly scheduled events, both religious and political. It cannot be overemphasized that this was a society where religion and politics were tightly intertwined, not divided into separate realms of life. Events that were overtly religious and dedicated to the gods often carried political overtones, and political occasions were frequently infused with religious meaning, symbolism, and legitimacy. These were theatrical and ostentatious events, and displays of every conceivable luxury heightened their impact.

Religious events conformed to specific calendrical dates. The featherworkers along with other artisans would have known which ceremonies were upcoming, and would have produced the specific godly and ritual arrays as needed. We read that some of the palace artisans fashioned the accoutrements of Huitzilopochtli, but manufacture of the attire of the other deities and their processional accompaniments might have fallen to the more independent featherworkers. Politically inspired events requiring feathered objects and array tended to be sporadic rather than continuous; in contrast to the religious ceremonies, these often occurred under less precise schedules. Rituals surrounding the death of a ruler, a grand feast sealing an alliance with other rulers, the return of an army from a lengthy but successful expedition – all of these required the handiwork of the featherworkers who had to be forewarned, methodically prepared, and, as was always expected, skilled and efficient workers.

The featherworkers present the appearance of exclusivity: they lived in their own *calpolli* (neighborhood) or in palace housing, revered their own patron deities, jealously guarded their specialized skills, and most surely maintained treasured trade secrets within the walls of their own households. Yet their lives were far from insular, as they required mutually beneficial and dependable relations with professional merchants, small-scale vendors, elite consumers, and a bevy of other specialists. These relations were integral to their ability to maintain their prestigious profession and elevated lifestyle, whether they worked in palace or *calpolli*.

## PALACE AND *CALPOLLI*

Featherworking was a highly skilled and complex craft specialization, so it should come as no surprise that the efforts of these elite artisans were divided up to serve specific purposes within the general featherworking enterprise. There were at least three categories of featherworkers, identified by the contexts in which they lived and labored and by the types of objects they manufactured. Two of them worked for royal patrons, the third lived in specific *calpolli* and were organized internally in a manner comparable to some Medieval European guilds.

## In the Palace

Some accomplished featherworkers, like Centzon ("400" or "Plenty"), were able to find relatively secure niches in the palaces of rulers (and perhaps other nobles). We do not know how these individuals were selected for these elite jobs. Were they sought and identified by palace officials? Did they offer themselves to royal service, carrying with them samples of their work as "portfolios"? Or were they the sons or other close relatives of featherworkers already or previously employed in the palace, naturally falling into the job if they were qualified? Whatever their path to the palace, these featherworkers must have been among the city-state's most accomplished. In Tenochtitlan at least, some of them fashioned the opulent array of the Mexica patron god Huitzilopochtli, while others manufactured the ruler's exquisite feathered clothing and adornments as well as gifts for his powerful

FIGURE 3.3. The ruler's military array. Sahagún (1950–1982: book 8: fig. 77). Firenze, Biblioteca Medicea Laurenziana.

guests (Figure 3.3). Their creations had to be of the very highest quality. Centzon was one such qualified artisan. After all, his name identifies him as one who has "achieved four hundred," that is, one who has grown to be a skilled master of his craft (Sahagún 1950–1982: book 6: 224).

Those known as *tecpan amanteca* ("palace featherworkers") were highly skilled artisans responsible for fashioning the feathered attire of the god Huitzilopochtli, constructed of quetzal, lovely cotinga, and hummingbird feathers (Sahagún 1950–1982: book 9: 91). Quetzal feathers flowed from Huitzilopochtli's headdress, his feathered cape was embellished with gold, and his shield featured five tufts of white feathers and a border of yellow feathers (Durán 1971: 73 and plate 3). The *tecpan amanteca* also manufactured splendid feathered objects that were bestowed on royal guests as gifts. Among these may well have been the "shields with their insignia done in fine featherwork" presented by Motecuhzoma Xocoyotzin to enemy rulers invited to his coronation, and also probably the "three loads of cloaks of rich feather work" presented by that same Mexica ruler to each of Hernando Cortés's captains (Díaz del Castillo 1963: 221; Durán 1994: 407). The hall in Motecuhzoma's palace where his royal guests were received was elaborately decorated with paintings as well as "magnificent shields hanging on the walls, and splendid featherwork" (Durán 1994: 405). It is probable that these works of art were created by palace-sponsored artisans.

Producing these various adornments and decorations would have required a diversity of featherworking skills: weaving feathered textiles, fashioning mosaics, and tying feathers into flowing adornments. There is very little documentation about how these artisans were organized for production, so we cannot say with any assurance whether a single household of featherworkers produced all of these types of objects, or whether there was specialization among households (with some making mosaics, others tying, and others producing the textiles). We suspect that any featherworking household was capable of producing all of these types of featherwork. Some extant pieces, such as the so-called Motecuhzoma's headdress and the coyote shield (both housed in Vienna), combine mosaic and tying techniques (Haag et al. 2012; Riedler 2015).

At least by the time of Motecuhzoma Xocoyotzin (r. 1502–1520), featherworkers were physically settled, or at least worked, at or near the royal palace. There must have been several of these elite artisans in order to keep up with the extensive ritual and royal demands emanating from that regal setting. The ruler provided these privileged artisans with a house of their own (*centetl calli*: "one house"). What was this "one house" like? Were all the featherworking artisans housed in a single dwelling, perhaps residing in rooms surrounding a single patio workspace where they could share resources and cooperate in producing individual objects? Or was each artisan family housed in its own dwelling in or near the palace? Were these units composed of complete households with husbands, wives, and children (as we suspect), or did the artisans work there and walk home at the end of the work day? And how do we interpret the statement that the featherworkers of "Tenochtitlan and Tlatelolco mingled with one another" (Sahagún 1950–1982: book 9: 91)?

Perhaps what is meant is the *totocalli* ("bird house"), a palace aviary full of all manner of captive birds, local and exotic. This area included designated workspaces not only for featherworkers but also for goldsmiths, painters/scribes, stone-cutters, stone mosaic-makers, and wood carvers (Sahagún 1950–1982: book 8: 45). Since, for instance, featherworkers relied on painters, used wood for backings, and often incorporated gold and fine stones in their mosaics, the close proximity of all these artisans made for a high level of efficiency, an ease of cooperation, and a degree of administrative oversight that would have been hard to match in any other setting. The presence of administrative oversight was especially meaningful here, where highly specific symbolic adornments with strong political and religious overtones were required.

This was not all the palace had to offer. It also housed *calpixcan amanteca* ("tribute featherworkers" or "mayordomo's featherworkers") who created the finery of the ruler when he danced. These artisans were especially adept and diversified, since they needed to produce quetzal feather headdresses, fans, banners (some embellished with gold), feather armbands with gold, and even headdresses of roseate spoonbill and quetzal feathers with gold attachments (Sahagún 1950–1982: book 8: 27–28). As their name suggests, these featherworkers had access to Motecuhzoma's ample storehouse – they could use materials acquired through tribute or other royal means, and the finery they produced belonged directly to the ruler and was stored and guarded in his coffers (Sahagún 1950–1982: book 9: 91). Nothing more is said about these artisans, but it is likely that their housing, labor arrangements, and range of skills resembled those of their palatial colleagues, the *tecpan amanteca* (who undoubtedly also drew on the ruler's abundant storehouse).

At least some of the feathered textiles produced in the royal palace may have been woven by noble women residing in the palace, perhaps in addition to the female featherworkers themselves. Women, nobles and commoners, were the weavers in Aztec society, and it stands to reason that they could also be engaged in this related activity. "Chieftains' daughters" and "daughters of other dignitaries" housed close to the Great Temple in Tenochtitlan wore gorgeous robes "entirely of featherwork." Women residing in Motecuhzoma's palace are specifically mentioned as producing "a huge quantity of fine robes with very elaborate feather designs" (Díaz del Castillo 1963: 230). These women may have woven their own garments, as Sahagún (1950–1982: book 8: 49) speaks of women spinning feathers all the while entertained by hunchbacks and dwarfs who sang and played music for them. It is difficult to envision commoner women being so entertained.

## In the *Calpolli*

Other luxury featherworkers, *calla amanteca* ("house featherworkers"), worked more independently in specialized neighborhoods where they manufactured feathered objects and adornments for sale in the marketplaces. These exclusive, specialized *calpolli* resembled rather closely the craft guilds of Medieval Europe. In that classic case, craft guilds developed as exclusive, specialized organizations largely to guarantee their own privileges and rights: they were highly protective and supportive of their own members. In that insular environment they were able to preserve trade secrets and maintain exclusive outside contacts. At the same time, they prevented others from encroaching on their manufacturing monopolies. They trained their own, assuring high standards and preventing poor workmanship. The Medieval craft guilds typically exhibited distinct hierarchies based largely on the attainment of skills and adherence to the guild's moral codes; an individual could rise from apprentice to journeyman and ultimately to master craftsman within the association. While there was considerable variation in these organizations throughout Medieval Europe, their members often established favorable relations with their host cities, sometimes becoming prominent and influential on the local political scene. In short, they diligently oversaw and protected their own interests, internal and external. This all sounds very advantageous to the artisan, yet the flip side of these arrangements was that each artisan was subject to the strict controls, rules, and restrictions of the guild and its leaders (Dyer 2002; Wood 2002).

It is likely that the Aztecs had craft associations rather like these: the featherworkers of Aztec Mexico fit within the wide range of associations called guilds during the long span of the Middle Ages in Europe. It is also probable that such arrangements were in force well before Aztec times. Admittedly, we do not know if such organizations applied to all artisans, or if all artisans of a particular craft *had* to be members of such associations. Yet for complicated and capital-intensive luxury crafts such as featherworking, goldworking, and fine stoneworking there were definite advantages to guild-type organizations. These artisans lived apart from others in exclusive neighborhoods or palaces, their insular living arrangements allowing them to guard and preserve their trade secrets. They trained and rewarded their own members, could maintain high and consistent standards, could pool capital and labor, and were capable of establishing advantageous outside contacts with merchant suppliers, noble consumers, and ancillary specialists such as painters/scribes and goldworkers (Berdan 2014: 100–102). They could therefore negotiate profitable and sustained relationships for acquiring raw materials and disseminating their finished objects. They also carried a certain amount of political clout as producers of symbolically important adornments and were capable of gaining the favor of powerful personages, even royalty. These sorts of arrangements were paralleled by the professional merchants (*pochteca*), whose collective importance eclipsed that of the featherworkers and other luxury artisans (see Chapter 4).

## DAILY ROUND IN THE WORKSHOP

Whether residing in palace or *calpolli*, the featherworkers undertook their daily round of work and other activities primarily within their household settings. Their place of residence was also their workplace.

It is unfortunate that, as yet, no actual Aztec featherworking workshop has been discovered. Therefore, this projected reconstruction of a workshop and its daily activities relies on ethnohistoric documentation and experimentation with featherworking techniques, combined with understandings of Aztec cultural priorities and some assumptions of practicalities.

Each household in the Aztec world conformed to seasonal and ritual rhythms, yet each developed its own pace and personality with respect to its production strategies. We have seen that the emperor and the priest each responded to different cultural, social, political, and religious demands and schedules; later, we will see the merchant, farmer, and slave adjusting their daily lives to their individual and collective goals and needs. Here, the featherworkers had their own adjustments to make.

FIGURE 3.4. Featherworker working in a residential patio. Sahagún (1950–1982: book 9: fig. 96). Firenze, Biblioteca Medicea Laurenziana.

   The featherworkers' domestic setting probably resembled other urban house sites: compounds with more than one room facing an enclosed patio. Most of the featherworking tasks would have taken place on the patio, as seen in the images from the later-sixteenth century *Florentine Codex* (Figure 3.4), so this patio workspace may well have been larger than that found in the usual urban house site. Working outside was not just convenient, but probably imperative: fires were needed, some work was carried out on sizable maguey leaves and wooden supports, and all of the tasks greatly benefited from working in natural outdoor lighting. After all, most of these exquisite objects would be carried in processions, displayed at temples and palaces, or worn at festive events and on the battlefield, primarily outdoor settings. This meticulous craft required a keen eye for color and luminescence, and the objects needed to be fashioned in the same light and other conditions in which they would be exhibited and admired. This requirement, however, inhibited featherworking on windy and rainy days, as such conditions would disperse the delicate feathers and interrupt the artisans' carefully orchestrated procedures.

Featherworkers used three basic techniques to produce their ornate objects: (1) they tied feathers together into long, flowing adornments such as headdresses, back devices, feathered armbands, banners, and fans; (2) they glued small feathers to firm backings to produce intricate mosaics on objects such as shields; and (3) they spun and wove tiny feathers into textiles, producing resplendent clothing, hangings, and warrior costumes. The feathers used in these several creations ranged from ordinary feathers of turkeys, ducks, grackles, and local water birds, to rich feathers of macaws, lovely cotingas, roseate spoonbills, hummingbirds, various parrots, and especially the highly esteemed quetzal birds. Specific types of feathers were applied to particular objects: long plumes were tied into banners, headdresses, and other flowing adornments; thousands of tiny breast, back, and neck feathers were layered and glued into mosaics; and very tiny feathers, including the white down of eagles, were applied to the manufacture of feathered textiles.

Acquisition of materials and tools was an ever-present concern, and featherworkers established sustained and predictable relations with others in order to acquire feathers and other tools of their trade. Chimalchiuhqui ("Shield-maker"), an "independent" featherworker, lived and worked in a district of Tlatelolco called Amantlan. This district, or *calpolli*, lay close to the *calpolli* of the long-distance professional merchants or *pochteca* (see Chapter 4). These merchants regularly undertook long and dangerous journeys in search of fine luxuries, including the many feathers required by the featherworkers in their luxury craft. It behooved Chimalchiuhqui and his colleagues to cultivate amiable relations with their merchant suppliers. These relations were mutually beneficial, since it likewise behooved the

FIGURE 3.5. Professional merchants in the Tlatelolco marketplace with feathers for sale. Sahagún (1950–1982: book 9: fig. 1). Firenze, Biblioteca Medicea Laurenziana. All rights reserved. Further reproduction in any print or digital format is forbidden.

merchants, such as Quetzalhua, to treat their featherworking consumers with proper consideration. Some feathers may have been transferred from merchant to featherworker through informal, even prearranged exchanges (after all, they lived in close proximity), but many others were sold in marketplaces by professional merchants (Figure 3.5).

In contrast to Chimalchiuhqui, Centzon worked in the Tenochtitlan ruler's palace. He and other palace artisans had access to the ruler's store of wealth – raw materials obtained largely through taxes or tribute. Annual deliveries of tribute from conquered provinces during the reign of the Tenochtitlan ruler Motecuhzoma Xocoyotzin (r. 1502–1520) included at least 2,480 quetzal feathers; four green/ yellow feathers; 800 handfuls of yellow (*Montezuma oropendola*) feathers; 8,800 handfuls each of blue (lovely cotinga), red (roseate spoonbill), and green (a parakeet species) feathers; and twenty bags of eagle feather down (Berdan and Anawalt 1992: vol. 1: appendix C). These figures are recorded in the tribute tally of the *Codex Mendoza*, yet they represent only a portion of the feather wealth obtained politically by the Tenochtitlan ruler. Additional feathers were acquired as immediate booty from successful military conquests. Others arrived in the imperial city from allied or dominated communities not listed in the *Codex Mendoza* tally, and still others may have been stockpiled from earlier occasions that required the delivery of luxuries to the imperial capital (such as a temple dedication or a ruler's coronation). And professional merchants (*pochteca*) were commissioned to bring feathers and other luxuries to the royal palace.

Palace featherworkers also had access to a whole host of birds, local and exotic, maintained in the palace *totocalli*, or aviary. There must have been a great deal of turnover of fine feathers, however, since the ruler, his patron god Huitzilopochtli, his high-ranking guests, and his valiant warriors required constant replenishment of impressive feathered objects. If royal stores ran low, palace featherworkers could obtain fine feathers in the larger marketplaces of the realm, although it is not known how (or if) these purchases might have been subsidized by the ruler.

Both Chimalchiuhqui and Centzon required more than feathers in their craft. Most of their other materials and tools were fairly mundane, cheap, and widely available: maguey twine, obsidian blades, animal hides, paper, cloth, cotton thread, raw cotton, wood, glues made from orchid roots, dyes, ceramic vats and bowls, and baskets. Any featherworker (including those attached to palaces) could find these materials and utilitarian objects in the many marketplaces, even small ones. Some other basic tools were even more readily available – bone picks, for instance, could easily have been retrieved from a recent meal. But overall, featherworkers in both settings were highly dependent on others for their acquisition of necessary materials, whether these "others" were an omnipotent ruler, a professional merchant neighbor, a more anonymous marketplace merchant, or a marketplace vendor of everyday goods such as pots, glues, or dyes.

Individuals' actual activities within their patio-workshops depended on gender, age, skills, and experience. All members of the household appear to have been involved in the craft, although adult women also undertook the household duties expected of virtually all Aztec women: cooking, weaving, child bearing, child rearing, and generally managing the efficiency and assuring the harmony of the household. Some women, whether or not belonging to featherworking households, spun feathers for textile manufacture. Women's crafting roles emphasized the dyeing of feathers and the sorting of feathers by type and color. Girls were trained from an early age to discern subtle variations in hues. One might visualize mother and daughters sitting in the patio, on a reed mat, some laying out and sorting all manner of feathers into discrete baskets, others dyeing feathers to the specifications required for the current object in progress. The sorting, at least, was an easily interrupted job, as these family members might be called away at any moment to tend to a boiling pot, a crying infant, or a minor quarrel.

Men were the primary featherworkers. Aside from women's work of dyeing and sorting feathers and probably feathered textile work, men were engaged in all stages of production (including some dyeing). Assuming that any featherworking household was capable of producing tied objects, mosaics, and textiles, boys mixed glues and the men's skills and duties ranged from delicate artistry to more mundane tasks such as dipping feathers in glues or arranging feathers for tying.

The production of a feather mosaic, a shield, for example, initially required the acquisition or manufacture of a wooden backing, supervision of the feathered design (coordinated with an invited painter or scribe), and selection of the proper feathers for their proper placement. The featherworkers continued by meticulously preparing backings of glue-reinforced carded cotton and papers. Designs on these carefully prepared backings were outlined in thinly trimmed feathers (usually black, and appearing to be paint to the naked eye) and filled in with layers of first inexpensive and then expensive feathers. All of the feathers were small and pliable, plucked from the birds' necks, breasts, and backs. The bottom-most layer of the mosaic consisted of glue-hardened feathers, produced by immersing less costly feathers (such as duck and molted feathers of the roseate spoonbill) in glue. These feathers were not chosen randomly, but rather selected to match the colors of the rich feathers (such as lovely cotinga and scarlet macaw) that would be layered on top of them.

The topmost feathers were glued only on their underside, leaving their visible side to catch the light and shimmer much like the

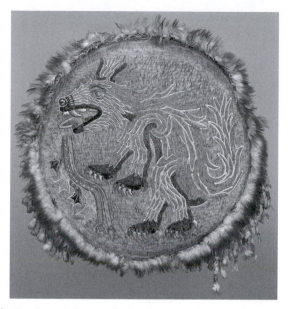

FIGURE 3.6. Feathered "coyote" shield with gold embellishments. Source: KHM-Museumsverband, Weltmuseum, Vienna; reproduced with permission.

exuberantly colored tropical birds from which they came (Filloy Nadal and Lourdes Navarijo Ornelas 2015; Sahagún 1950–1982: book 9: 93–97). A close look at existing feathered mosaics reveals pattern segments sometimes cut out separately and reassembled rather like a jigsaw puzzle (Figure 3.6). The master artisan would have been responsible for the final assembly, which may include gold or stone pieces as well. Close supervision and quality control were the order of the day, as "the feathers were repeatedly laid out in trial designs, matched, trimmed, arranged, rearranged, and at last attached to finalize the exquisite creation" (Berdan 2014: 101–102).

If a tied featherwork piece was being produced, again the feathers were selected for appropriate quality, size, and color, although this time the long, flowing tail feathers of quetzal birds and the primary feathers of scarlet macaws and other large birds were added to the mix. The goal was to assemble these feathers into a banner, head-dress, back device, or similar flowing masterpiece. The artisans tying the plumes into a dazzling ensemble needed to meticulously loop threads over and around the feather shafts, repeatedly arranging,

FIGURE 3.7. Featherworker tying feathers. Sahagún (1950–1982: book 9: fig. 86). Firenze, Biblioteca Medicea Laurenziana.

lining up, shaking out, rearranging, reselecting, lining up again, and so on tirelessly until the object was, in their eyes, perfect (Figure 3.7). One such existing piece, "Motecuhzoma's headdress" in the Weltmuseum Wien (Worldmuseum Vienna, Austria) is complex: it is partly mosaic, partly tied, and embellished with 1,544 gold pieces: 194 round disks, 1,313 rectangles, and 37 half-moons (Moreno Guzmán and Korn 2012: 72; Figure 3.8). Its technology suggests that skills needed to produce such a complicated, multifaceted object

FIGURE 3.8. Feather headdress known as "Motecuhzoma's headdress."
Source: KHM-Museumsverband, Weltmuseum, Vienna; reproduced with
permission.

would have all been present in one place, at one time – that is, in one
crafting household.

Less is known about the production of feathered textiles. Small and
pliable feathers (perhaps down) were spun, perhaps twined with
cotton, using tiny spindles (McCafferty and McCafferty 2000: 47;
Phipps and Commoner 2006: 486; Sahagún 1950–1982: book 8:
49). These feathered threads were then woven into luxurious (and
cozy) capes and other textiles for use by the elite. Alternatively,
feathers may have been tied to the threads of already woven textiles,
as produced in ancient times in both North and South America.
Unfortunately, no pre-Hispanic Mexican feathered textiles have yet
been found for us to examine. Who spun and wove these high-end
fashions? In one case we are told that women who owned birds
(ordinary ones) spun feathers in the Tlatelolco marketplace (Sahagún 1950–1982: book 10: 92). These were most likely commoner
women. We have already seen that noblewomen produced feathered
robes in Motecuhzoma's palace and spun feathers while being entertained with song and dance (Sahagún 1950–1982: book 8: 49). And it
is not at all unlikely that women of featherworking households also
undertook this activity.

Other tasks fell to various workers in the household: assuring that
tools and equipment were available and in working order, selling

finished goods in the marketplaces or delivering them to the palace overseer, obtaining materials and tools in the marketplace or from neighbors (in a pinch), and negotiating necessary (and favorable) dealings with merchants, painters/scribes, goldworkers, stone mosaic workers – anyone whose own labors contributed to these glamorous feathered objects. We can only guess how many such objects were underway, in various stages, at a single time within any feather workshop.

The final, artfully designed, and meticulously executed feathered object was the end result of a well-managed production process requiring the input and commitment of different members of the household. Each understood his or her role and responsibility. Tasks were either ongoing, sequential, or on-call. Ongoing jobs could be undertaken at almost any time, irrespective of other featherworking activities. These included sorting, trimming, and dyeing feathers; manufacturing feathered textiles; and maintaining or upgrading tools. Other tasks, especially those involving the assembly of the over-all piece, were sequential in nature, each stage depending on the prior completion of other tasks. For instance, the arranging of feathers followed the drawing of the design, and the finer feathers were laid atop the ordinary, glue-hardened ones. Still other activities were undertaken on a more situational and sporadic basis; the best example of an on-call activity is the mixing of the glues, which allowed only a short window of time before they hardened.

In this industrial setting, each worker depended on the others. Men selecting the feathers to be applied to a mosaic would have worked closely with the girls and women dividing the feathers by size and color. Boys had to be available on short notice to mix the appropriate amounts of glue at the appropriate times for the master and his other workers. Different individuals, if fashioning discrete segments of the final object, needed to coordinate their efforts to assure the integrity of the piece; for example, on the coyote shield (see Figure 3.6), the feathers on all of the individual blue "fur" segments face in the exact same direction, regardless of the shape of the pieces.

Featherworkers were also dependent on others in the broader Aztec world. For instance, they characteristically invited a painter or scribe to prepare the design of a planned feathered mosaic (Riedler 2015). And few feathered objects, whether flowing headdresses or regal fans, were made solely of feathers. A great many of them incorporated decorations of gold and precious stones. As examples, among the precious objects sent from Mexico to Spain shortly after the Spanish conquest were "three shields, one the field green with some serpents of gold and blue in the center; the other, the field green with the head of an owl in the middle; the other, the field red with some fancy work of gold" and "a feather-piece, the center blue with stone mosaic-work, with other colored feathers, the border of green feathers, and lined with a jaguar skin" (Saville 1920: 62, 72). Those exact objects have not yet surfaced, if they are not altogether lost. In fact, we can count only seven ancient Mexican feathered objects currently housed in museums. One of these, the ornate feathered shield in the Weltmuseum Wien, is embellished with hammered gold pieces forming the coyote's claws, teeth, and nose (see Figure 3.6), and the exquisite feather headdress ("Motecuhzoma's headdress") in the same museum is artfully decorated with numerous small gold pieces (Moreno Guzmán and Korn 2012: 65; see Figure 3.8). The featherworkers who made these objects did not work alone in their manufacturing enterprise – either they commissioned goldworkers to fashion specific pieces and then incorporated them into the feather-working themselves, or the goldworkers worked hand-in-hand with the featherworkers. In the end, we do not know exactly who attached the gold pieces to objects such as these – in some cases it may have been the goldworkers, in others, the featherworkers, or in others, they may have worked in concert.

Featherworkers may also have been kept busy with orders for repairs. By their very nature feathers are fragile, and much feathered finery was carried into ferocious and demonstrative situations. Accomplished warriors wore feathered costumes and carried cumbersome feathered back devices and shields into hand-to-hand combat – feathers must have been flying everywhere. Many religious processions were less than tame, and the lifespan of feathers adorning deities and platforms was probably quite short. In one documented colonial Mexican procession, excited observers needed to be restrained from dancing with the feathers adorning the processional display (and possibly damaging them) (Lockhart et al. 1986: 70–71). It is entirely possible that this behavior derived from pre-Spanish times.

Deities were even more demanding of perfection than mortals, and their adornments needed to be frequently revived and renewed.

Motecuhzoma would not tolerate wearing a cloak more than once; it is inconceivable that the gods were any less exacting. The featherworkers might well have needed to attend to matters of repairs as well as production of pristine objects, but repairs may have fallen most often in the laps of the independent (guild) featherworkers, since non-pristine adornments surely would have been an affront to rulers and gods. In truth, we do not know for sure who made repairs to feathered objects, although we have one brief statement that individual warriors were responsible for repairing their own weaponry, including their shields (Durán 1994: 167).

Both men and women went to market to buy and sell, and children would be sent for small errands for household and workshop. Even the master featherworker may have been seen in the marketplace, seeking the finest feathers, selling his wares to best advantage, or chatting with traveling merchants to check on the latest news from the lowlands – Was the rumor about that nasty rebellion true, and the feather supplies cut off? Did a new source of quetzal feathers open up (perhaps he should spend more time making headdresses and banners)? Information was as important a resource as any to the master featherworker.

Featherworking, like so many other economic enterprises, experienced peaks and lulls in activity. The approaching flurry of a major religious festivity, the arrival of merchants laden with loads of precious tropical feathers, the return of weary warriors in need of replacement or repaired feathered costumes and shields – these and other predictable and unanticipated events all contributed to the spurts and rhythms of featherwork production. And, like everyone else, the featherworkers had public ceremonies to attend to:

*No work would be done today in her father's workshop, thought Xochitl. She had spent a restless night, anticipating today, the feast day of Tlaxochimaco. It was the Distribution of Flowers, and women in all parts of the city were already singing, dancing, feasting, and giving away their garlands of colorful and aromatic summer flowers. She was proud of her garlands. For the past two days, she and other girls her age, at fourteen, had enjoyed the camaraderie of stringing the beautiful flower strands. She knew hers were especially lovely – as a featherworker's daughter, she knew her colors and how to arrange them to best effect. Her garlands would be among the first to adorn the goddesses this morning, and later her arms and legs would be pasted with bright feathers and she would sing and dance with the other girls and women. No wonder she was eager for the day to begin.*

## LIFE CYCLE

Featherworkers were commoners, and children in commoner households were expected to engage in productive, often manual labor from an early age. Young boys grew up with domestic chores such as toting water and firewood, gradually moving into chores requiring more strength, dexterity, and judgment. At some undisclosed time, boys in featherworking households were taught to make glues, thereby entering into a kind of apprenticeship (Figure 3.9). Exposure to the bustle of the workshop introduced the boys not only to essential

FIGURE 3.9. Boys making glue for featherworking. Sahagún (1950–1982: book 9: fig. 99). Firenze, Biblioteca Medicea Laurenziana. All rights reserved. Further reproduction in any print or digital format is forbidden.

skills but also to the underlying bulwarks of the craft: cooperation, efficiency, reliability, and predictability in the workplace and pride, care, and meticulousness in workmanship. While we have no specific documentation, boys most likely graduated to more skilled tasks such as making glue-hardened feathers, and then on to more complex contributions like laying out feathered designs. They probably accompanied the household's master artisan from time to time to trade in the marketplace, negotiate with neighboring merchants, or stave off the demands of a palace overseer, learning by observing. If a boy was seen to be adroit as an artist and committed to the enterprise, he would be groomed to take over as the household's master featherworker. But there was probably room for only one master artisan per household. The heir's brothers probably had options: they could remain working in subsidiary positions in the household, move to another household needing their particular skills, or perhaps even move to another community to find a suitable position. But at bottom line, he was trained as a featherworker, and it would be difficult for him to change professions. One exception was that, early on, a son could be dedicated to the priesthood.

Girls were likewise raised in a working household, initially engaging in light domestic chores. As they grew up, girls were prepared for their future lives by learning to cook, spin, weave, and care for younger siblings. They also contributed to featherworking by sorting, trimming, and dyeing feathers, tasks that many would carry into their adult lives.

Upon marriage, the young men would most likely remain in their natal homes, but the girls would leave to live with their new husbands. Ideally, the girls would marry into other featherworking households where their skills would be welcomed and useful. Marrying into another type of household (e.g., farming, fishing, merchant) would require some adjustments on the bride's part; but she would already have her essential lifelong skills at hand, especially cooking, spinning, and weaving. On the flip side, the entry of an untrained bride into a featherworking household was not necessarily welcomed – think of the investment in training required to bring the young woman up to speed in a household accustomed to its own working relationships, routines, and expectations.

A featherworking household may be more or less successful depending on the skills, attitude, and reputation of the workshop.

In the Aztec world view, fate and diligent care of the patron gods also contributed to the prosperity of the household. Like the professional merchants (Chapter 4), featherworkers had opportunities to buy, bathe, and offer slaves for sacrifice during the month of Panquetzaliztli. Acceptance of this responsibility demonstrated the artisan's commitment to guild and god and, like the merchant, surely contributed to his prestige among his associates. These rituals, at the *calpolli* level, were overseen by respected elderly featherworkers who surely themselves had offered slaves to the gods. Sponsorship of a sacrifical offering, in this ritual, was indicative of the wealth that could be accumulated by featherworkers, for these were expensive undertakings.

Yet another factor, the household's life cycle, entered into the artisans' success at any moment in time. Like individuals, households went through life cycles. Where division of labor was at least to some extent dependent on age and gender, each household at any point in time was either favorably or unfavorably poised to fulfill its labor requirements. With a multitude of related tasks and responsibilities, and especially the periodic bouts of intense activity, lack of sufficient and appropriate labor could lead to bottlenecks and disorder (e.g., not enough adult men to keep up with assembling the pieces, too many boys stumbling over one another to make the glues, only one frazzled girl trying to keep up with the feather sorting, trimming, and dyeing). The feather workshop required at least one, and preferably more than one, adult of each gender, and children of both genders performed essential tasks.

Since households changed in composition over time, acceptable and accessible strategies needed to be available to deal with these expected changes. Children, those of relatives or neighbors (with too many children at the moment), may be incorporated into a child-depleted household. An elderly but accomplished master artisan, whose eyesight is failing, could instruct neophyte featherworkers, massage relations with ambitious merchants, and oversee periodic rituals, leaving the everyday crafting to his well-trained sons. With the eventual loss of their father, one or more sons must be prepared to manage the household's external relations. And on it went in the workshop generation after generation, at times stable and steady, at times requiring adjustments to achieve a workable balance.

FIGURE 3.10. Colonial feathered triptych made by at least three artisans. Metropolitan Museum of Art, New York City; image is in the public domain.

One buffer against periodic labor shortages was extended (rather than nuclear) households. These enlarged groups would be able to provide a relatively large and diversified labor pool for featherworking needs. In this vein, the possible combining of households in palaces may have been an especially effective labor strategy. Alternatively, it is possible that portions of some feathered pieces were fashioned by different featherworkers in separate households and assembled later (Figure 3.10).

## IN AND OUT OF TROUBLE

No matter how skilled the workers in artistry, and no matter how well-organized the household in business, some things were simply beyond their control. Prominent among these were access to raw materials (especially exotic feathers), "cash flow," and maintaining a balanced labor force for the *calpolli* featherworkers. Also serendipitous were unexpected demands, deadline pressures, the whims of ruler and royal majordomos, and the always-lurking labor imbalances for the palace artisans. These constituted the featherworkers' greatest worries.

While the *calpolli* artisans may have enjoyed more overall independence in pursuing their craft, that independence had its drawbacks. None of the most colorful feathers (except those of migratory hummingbirds) was native to the central highlands of Mexico, and they therefore had to be obtained from great distances. The featherworkers therefore depended on establishing and maintaining good relations with their neighbors the long-distance merchants (*pochteca*) (see Chapter 4). These merchants could carry large quantities of feathers to the artisans. And the featherworkers needed enormous quantities of feathers – thousands and thousands of them (see Filloy Nadal and Moreno Guzman 2017).

Even with amiable relations between merchant and artisan, some things were beyond the control of the merchant as well: rebellions in source areas, natural travel impediments, or attacks on the road. All of these could hinder or even halt production in a featherworking workshop. Still, some feathers also probably arrived in the featherworkers' vicinity through down-the-line trade, changing hands from vendor to vendor and market to market until arriving in a marketplace near them. But this too was somewhat unpredictable. Whether receiving their feathers directly or indirectly, supply lines would have been a cause of almost-constant worry. Cash flow was also an issue: the featherworker needed to sell his work to obtain the resources to purchase more feathers for continued manufacturing. One wonders (but can only wonder) if some form of credit was in operation here to offset slow times. Irregularities in supplies of raw materials as well as labor imbalances might be relieved by the broad base of cooperation within the featherworking *calpolli* where both materials and people could be shared across households.

The palace featherworkers had other issues. While they typically would have access to abundant raw materials, including precious feathers, their manufacturing activities and artistic output would have been closely scrutinized by palace officials. After all, their prized

FIGURE 3.11. Merchants bestowing captured feathered devices on Ahuitzotl. Sahagún (1950–1982: book 9: fig. 6). Firenze, Biblioteca Medicea Laurenziana.

feathered creations would adorn the very gods, bedight the ruler as he danced, and be bestowed on royal visitors. These were very specific adornments, with highly charged symbols – their production left little room for creativity on the part of the artisan-artist. Some new designs did occasionally appear. For instance, in his wars on the southern Pacific coast (Xoconochco), Ahuitzotl's merchants captured some local war regalia which they passed on to their ruler (Figure 3.11). Ahuitzotl so liked them that he had them reproduced at home, certainly by his palace featherworkers, who would have copied the new styles.

The palace artisans had little artistic freedom; their *calpolli* counterparts may well have had more. Feathered objects for palace use also needed to be of the highest quality. Of course, in all events the featherworkers held themselves to the highest standards of workmanship and managed their own quality control, but the political pressures to produce perfect godly and royal adornments were surely heavy. Beyond quality, quantity and speed would also have pressured the palace artisans, who had to attend closely to political and ritual schedules. In such a meticulous craft as featherworking, speed and quality do not match up well. As for labor imbalances, these could be offset by the collective labor force housed in the palace setting.

It is worth considering what the featherworkers did *not* worry about. It was less the feathers and featherworking materials themselves than the artisans' extraordinary artistic skills and production abilities that

set the featherworkers apart. Successful featherwork required specialized knowledge, well-honed skills, extensive cooperation, capital
investments, a meticulous work ethic, and an understanding of cultural symbols and stylistic nuances. Whether creation of feathered
objects was carried out in palace or *calpolli*, the complicated nature
of the craft contributed to its exclusivity and hence the ability of the
featherworkers to monopolize production in this arena of life. They
taught their own and had captive consumers, and competition only
among themselves. They also developed a lifestyle a notch above most
other commoners in terms of political privilege, potential wealth, and
job security.


## REFLECTIONS AND PROSPECTS

Chimalchiuhqui was walking to the market with his young son when
his friend Centzon fell into step beside him. They greeted each other
companionably and began a familiar conversation:

*Centzon: I have not seen you in a while, my friend. What brings you to the*
   *market today?*
*Chimalchiuhqui: Hello, my friend. We have run out of glues. My son here*
   *bought glues last week, but they were bad.*
*Centzon: How so?*
*Chimalchiuhqui: The usual. The thieving gopher threw in pieces of ground up*
   *maize and beans. You can't make a good shield without clean glue. My son*
   *will point him out if he's here. How is life in Ahuitzotl's palace?*
*Centzon: Busy. Hectic. Rushed. Ahuitzotl has decided to have a big feast,*
   *again, and we're all scrambling to make too many gifts for the guests. You*
   *know Ahuitzotl, he's beyond generous and it all falls on us to keep up.*
*Chimalchiuhqui: I don't think he realizes how slowly and carefully we must*
   *work ... we're artists, after all. I guess that's a good thing: as long as we*
   *teach our children well, we will always be needed. Always.*
*Chimalchiuhqui's son: Wait! There he is! The bad glue-seller!*
*Chimalchiuhqui: Excuse me, my friend. I have some personal business to*
   *attend to ...*

Chimalchiuhqui's words were prophetic. In his own and his son's day,
Spanish invaders would replace Aztec rulers. In his grandson's day,
featherworkers would still learn and practice their intricate craft.

But then, under the new lords of the land from across the sea, they would fashion different types of objects with different themes and symbols inconceivable to Chimalchiuhqui and Centzon (see Figure 3.10). Still, they would continue to use their fathers' and grandfathers' and great-grandfathers' methods, and their fine art would thrive.

# 4

## The Merchant

*Quetzalhua was nervous. This was the final day of a journey that had taken him and his caravan months to complete. Luckily, the lake was calm in the shining moonlight as he and his companions paddled to the looming island from the southern lakeshore. They had begun their journey on the day Seven Serpent, and surely that had contributed to their great success. Yet he knew he also had a keen sense of opportunity, and he had taken advantage of gaining wealth in every distant market.*

*Now, traveling at night, they had managed to avoid the dreaded night axe, the frightful shamans who transformed themselves into dangerous nocturnal creatures, and the unpredictable but always feared spirits of women who had died in childbirth. Yes, he was grateful to at last be on his familiar lake.*

*He wished it had been darker. After all, that was the point: to enter his home city of Tlatelolco undetected. His string of canoes rode low in the water, heavily laden with valuable goods: cacao, precious stone beads and necklaces, shells, and piles of beautifully decorated clothing. And shimmering tropical feathers for his friends and neighbors the amanteca. He knew his feathers, living up to his name of Quetzalhua, "Owner of Precious Feathers."*

*He would secretly deposit all of this at his uncle's house. It was important that the city's nobles did not learn of the extent of his wealth, he thought nervously. Yet he smiled inwardly, knowing that now he could sponsor a sacrifice, bathing and offering a slave in the coming months, and gain the respect of his fellow merchants. Yes, he was proud. But still nervous.*

Quetzalhua is fictitious, but his journey is not and his worries are reasonable inferences. His immediate life was woven around the well-established and demanding organizations of professional merchants (*pochteca*). Yet his profession, by its very nature, required him to pursue activities beyond his comfortable "in-group": he frequented local and distant marketplaces and, if successful, might engage in amicable relations with craft specialists, offer slaves for sacrifice in public ceremonies, act as a warrior in distant lands, and serve even royalty itself. With these opportunities came stresses. He lived in a complex world, competing and collaborating with other merchants, and balancing entrepreneurial interests with political savvy. In Aztec terms, he walked along a cliff's edge, from which he could plummet with any misstep.

### OPPORTUNITIES ABOUT AND ABROAD

Quetzalhua and his *pochteca* associates played strategic economic and political roles in the dynamic Aztec world. They were economic entrepreneurs and astute political players par excellence. Their name, *pochteca*, derived from the Tlatelolcan district or *calpolli* of Pochtlan. Apparently, the merchants residing in that neighborhood had become sufficiently famous (at some unknown point in highland history) to lend their name to other merchants in the Basin of Mexico, much as a Kleenex can refer to any tissue in our daily lives. By the time of the Spanish arrival, twelve documented Basin of Mexico city-states boasted *pochteca*, each with intimate affinities to their own political rulerships (Figure 4.1).

The *pochteca* were purveyors of the finest materials and goods available in the empire and beyond. They trafficked in shimmering tropical feathers, precious stones, shells, jaguar pelts, fine decorated textiles, and slaves. Stationed in the highland Basin of Mexico, they needed to travel far beyond their homes to obtain these exotic goods and then deliver them to rulers, nobles, and artisans in highland cities or use them for their own economic and ritual purposes. In exchange, they carried a variety of goods from their homelands: fine decorated textiles from their ruler; golden and rock crystal ornaments for distant nobles; and obsidian ornaments and tools, rabbit fur, sewing needles, shells, alum, cochineal, and various herbs for commoners in far-away trading centers (Sahagún 1950–1982: book 9: 8, 17–19). Many of these export goods were surely produced locally or nearby: for instance, Otompan's workshops (northeast of Tenochtitlan) produced "obsidian knives and blades, earspools, lip plugs of obsidian and rock crystal, other ornaments, cochineal, and textiles" (Nichols 2013: 74).

This surely is only a partial list, as these merchants made frequent trading stops in markets along their routes to the distant trading

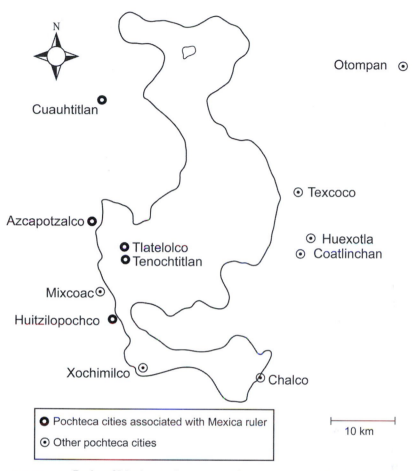

Otompan ⊙

Cuauhtitlan ●

N

Azcapotzalco ●

Texcoco ⊙

● Tlatelolco
● Tenochtitlan

⊙ Huexotla
⊙ Coatlinchan

Mixcoac⊙

Huitzilopochco ●

Xochimilco ⊙

Chalco ◉

● Pochteca cities associated with Mexica ruler
⊙ Other pochteca cities

10 km

FIGURE 4.1. Basin of Mexico *pochteca* towns. Source: Jennifer Berdan Lozano; reproduced with permission.

centers, and their specific commodities undoubtedly changed opportunistically with every stop. They became wealthy by moving expensive goods from market to market throughout the empire, traveling "to all the markets of the land, bartering cloth for jewels, jewels for feathers, feathers for stones, and stones for slaves" (Durán 1971: 138; Berdan 1978, 1988). Quite simply, they gained their livelihoods through commercial profit, and that profit was achieved primarily through shrewd and fortuitous exchanges in the many marketplaces within the empire and beyond (Figure 4.2). All the while, they were not the only merchants in the economic landscape – they faced competition

FIGURE 4.2. Merchants with luxury goods in the Tlatelolco marketplace. Sahagún (1950–1982: book 9: figs. 3, 4). Firenze, Biblioteca Medicea Laurenziana.

from local and traveling merchants from other city-states throughout central Mexico. Risk and profit were the order of the day (Hirth 2013: 88; 2016: 96–98, 210).

Many of the Basin of Mexico *pochteca* were restricted to trafficking within the Aztec imperial domain, but they may have found nice opportunities in moving their wares to and from marketplaces in conquered provinces. *Pochteca* from seven Basin of Mexico city-states were required to trade only within the imperial bounds, and increasingly far-reaching conquests into lowland environments allowed these merchants to acquire exotic tropical goods and become rich by moving them into highland regions. Some intra-empire marketplaces seemed to cater especially to these merchants – the one at Tepeacac, for example (Figure 4.3). One condition of Tepeacac's subservience to the empire was its requirement to hold a market on a designated day, making available all kinds of precious goods (Durán 1994: 159). This requirement may well have been instituted to make rich commodities available to the intra-empire *pochteca*, who could then distribute them in markets throughout the imperial domain and, importantly, deliver them to nobles in the Basin of Mexico cities (see Berdan 1988: 644).

Exotic tropical goods probably arrived in the Tepeacac market in the first place through the efforts of the extra-empire *pochteca* and other merchants who also frequented this marketplace: Tepeacac was required to assure the safety and well-being of traveling merchants,

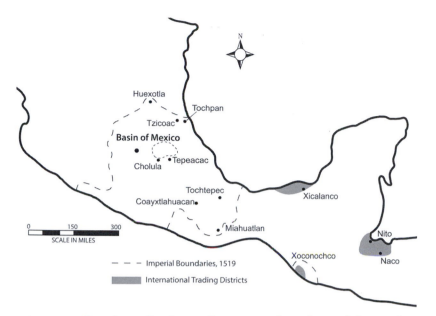

FIGURE 4.3. Locations of major trading centers, in and out of the empire. Source: Jennifer Berdan Lozano; reproduced with permission.

those "who trade with Xoconochco and Guatemala and all the land" (Durán 1994: 158; Figure 4.3). Similarly, and geographically close to Tepeacac, "it was ordered" that commodities at the Cholula marketplace must include "jewels, precious stones and fine feather-work" – although we do not know who made the order (Durán 1971: 278). Cholula was an on-again/off-again ally of the Aztec Triple Alliance, so it may have been an imperial command or a local edict at any point in time.

Business was brisk. Almost-constant warfare fed a continual demand for fine feathers to adorn damaged or lost warrior parapher-nalia. Diplomatic engagements and missions required increasing quantities of exquisite clothing and precious stone, metal, feather, and shell adornments to impress enemies, intimidate potential allies, and solidify always-tenuous alliances: more feasting, more flamboy-ance, more gifts. In addition, many valuable items were dedicated to ceremonial events, some of them buried in ritual caches (López Luján 2005), and slaves were sometimes sacrificed. All of these practices necessitated a constant replenishment of the kinds of materials and goods carried by the *pochteca.*

Some of the merchants' cargo was their own, but some was the property of their ruler. Merchants were convenient instruments of the state. Some of them carried their ruler's goods to extra-empire trading centers, offering them to the local rulers in exchange for their exotic goods – all of this with distinct political overtones. While appearing as economic dealings on the surface, these exchanges served to convey diplomatic messages and establish political relations. Other professional merchants, called *nahualoztomeca* (disguised merchants), served as spies rooting out potential rebellions and reporting on desirable resources as targets for military conquest.

All of these merchants were rewarded for their services as diplomatic ambassadors and spies. Returning from one distant trading expedition, the Mexica ruler presented each of his *pochteca* emissaries with decorated cloaks and loincloths, a bundle of rabbit fur cloaks, and a boatload each of maize, beans, and *chia* (Sahagún 1950–1982: book 9: 5–6). That said, in many cases these gifts paled against the merchants' personal entrepreneurial gains.

Theirs was not a cushy life. Their routes were dangerous, and their political assignments could be tricky. As spies in distant lands, they needed to disguise themselves as local or regional merchants – the potential for tripping on a local accent or misinterpreting a local custom made their jobs dangerous. The popularity of all *pochteca* was generally low. They were accused in distant markets of unfair trading practices and taking advantage of local vendors. They traveled in great caravans partly to tote their enormous quantities of goods, and partly for safety. They went armed. Even so, they were set upon often enough by disaffected locals who robbed and sometimes killed them (Figure 4.4). Although their overbearing demeanors no doubt contributed to these attacks, their known affiliations with dominant and hated polities probably were more weighty motivations. Such assaults were more than just violations against the individual merchants; they were attacks on the rulers that supported the expeditions. For their part, the offended imperial rulers were provoked to retaliate and either conquer or reconquer the malefactors. It was an accepted, expected, and frequent excuse for imperial expansion.

FIGURE 4.4. Merchants killed on the road. Reproduced from Berdan and Anawalt (1992: vol. 4: f. 66r), with permission.

The merchants' determination to control lucrative trading centers can be seen in their military role in the reported conquest of several city-states along the southern Pacific coast (in the region of distant Xoconochco). When the *pochteca* defeated these distant peoples after four years of incessant warfare, they absconded with their enemies' fancy feathered warrior regalia, wearing them in battle and then bestowing them on their ruler Ahuitzotl. The merchants were wealthy, but not sufficiently privileged to permanently possess these symbols of battlefield courage, achievement, and victory. The merchants did, however, receive gifts (including decorated cloaks) from Ahuitzotl in recompense. While this report of the military importance of the *pochteca* may be somewhat exaggerated, another record of Nahua merchants engaging in warfare on behalf of a Tarascan king lends credence to this account (Pollard 2017: 19).

The *pochteca*'s successful trading ventures not only contributed to their own prosperity, but importantly provided nobles with wealth and status symbols, and supplied artisans with raw materials for their exquisite creations. These merchants also stimulated the economy with extraordinary levels of consumption within their own professional associations centered in *calpolli*.

## IN THE *CALPOLLI*

It is difficult to separate the merchant's society-wide obligations from his roles within his neighborhood, nor would any self-respecting

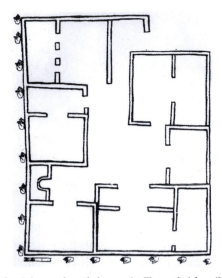

FIGURE 4.5. A colonial merchant's house in Tenochtitlan/Mexico City. AGN, Tierras, 38.2. Source: Edward Calnek; reproduced with permission.

*pochteca* entertain such a thought. Their city-state and neighborhood lives overlapped. At their most significant level, *pochteca* lived relatively exclusive lives in specific *calpolli*, or neighborhoods. Any Aztec individual's life was centered on his or her *calpolli*. People's daily lives and life histories were played out on this stage: family, school, patron deity, many ritual activities, and sometimes a specialized occupation consumed their attention and directed their priorities. This focus on the *calpolli* was especially intense for the *pochteca* – to the extent that we might liken them to guilds. Training, opportunities, wealth distribution, and luxurious displays of wealth, primarily in the form of prescribed and often extravagant feasts, took place within the confines of the merchants' homes and in the broader context of their *calpolli* (Figure 4.5). This is documented for Tenochtitlan and Tlatelolco and was probably also the case in the other Basin of Mexico cities housing *pochteca*.

The concept of guilds was introduced in the preceding chapter, where we saw that the internal organizations of featherworkers resembled some of the craft guilds of Medieval Europe. In general, the exclusive Medieval merchant associations guaranteed and controlled rights, privileges, and employment for their members. They set high professional standards, assured proper training, guarded trade secrets, and supported their own. Members of merchant guilds engaged in long-distance commerce (even at times monopolizing it) as well as more local trading activities. They were influential in international commerce and politics, and sometimes established colonies of their own in distant areas. Leaders emerged among them who also became important figures in the civic life of the community. Based on these criteria but still recognizing notable variations among such associations even on the Medieval European stage, we have no problem including the *pochteca* under the broad umbrella of guilds (but see Hirth 2016: 192–193).

For the *pochteca*, the *calpolli* was not just a place of residence. It served as a base of operations for their profession: as *pochteca* they enjoyed commercial privileges that included access to distant trading venues and the opportunity to carry their ruler's goods abroad and represent him in diplomatic exchanges. Their tightly knit relations were reinforced by repeated and overt expressions of a particular moral and social code. They were constantly harangued to obey their elders and higher-ups, appear humble in public, and contribute unstintingly to all necessary rituals. There were well-established hierarchies within the merchant associations, and individual *pochteca* answered to *pochteca* authorities rather than to state and imperial ones (at least in Tlatelolco). They were expected to participate in the training of young *pochteca* and care for merchant neophytes on their initial expeditions. The travelers journeyed in large caravans for support, safety, and probably comradeship. They carried not only their own and their ruler's goods, but also the goods of others in their association who did not join them on this particular trip. This included merchant women, who could be important personages but probably did not actually set out on the road (at least we do not hear of any who did). In addition to their home bases, the *pochteca* established a strong merchant colony at distant Tochtepec. This *pochteca* center was conveniently located well along the routes to lucrative Gulf and Pacific trading locales (see Figure 4.3) and afforded them some privacy in conducting their exclusive affairs and rituals.

Those who stayed home supported the traveling merchants in rituals before, during, and after their journeys and, as in the case of

Quetzalhua, protected their goods upon their return. All members of the guild were reminded (indeed, frequently reminded) that they would surely suffer hardships and dangers, but even so they were expected to fulfill their responsibilities as proper *pochteca*. These communally oriented ethics were instilled in each and every merchant, presumably in each and every guild.

There were personal incentives as well. The merchants' goals were profits and the investment of those profits in personal advancement. Their ambitions were sought and achieved within their *pochteca* organizations; it was imperative that aspiring merchants impress their elders by committing their hard-earned wealth to sponsoring lavish and expensive banquets within their guild – even to the point of sacrificing one or more slaves at a public ceremony. There were many opportunities for hosting feasts and demonstrating one's generosity to other (especially senior) members of the guild. They were performed when a merchant prepared to leave on a long journey and upon his return; they were imperative on the ritual days Four Wind, One Dog, and One Serpent. It was fitting that merchants folded some of their economic gains back into the guild through these feasts, since the guild trained and supported them and they sometimes carried goods of their co-members on their dangerous treks. These expensive gestures not only offered the sponsor of the feast enhanced status in the merchant hierarchy, but also provided repeated examples of the *pochteca*'s willingness to contribute to the spiritual well-being of the community at large.

The merchants of these *calpolli*-based associations accomplished all of this so well that they managed to gain the favor of their city-state rulers. They not only acquired prodigious wealth; they also enjoyed a surprising amount of power in this hereditary caste-like world. The most esteemed *pochteca* served as marketplace judges and enjoyed royal trading commissions to distant trading centers. The imperial ruler at Tenochtitlan even ordered the protection of merchants in outlying marketplaces, as at Tepeacac. These favorable political relations assured the security of their status vis-à-vis the state, empire, and possibly jealous nobles. It must be remembered that the *pochteca* were commoners, not hereditary nobles. But they were extra-ordinary commoners: very wealthy and very privileged (Berdan 2014: 186–187).

These professional merchants lived their unusually wealthy and privileged lives within their *calpolli* and on treacherous roads, always supported by their collective strength. Their daily round and life histories were largely defined, composed, and regulated by these collectivities.

## DAILY ROUND

Like other people in the Aztec world, the merchants filled their days tending to personal needs, making a living, carrying out family and neighborhood duties, and fulfilling religious obligations. And as was usual, these individuals' specific activities varied according to their gender and age. As *pochteca*, their daily lives encompassed additional activities and responsibilities, depending on their social position within the merchant hierarchy and on whether they were at home or on the road.

### Life at Home

When at home a man's daily activities would include managing the family wealth, negotiating with luxury artisans, trading in nearby marketplaces, and, less frequently, making elaborate preparations for a feast (Figure 4.6). If the merchant enjoyed particularly high

FIGURE 4.6. Preparations for a lavish feast among the merchants. Sahagún (1950–1982: book 9: fig. 27). Firenze, Biblioteca Medicea Laurenziana. All rights reserved. Further reproduction in any print or digital format is forbidden.

status, he might spend much of his day serving as a marketplace judge or, on sporadic occasions, arranging future expeditions with his ruler or perhaps other patron. If the merchant was a *nahualozto-meca*, a spying merchant, he would undoubtedly spend a good deal of time becoming proficient in the language and customs pertinent to his next assignment. Rituals and social events were frequent and adhered closely to prescribed formulae and schedules; these dictates included calendrical timing, sequencing, involvement of proper participants, and the use of prescribed materials (such as copious quantities of food, fine copal incense, and a slave who could dance well).

We know less about a *pochteca* woman's daily round, but in large part it may have differed little from other women in Aztec society. All women were expected to spin fibers and weave cloth, buy and sell in marketplaces, cook food, bear and rear children, and generally keep the house clean and in order. These were extremely time-consuming tasks, and their importance in household maintenance should not be underestimated. Beyond these general duties, *pochteca* women were essential actors in ritual events performed at the household and *calpolli* levels – especially where massive amounts of food were required. In addition to onerous cooking duties for these lavish events, women probably were also largely responsible for acquiring the assorted feasting goods in a nearby marketplace (from beans and turkeys to flowers and charcoal). It would be a near-impossibility for a *pochteca* man to rise in the merchant guild's hierarchy without the dedicated efforts of an energetic wife (as well as the services of other female relatives at particularly strategic and stressful moments).

The merchants' lives were governed by both predictable and unpredictable events. Market days were set by the calendar, and the merchants were especially adept at knowing where and when they would gain the greatest profits. It was their job, after all. They also participated in ritual events that were strictly fixed by calendrical scheduling. Some life-cycle occasions (such as those commemorating births) and elaborate banquets validating an individual's rise in the merchant hierarchy were anticipated months in advance.

Other rituals punctuated daily life in the *pochteca calpolli*. Some of these announced the departure and arrival of merchant caravans. The departure of a long expedition affected not only the travelers. Those left at home joined the leave-takers prior to their departure in performing required rituals assuring the travelers a safe and prosperous journey. And when a merchant such as Quetzalhua arrived home at night from a long expedition, he delivered his goods to the house of a relative, and then immediately presented himself to a *pochteca* leader where formulized pleasantries were exchanged. At midnight he made offerings to the merchant god Yacatecuhtli, and just before dawn he and other merchants laid out food, chocolate, and tobacco offerings for the gods Yacatecuhtli and Xiuhtecuhtli. The host then distributed costly gifts to guild members, the quantity and quality of the gifts appropriate to each guest's position within the merchant hierarchy. This was followed by oral presentations where the host assured his higher-ups that he had performed well on the road; his august guests then admonished him to "not be presumptuous nor proud" (Sahagún 1950–1982: book 9: 29). With these rituals, sacred offerings, and generous feasting the recently arrived merchant was folded back into the home life of the guild. Secure at home, a successful merchant might host extravagant banquets to establish and confirm his rise in the merchant hierarchy. These were no ordinary parties: they all required strict adherence to ritual protocols as well as substantial outlays of the merchant's resources. In Kenneth Hirth's words, "Ritual ... was a constant aspect of merchant life" (2016: 225).

The merchants' rhythms of life were sometimes interrupted by unscheduled happenings. The death of a merchant while on a trading expedition, for instance, required his relatives at home to commit themselves to elaborate mourning rituals for several days. In another example, the death of one ruler and the coronation of another would have required the merchant associations to reestablish their favored political status within the city-state. Aztec conquests impacted the merchants, especially in opening up markets within the imperial domain and perhaps motivating them to reassess their commercial priorities and redirect their entrepreneurial expeditions. Aztec armies

were sometimes defeated abroad; this also could realign political
borders and necessitate adjustments by the merchants in their quest
for valuable resources. Such occasions as these interrupted or shifted
the merchant's daily flow of life.

### Life on the Road

The *pochteca* lifestyle necessarily took these entrepreneurial individuals
far from home (Figure 4.7). Their treks might include months-long
mercantile journeys, military engagements, and political negotiations.
Although the merchants liked to portray themselves as humble and
self-sacrificing while in Tenochtitlan and Tlatelolco, people in outlying regions saw them quite differently. As the *pochteca* passed through
their territories, selling dear and buying cheap (according to local

FIGURE 4.7. *Pochteca* on the road. Sahagún (1950–1982: book 9: fig. 13).
Firenze, Biblioteca Medicea Laurenziana. All rights reserved. Further reproduction in any print or digital format is forbidden.

perceptions, at least), the local people thought the merchants haughty and arrogant with no qualms about taking advantage of them. They were not popular.

Their lives on the road were a mix of adherence to established norms and responses to unpredictable circumstances. The merchants conformed to the dictates of the fate-driven ritual calendar, being sure to depart on a trading expedition on the day One Serpent and return on the days One House or Seven House. On their return journey, they would lay over at the city of Itzocan (a convenient transportation hub linking the Basin of Mexico with points south) until the onset of one of these favorable day signs for their stealthy entrance into the home city. This may have required a delay of many days. The merchants also adhered to expected behaviors by performing penances at temples they encountered along their routes. If their expedition included a commission from their own rulers, they knew they would meet with the rulers of distant city-states, performing a set of formalized interchanges involving diplomatic overtures and reciprocal exchanges. Predictable events and behaviors such as these were balanced against less predictable ones such as a spate of inclement weather or a well-planned deadly ambush.

Traveling merchants were not without assistance and resources during their treacherous journeys. The Basin of Mexico *pochteca* were well-established at Tochtepec, partway between their home cities and diverging routes to the Gulf and Pacific coasts. Tochtepec was included in an Aztec conquered province and from there the merchants could travel directly to either coast in search of exquisite and expensive luxuries (see Figure 4.3). This important center furnished storage and residential facilities; it offered a relatively safe and convenient way station for exhausted merchants. Tochtepec was a place where they could openly display their wealth without risking the jealousy of their home city's nobility. Upon heading south from Tochtepec, the merchants soon entered "foreign" territories beyond the thrall of the Aztec Empire. On such journeys – at least to the Gulf coast (Xicalanco) – they were escorted by an armed contingent sent from Xicalanco for protection. Apparently, the people of the coast were as interested in the *pochteca*'s wares as the *pochteca* were in theirs. Or the coastal peoples' concern for the *pochteca*'s welfare had a political motivation – it was to their advantage to mollify the merchants and keep the Aztec military at arm's length.

FIGURE 4.8. A merchant accepts the admonitions of his elders. Sahagún (1950–1982: book 9: fig. 34). Firenze, Biblioteca Medicea Laurenziana. All rights reserved. Further reproduction in any print or digital format is forbidden.

There were probably few "typical" days on the road. Some days would be consumed by travel, others by trading, others by fending off attackers, others by resting and feasting at Tochtepec or other merchant center, and still others by negotiating with local rulers or nobles. Many days would combine these activities. Some days would be easier (a day of boat travel, for example), others more difficult (such as crossing a menacing river or a craggy mountain on foot). The elders had warned that there would be days like that: they would suffer starvation, fatigue, and general misery; they would encounter afflictions, ambushes, and hazardous rivers (Figure 4.8). It is not known for sure how often this rather dismal picture painted by the elders was actually played out on the road. There were probably pleasant, fulfilling, and successful days as well.

LIFE CYCLE

At least some of the merchants' personal histories conformed to the more general patterns of life in the Aztec world. They were born, grew up, learned their trade, began their own families, took on larger responsibilities, aged, and died, much as did all Aztecs. Yet the specifics of their occupation and peculiar status set them apart.

Rituals surrounding the birth of a child most likely resembled those of other people in Aztec society – involvement of a midwife, a washing and naming ceremony, celebratory feasting, and incessant harangues of the parents' elders to assure the parents take proper care of their new arrival (see Chapter 7). It was usual for infants to receive miniature symbols of their anticipated futures, such as weapons for a boy and spinning equipment for a girl. While these same symbols may have also pertained to the merchants (since men were also warriors, and women spun and wove cloth), they might also have been given, perhaps, a diminutive staff, representing the larger staffs without which no self-respecting merchant would travel.

A girl growing up in a *pochteca* household would have been instilled with the Aztec virtues of diligence, modesty, and forbearance. As a child she learned to spin and weave cloth, cook food, and generally maintain a prosperous and harmonious household. Upon marriage her duties became more onerous: the house's storerooms may have been full of merchandise from time to time, and she may have been given some responsibility to oversee this wealth. More demanding would be her role in supporting her husband's rise through the merchant hierarchy – the hosting of extravagant feasts gave her husband honor and status, but much of the preparations were in her capable hands. We know little of *pochteca* girls and women, but can reasonably suggest that as a woman's husband rose in status and admiration, so did she.

As a boy grew and absorbed the requisite knowledge and morals of a proper merchant, he was allowed to go on his first trading expedition. He was now a *telpochtepitoton*, or "small youth." Before embarking, he sat through long lectures by his elders warning him of dangers and encouraging him in his life's work. On the road his safety and instruction were in the hands of more experienced and well-traveled merchants who were expected to bring him home safely. With each subsequent successful expedition, the maturing merchant gained the confidence of his elders and the harangues became shorter and less stern. At some point, although we do not know specifically when, he married and began a family. The teamwork of man and wife was essential for the next stages of life, especially if he (or they) were ambitious. In a series of rites of passage, he would sponsor feasts, displaying and generously heaping his hard-earned wealth on his elders, seeking and hopefully gaining their support and admiration. With each performance he gained position and prestige in the hierarchy.

Wealthy, established merchants could offer slaves for sacrifice at large public ceremonies, contributing to the ritual life of the community at large; they committed their hard-earned resources to publicly displaying their wealth while at the same time contributing to the city-state's spiritual well-being. Both goals enhanced the well-heeled merchant's prestige – within his *calpolli* and in the eyes of the dynastic and priestly authorities.

*Quetzalhua had never been so excited in his life. It was some time since he returned from his long journey, and he was now preparing to purchase and bathe a slave as a sacrificial offering. It would be during the festival of Panquetzaliztli, only a few months away. But the preparations! He knew he could buy the necessary foodstuffs and containers in the market, and his wife and her close female relatives would cook the meals. But the slave – he would have to go to nearby Azcapotzalco to find a really good one. One who could dance lightly and gracefully. Perhaps he would take his older brother and uncle with him. They had a good eye for such things.*

Quetzalhua's preparations were protracted, complicated, and expensive. First, he must purchase one or more slaves. The slave dealers were crafty: they lavishly adorned their slaves and hired men to play music to which the slaves danced, showing off their "wares" to their best advantage. But the purchasers were knowledgeable, too, and bargaining was probably brisk and lively. A buyer would expect to pay thirty to forty large cotton capes (*quachtli*) for a slave, depending on the slave's appearance, health, and dancing skills. There was certainly pressure to pay more, for if the buyer skimped, all attending the ceremony would know.

This was but the beginning of a long string of expenses. He must build platforms on which the slave(s) would dance, he must assemble from 800 to 1,200 fancy decorated capes and 400 loincloths as gifts to exalted warriors, members of the city-state's dynasty, and high-ranking merchants from other city-states in the Basin of Mexico (Sahagún 1950–1982: book 9: 47). He needed to offer gifts to the women who would bathe the slaves. He was required to undertake a journey to the merchant headquarters at distant Tochtepec. There he solicited the approval of resident or transient high-ranking merchants by offering them gifts along with food, chocolate, and tobacco, thereby announcing his intent to offer his bathed slave or slaves in sacrifice. The merchant was also expected to offer quail and incense to the merchant god Yacatecuhtli in these social-political-religious events: the ritual side of these formulized occasions was never neglected.

The merchant's return to Tenochtitlan-Tlatelolco from Tochtepec heralded a new round of feasting and rituals. In a series of prescribed feasts, the merchant offered massive quantities of food, flowers, tobacco, and other materials, making sure that there was an overabundance of these – if all was used up, it was considered an ominous sign that there would be no more feasting in the future. Therefore, the merchant was obligated to stock up on at least eighty to a hundred turkeys, twenty to forty dogs, forty to sixty jars of salt, twenty sacks of cacao beans, and enormous quantities of tomatoes, maize, beans, chia, squash seeds, and water. He also needed large numbers of baskets, cups, dishes, and plates to properly serve these foods, and charcoal and wood for their preparation (Sahagún 1950–1982: book 9: 48).

At a final series of feasts the merchant displayed his lavishly arrayed, dancing slave(s). Following these events, the slave(s) were committed to the care of priests, who prepared them for sacrifice (and who were also suitably compensated). Finally, the day to offer his slave(s) arrived, and he gained public honor by his generosity and commitment. The body of his sacrificed slave was returned to him, to be ritually consumed at his home in a feast with important *pochteca* personages in attendance. This sacrifice, performed publicly in Tenochtitlan, honored the Mexica patron god Huitzilopochtli. Similar ceremonies, with local variations, were perhaps performed by wealthy merchants in other highland cities. For example, the ceremony had its counterpart among the professional merchants of Cholula, where wealthy merchants dedicated their bathed sacrificial offerings to their paramount deity, Quetzalcoatl. Diego Durán tells us that the merchants of that important city "spent all they had earned during the year to surpass the other cities and to show and make evident the grandeur and opulence of Cholula" (1971: 129). One detects a strong competitive edge to these ceremonies (reaching to the city-state level), complementing their religious purposes.

As a merchant climbed the hierarchy, *pochteca* superiors were carefully watching and checking on him to make sure he had sufficient resources to complete the expensive and high-profile feasts in a manner that would not shame his merchant associates. And despite his extraordinary displays of wealth, the merchant was exhorted by his elders at each feast to be humble, respectful, and generous, and to adhere to the proprieties of established social and political hierarchies. These were expensive and economically draining enterprises, but rewarding. For he was exchanging wealth for prestige and standing among his peers, at the same time promoting the political position of his *pochteca* guild vis-à-vis his and other city-states.

Elderly merchants who had traveled extensively and become wealthy promoted the status of their guild in the eyes of their ruler. They also upheld the demanding precepts of *pochteca* life and were accorded great respect. With this respect came great responsibilities. While they no longer traveled long distances, they shared their valuable experiences and knowledge by educating and exhorting younger merchants who did. These lectures were expounded by both men and women. It was said that the neophyte and maturing merchants alike placed great store in securing the approval of these respected *pochteca* (e.g., Sahagún 1950–1982: book 9: 30). And although they now stayed at home, elderly merchants were standard invitees to *calpolli* banquets, receiving an abundance of gifts. They still accrued wealth, but now without the dangers of toilsome and risky journeys.

A merchant's death required much on the part of the living. A merchant dying in his home city or region was wrapped in the customary mummy bundle and cremated with his wealth (or at least some of it). The *Codex Magliabechiano* (Nutall 1903: 68) depicts just such a deceased merchant surrounded by greenstone beads, gold ornaments, precious green feathers, a jaguar skin, and cups of food and drink. The mummy bundle itself (wrapped in white cloth tied with rope or twine) is further enveloped by a decorated textile and is adorned with a golden necklace and feathered headwear (Figure 4.9). He was sent on his way accompanied by the evidence of his achievements and prosperity. If a merchant died on the road, far from home, his body was not returned and the household members fashioned an image of bound pine torches to represent him. After being decorated and revered in the house, the image was moved to the *calpolli* center to

FIGURE 4.9. A deceased merchant, surrounded by his wealth. Reproduced from *Codex Magliabechiano* (1903: f. 68r).

be burned at dusk or midnight. Thus, the merchant's *calpolli* as well as his immediate family recognized his efforts and revered his memory.

### IN AND OUT OF TROUBLE

The lives of the *pochteca* may seem glamorous and exciting, but they were also fraught with risks and hardships. First, their wealth was gained at the expense of arduous and stressful treks to distant regions, often lasting months at a time. They needed to be vigilant on these journeys, as they were not very popular beyond their home bases and were attractive targets for robbery and assassination. But merchants were well-trained, well-prepared, and capable of spontaneous responses. Since trips abroad often brought precipitous turns of events, the merchant's training prepared him for a life of deprivation, danger, and surprises on the road. His elders forever entreated him to never lose heart; these were expected travails. Yet he still needed to keep a keen eye out for an unexpected ambush. *Pochteca* traveled in large caravans, partly for transporting large quantities of goods (all on foot or in canoes where possible) and partly for safety. They went armed, also arming any slaves in the party, including female slaves. Their entire entourage must have presented quite a formidable appearance, although rigorous training and preparations did not protect them from all contingencies.

Assaults on traveling merchants were quickly reported to the merchants' rulers, who responded with swift and deadly military force. The local people knew this was likely, and it may have served as a small deterrent to the molestation of these entrepreneurs. Nonetheless, merchants continued to be accosted by disaffected locals. A direct response by the merchants themselves was aggression: the *pochteca* trading expedition to cities on the southern Pacific coast that became transformed into a war of conquest has already been mentioned. Even if this account is overblown, it strongly suggests military capabilities on the part of the merchants. With high risk came great rewards, and these particular merchants achieved renown and gained wealth from their grateful ruler Ahuitzotl. The merchants and their caravans responded to their difficulties with fortitude and creativity.

Was this their greatest concern? It certainly was a periodic, situational, and dramatic one, but the merchants were on the road for only a part of their lives. More pervasive and subtle may have been a second worry: the looming jealousy of the hereditary elite. The *pochteca* were clearly concerned about this, as many of their behaviors were geared toward secretly protecting their wealth and privileges. Like Quetzalhua, they concealed their wealth, even returning from expeditions in the deepest night and delivering their goods to the home of a relative. They also minimized their public exposure, "wearing only their miserable maguey fiber capes" in their home cities, since "they greatly feared notoriety, the praising of one" (Sahagún 1950–1982: book 9: 32).

Their entrepôt at Tochtepec must have provided them with welcome relief from these stresses. There, merchants could freely regale one another about their adventures, far from the prying eyes of sometimes-edgy and often-competitive nobles. Professional merchants also contributed generously to religious ceremonies, making it difficult for any envious nobles to complain about their wealth and its disposition. And they cultivated political favor. It was said that Motecuhzoma Xocoyotzin made the accomplished merchants "like his sons" (Sahagún 1950–1982: book 9: 32). In many ways they became indispensable to their rulers, trading royal goods in distant lands, making diplomatic contacts, spying in outlying marketplaces, and serving in Tlatelolco (at least) as marketplace judges. Additionally, the Aztec aristocracy became increasingly dependent on the efforts of the *pochteca*. It was these stalwart travelers who brought them the exquisite and essential symbols of their exalted status from distant lands. While we might consider gold ornaments, flowing tropical feathers, and greenstone beads as luxuries, it is a good bet that the Aztec nobility considered them necessities. And they acquired them through the exertions of knowledgeable and committed merchants (for a price, of course). A noble might feel jealousy, but it is unlikely that he would openly express it or act on it.

## Reflections

*I am an old man now, Quetzalhua mused. I used to sit dutifully through the long and (it seemed at the time) boring and interminable harangues of my elders. But now I deliver those same endless lectures! In truth, I enjoy them now more than I did before! And I understand their value now – if we pochteca did not hold to our code, if we did not stick together, if we strayed from the known and disciplined path, we would become weak and vulnerable. Sometimes I see the nobles eying our wealth. Don't mistake me. I'm not apprehensive. Or maybe I am.*

Quetzalhua was born during the reign of Motecuhzoma Ilhuicamina of Tenochtitlan (r. 1440–1468). The world into which he was born was quite different from the one he lived in more than fifty years later. Naturally, he too had changed over the course of his life. But so had the empire. The empire had expanded, as had his own opportunities and wealth. The nobles, his clients and sometimes patrons, had likewise expanded in numbers, providing him with a more than comfortable living. But the dangers in his life had also grown, both at home and abroad. Rebellions against Aztec rule had become more common, and attacks against Aztec-sponsored merchants more bold. As long as he maintained his profitable trading acumen, adhered to the elders' teachings, observed the calendrical dictates, and honored gods and men with generous offerings and gifts, he would survive. He took comfort in knowing that he was a proper Aztec, and a quintessential *pochteca*.

# 5

## The Farmer

*Icnoyotl stopped to rest in the shade of a copal tree. His dogs were already sleeping nearby. Icnoyotl was repairing one of the stone field walls damaged in last night's rainstorm. This set of agricultural terraces was farther from the house than the others, making it difficult to keep up with the constant maintenance that was needed. Rain, wild animals, and clumsy farm hands conspired to dislodge stones more often than Icnoyotl would like. He needed someone reliable who perhaps could stay out here and keep the walls intact. They could also scare the deer and birds away from the growing maize and cotton.*

*This flat stone under the copal tree afforded a nice view down the mountain to the river below. The main trail running through the province ran alongside the river. This trail connected Tenochtitlan to the north with distant parts of the empire and beyond to the south. Icnoyotl liked to watch people walking along the trail. He envied those who got to travel to distant lands, leaving farmers like him stuck at home. Just now a large group is trudging by, obviously some pochteca merchants heading back to Tenochtitlan. He makes out several warrior-merchants accompanied by ten or twelve bearers, each loaded down with big baskets or packs. Three or four dogs – probably owned by the merchants – trot along with the group.*

*As Icnoyotl stands up to resume moving large rocks around his fields, he reflects on the unfairness of life. While the gods presented good people like himself with a hard life of rain, dirt, weeds, and rocks, stuck here in the village, some of those lucky city-dwellers got to head off to adventures in Huaxacac [Oaxaca], the western [Pacific] coast, or even distant Xoconochco. It might even be fun to be a professional bearer – in spite of the heavy loads – if you got to see foreign lands. As Icnoyotl's two dogs woke up and stretched, he mused that even the pochteca's dogs probably had more fun than his own pets.*

This description of the farmer Icnoyotl brings us to the mass of the Aztec people. Earlier chapters described the emperor and three special categories of people who had more wealth and status than most. But we now reach into lives that pertain to the bulk of the Aztec population. Our focus on regular people will then continue in the following chapter on slaves.

## AZTEC FARMERS

Most Aztecs were farmers. It took a lot of maize and beans to feed the several million people who lived in central Mexico in the final centuries before the Spanish conquest. Even though the Aztecs and their ancestors had devised some very innovative and productive methods to cultivate crops, agriculture still commanded the labor of most people. Many city dwellers had to work the fields, walking out from their urban house each day. But most farmers lived in villages and hamlets, close to their fields.

Farming peoples had lived in central Mexico for thousands of years before the rise of Aztec society. Early villages gave way to the huge metropolis of Teotihuacan, which was in turn followed by several smaller urban societies. Over this long period of occupation, there had never been as many people as in the Aztec period. The four centuries of Aztec society was a time of major population growth throughout central Mexico. By 1519 more Aztec cities had been founded than had ever existed in earlier times, and the countryside had more villages and hamlets than previously. Both absolute population numbers and population density (people per square kilometer) were at their maximum level in late Aztec times. After the colonial period population collapse, caused by European diseases, central Mexican populations would not reach Aztec levels until the second half of the twentieth century (Sanders et al. 1979).

This population explosion had a number of consequences for Aztec farmers. To start, they had to devise ever-improving methods to squeeze more maize and other crops from their fields, just to feed all the people (including themselves). Those methods – called intensive farming methods – required ever-increasing amounts of labor time, which affected the lives and families of Aztec farmers. And even though central Mexican agricultural productivity was at an all-time high, food production was not enough to keep up with the growing population. We know this because a series of serious droughts

FIGURE 5.1. A modern agricultural terrace with maize in Tepoztlan; Aztec terraces were identical. Reproduced from Lewis (1951: 10).

and crop failures plagued the final century before the arrival of Cortés. It is perhaps surprising that agriculture managed to flourish at all during the early sixteenth century given this sampling of catastrophic episodes: 1500, a great flood; 1502, drought and famine; 1503, heavy snowfall; 1505, famine; 1506, a rat plague; 1507, earthquake; 1511–1512, heavy snowstorms; 1512, three earthquakes; 1514, drought. Imagine facing these stressful events year after year.

While some Aztec farmers probably used simple techniques, based mostly on rainfall, most used one of several methods of intensive agriculture to increase their yields. The three most important were canal irrigation, terrace cultivation, and raised fields, or *chinampas*. Each of these methods requires more labor than simple rainfall agriculture. Dams must be built and canals excavated for irrigation; walls are constructed on slopes for terracing (Figure 5.1); and swamps are modified to create new planting surfaces for raised fields (Figure 5.2). Once these landscape features were built, they had to be maintained. Icnoyotl, for example, had to keep a close eye on his stone terrace walls and rebuild them several times a month in the rainy season if he didn't want them to tumble down the hillside. The

FIGURE 5.2. An Aztec *chinampa* still being farmed in 1905. Reproduced from a old postcard.

greater effort needed to farm intensively usually paid off with much higher yields, which were needed to feed the growing population (Doolittle 1990; Evans 1990; Morehart 2016; Smith and Price 1994).

Why would Aztec farmers want to put extra effort into their farming? It meant longer hours in the field and the bother of finding field hands to help for harvest or wall-building, while leaving less time for other activities. The answer is rent and taxes. Most farmers had to pay some kind of rent to a noble for use of the land, and they all had to pay taxes to their local king and to the distant emperor. The most common forms of payment were money (in the form of cotton textiles) and labor. Farmers and other commoners did not have a choice about the matter. As populations grew, city-state kings and nobles increased taxes and rents, which forced farmers like Icnoyotl to increase their production, either by bringing new land under cultivation or by building the landscape features of intensive agriculture.

Some farmers had more say over their own lives than others. At the top of the scale of farmers were people sometimes called "free commoners." These individuals belonged to a rural *calpolli*, which gave them access to land and the right to decide how to work the land. Next on the scale were dependent laborers. Not having a *calpolli* to back them up, these farmers depended on a noble for their lives and livelihoods; they worked his land or served in his household. This category is similar to the well-known category of serf in medieval Europe. At the bottom of the commoner scale were the slaves; these are the subject of the next chapter (Smith and Hicks 2016).

## LIFE IN THE VILLAGE

Two short decades after the Spanish conquest, a Spanish administrator sent a team of Nahuatl-speaking scribes to take a census of a series of communities in what is now the Mexican state of Morelos (Carrasco 1964; Cline 1993; Díaz Cadena 1978; Hinz et al. 1983). The scribes asked a series of standard questions, including: Who lives in this house (names, ages, and relationship to the household head)? How much agricultural land does the household work? and What does the household pay in rent and taxes? The entries for each house, recorded in Nahuatl, are a gold mine of information on families and households and some aspects of local life in farming communities. The only major change since the Spanish conquest was that some people (but far from all) had been baptized. Also, it is likely that a good number of people in these communities had died of epidemic diseases introduced after the conquest.

Here is a typical entry, for a household in the community of Quauihchichinolla:

Here is the home of some people none of whom is baptized. The tribute payer is named *Epcoatl*. His wife is named *Centehua*. He has four children. The first is named *Yaotl*, married. His wife is named *Tlaco*. They have been married 160 days. The second of his children is named *Xochihua*, now 30 years old. The third is named *Teicuh*, now 15 years old. The fourth is named *Necahuatl*, now 6 years old. Here is Epcoatl's nephew named *Telpoch*, who is blind. His wife is named *Teicuh*. He has three children. The first is named *Huehuel*, now 15 years old. The second is named *Cihuacocozqui*, now 10 years old. The third is named *Tepiton*, born 80 days ago.

Here is Epcoatl's field: 15 *matl* [one *matl* = 1.67 meters] long and 10 *matl* wide. Here is his tribute: every 80 days he delivers one quarter-length of a Cuernavaca cloak, one quarter-length of a tribute cloak, one quarter-length of

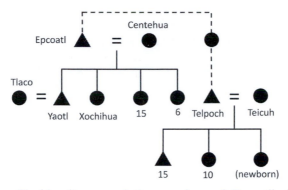

FIGURE 5.3. Kinship diagram of the members of Epcoatl's household. Source: Michael E. Smith.

a narrow cloak, and two turkey eggs, so that in one year it is one Cuernavaca cloak, one tribute cloak, one narrow cloak, one turkey hen and 8 turkey eggs. That is all of this tribute; no cacao. At his home here there are eleven included in just one house; that is all of them. (Cline 1993: 155)

The kin relations in this household are illustrated in Figure 5.3. This house has two nuclear families: that of Epcoatl, who is head of the entire household, and the family of his nephew Telpoch. Telpoch's newborn son is not included in the count of people living in one house; little Tepiton was not yet considered a full person. Epcoatl is in charge of the agricultural fields, and he is responsible for the tax/tribute payments. In addition to the payments of cloaks, Epcoatl also owes a turkey hen and eight eggs. The fact that the document says "no cacao" indicates that many other households did pay their tax/tribute in cacao beans. While eleven people may seem like a large group to be living in one house, many houses had even more people. In this warm climate, most activity took place outside, in the patio or near the house, and the house was probably full only at night for sleeping.

Only a few households in these communities consisted of a simple nuclear family (parents and children). Most were extended-family households, meaning they contained adults from two or more generations (Figure 5.3). Also, many households included unrelated boarders. These were poor or dispossessed individuals who did not belong to the local *calpolli*. Usually single, dependent laborers resided with a *calpolli* household and helped with agricultural work and/or household chores and textile production. When people found

FIGURE 5.4. An excavated house at the rural Aztec village of Capilco. Source: Michael E. Smith.

themselves in economic difficulty, they could just pick up and move to try their fortunes elsewhere. This is one way that Aztec landless workers differed from Medieval European serfs, who were not free to leave if they became fed up with their situation or overlord. When such newcomers arrived in an Aztec village, they would petition the *calpolli* council, and, if approved, they would move in with a family looking for help with economic activities. In the census entries, these newcomers are described as having no land themselves because they just arrived; they are said to have helped the household head.

Because the people living in a house often included unrelated individuals, it is better to refer to these groups as households rather than families. Most rural households lived in a small, one-room house (Figure 5.4). At approximately 4 × 5 meters, this is the most common type of structure at Aztec-period archaeological sites throughout central Mexico. While such houses may seem small to us today, they were primarily sleeping places; most work – including cooking and serving food – took place outside the house (Smith 2016).

Nobles, on the other hand, had much larger houses. Rooms and courtyards were built on platforms that elevated the house above the level of the ground. Noble males frequently had more than one wife, and each one would have a living space in the palace. The more powerful and wealthy the noble, the larger and more sumptuous the residence. Nobles comprised only 2–5 percent of the Aztec population, but their influence – of course – was much greater. They owned the land, they ran the city-states (as the king and royal council), and they received the most income in Aztec society (Evans 2004; Smith 2012: 134; Smith and Hicks 2016).

In some farming communities, many houses were grouped into two to four dwellings arranged around a common patio. The term for these units in the documents – *ithualli* – means "those of one yard"; archaeologists call these units "patio groups." The nature of the relationship among the houses in these patio groups is not clear in the documents. These differ from the patio groups of the Classic Maya, each of which was occupied by a single household. Maya patio groups contained specialized structures, including living quarters, a kitchen, shrine, and sometimes a storehouse. The houses in an Aztec patio group, on the other hand, were all houses for single households. Even where patio groups were the usual arrangement, not all houses were part of such a group (Smith 1993).

As we move up the settlement hierarchy, the next two levels are groups of nearby houses and both are called *calpolli* or *tlaxilacalli* in the documents. Some writers use the terms "small *calpolli*" and "large *calpolli*" to distinguish these. We use the term "house cluster" for the smaller of these units and "*calpolli*" for the larger unit. A *calpolli* was a group of households whose members lived near one another and typically shared some key economic characteristics and social relations. In cities *calpolli* served as spatial divisions, or neighborhoods. *Calpolli* often featured specialized craft occupations and their members shared a common patron god. A house cluster typically had some twenty to twenty-five households, situated near one another. A *calpolli* would contain several house clusters, and contain fifty to a hundred households. The (large) *calpolli* usually had a common temple, perhaps dedicated to a patron god. The *calpolli* also had its own school. In rural areas, a *calpolli* was usually an entire village or a town, with its temple and school, as in the urban setting (Lockhart 1992: 16–19; Reyes García 1996; Smith 1993, 2016).

This four-level hierarchy of settlement is shown in Figure 5.5. We call it a settlement hierarchy because each level incorporates units

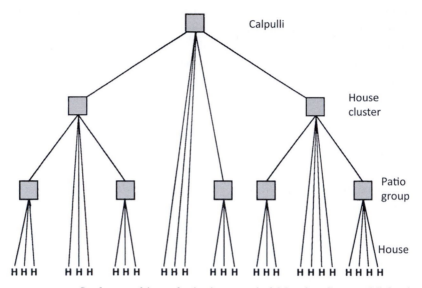

FIGURE 5.5. Settlement hierarchy in Aztec-period Morelos. Source: Michael E. Smith.

from lower down. But it is not a political or an administrative hierarchy. That is, the *calpolli* does not control the house cluster, and the patio group does not control the households. The political hierarchy, which focused on the city-state and the nobles, was separate, and all of these settlement units had to make payments to nobles and to the king.

## DAILY ROUND

Like farmers everywhere, Icnoyotl and other Aztec farmers got up early each morning. But however early an Aztec farmer may rise, sometimes long before dawn, his wife will already be working at the *metlatl* (Spanish *metate*, grinding stone), grinding maize flour for tortillas. The tortilla was the basis of the Aztec diet. Most calories and protein in the diet came from maize, and most maize was eaten in the form of tortillas. People ate maize in other forms as well (tamales, corn on the cob, pozole). The tortilla has two big advantages over other forms of maize for farmers: it can last all day, and it can hold beans and other ingredients as a taco.

Grinding maize for a day's ration of tortillas for the entire family was a big job. In the 1950s, before mechanical mills were introduced into small Mexican villages, ethnographer Oscar Lewis estimated that it took more than five hours to hand-grind enough maize for a family's daily tortilla needs (Lewis 1951). And this does not count the time spent shaping the tortillas (by hand) and then cooking them on the clay griddle (*comalli*). If a farmer was going to take his lunch to his fields, then someone had to be up early grinding maize and making the tortillas. Tortillas were eaten at every meal, as were beans.

For the most part, men were the primary household members engaged in farming. During busy agricultural times, the women of the household would sometimes lend a hand in the field, but for the most part their contribution to the household took place in and around the house. In addition to grinding maize, cooking meals, and caring for children, women spent many hours spinning thread and weaving cloth. These cloth-making activities took place on and off during most days, between household chores, childcare, and tending a small kitchen garden and turkeys, if the household was fortunate enough to have these resources. Women were also the primary marketers in each household: they went to the marketplace regularly to sell any of their small surpluses and purchase food and other needed goods. And if household members produced any craft goods, the women of the household would contribute to those activities and spend time at the marketplace selling these items (Figure 5.6).

Terrace farming was the most widespread form of intensive agriculture in the central Mexican Aztec heartland. The remains of old Aztec terrace walls can still be seen on many central Mexican hillsides today. The agricultural season corresponds to the rainy season in central Mexico: June through October. During that time farmers must visit their terraces at least several times a week, if not every day. It rains five or six days per week in the rainy season. While those rains bring water to the fields, that same water loosens the stones in the walls. If such a breach is not fixed immediately, it will grow rapidly with each rainfall, and an entire terrace can wash away in a week. Terrace farmers had no choice but to load up on tortillas and beans in the early morning and trudge out to their fields each day to work on their fields and terraces all day long.

FIGURE 5.6. Stalls for pottery in a street market in Cuernavaca in 1980. Aztec market stalls were almost identical to these. Source: Michael E. Smith.

Farmers usually took their dogs out with them each day. The dogs would enjoy chasing away any small animals that happened to approach the fields. They could warn the farmer when someone approached, although in reality they slept in the shade most of the time. For the most part, each farmer worked on his own field. Although they did not "own" the land, they were given regular use of the same plots year after year through the *calpolli* system. Thus it was worthwhile to spend the effort to develop their fields, knowing that any improvements would pay off in the future.

Nearly all Aztec farms were small, household plots. A farmer's sons would start helping at a young age. At harvest time, there was some-times a need to get the crops in quickly, and the women of the family would come out to help as well. But the intensive methods that had to be used – in order to produce enough to pay rent and taxes – seemed to require more and more labor each year. This is where a dependent laborer could really make a useful contribution to the household effort. In particular, he could extend the number of fields that could be checked each day during the rainy season, and help out in numer-ous other ways.

Once the crop was harvested, in the fall, a farmer's daily round changed greatly. Some farm work remained. The crops had to be processed and stored properly, and basic maintenance activities were done throughout the year. Terraces and other fields had to be checked periodically, storage buildings built or repaired, and of course there were many small but continual acts of maintenance needed in and around the house and yard. But these activities did not take up all of a farmer's time. Between November and April, they had time for other activities.

Many Aztec farmers worked on handicrafts during the agricultural off-season. Ceramic vessels, obsidian tools, grinding stones, mats and baskets, all kinds of items for everyday use were produced by farmers working during the dry season. This kind of domestic craft activity was so prevalent that it comprised the primary way that these products were made. Potters, mat-makers, and paper-makers were all part-time specialists, working on their crafts when they did not have to be in the fields. They worked at home, rather than in specialized workshops or factories.

Potting was one of the major craft activities among the Aztecs. Men would usually be the ones to find good clay deposits, dig out the clay, and lug it home. The clay was then mixed with sand, plant fibers, or other materials – these are called temper – to make it easier to form and to fire. Many ceramic items, from cooking pots to small figurines, were fashioned using molds of fired clay. Other items were fashioned by hand, and some vessels were made using the coiling method. The Aztecs did not have the potter's wheel, which was introduced only after the Spanish conquest.

Once the vessels or other items were formed, they needed time to dry thoroughly before firing, and this was much easier to do in the dry season. After drying, various decorative techniques might be used, from smoothing and polishing the clay to painting colorful designs. Then the vessels were fired, usually in a pit or on the ground in the house lot; the Aztecs did not use kilns. Vessels and firewood were piled up, and the fire lit. The potter tended the fire closely to make sure vessels did not get too hot or burn. Then the finished items had to be stored somewhere before bringing them to market. The entire operation – with the exception of digging the clay – was done in and around the house. Many family members must have participated in various aspects of the production process.

Other crafts were similar to potting in that items were produced by farmers in the dry season, working around the house and yard. We have little idea of just how specialized these part-time producers were. Was "general potter" the basic occupation, with one household producing vessels, ceramic figurines, incense burners, and other items? Or were there specialists within the ceramics industry? Sahagún (1950–1982: book 10: 83) talks about a "clay worker" who dealt in a variety of ceramic wares in the grand Tlatelolco marketplace, including *comallis* (griddles), cooking pots, water jars, braziers, ladles, sauce bowls, and the like. It is not clear if these were the product of this single potter or if he was selling the goods of several specialist producers. Either way, Sahagún's descriptions were made by young nobles who described crafts in very general terms. A suggestion that these highly specialized potters really existed comes from mid-sixteenth-century market tax records from the town of Coyoacan where we find separate clay-vessel makers, *comalli*-makers, stewpot makers, and spindle makers (Anderson et al. 1976: 138–149).

Some part-time specialists – farmers in the dry season – worked on several related tasks within the household. For example, households that specialized in making baskets from reeds probably also made mats (*petlatl*; Spanish *petates*) from reeds – used as beds for sleeping and as floor-coverings – when needed. Excavations at the site of Cuexcomate in Morelos found that the houses in one patio group had high concentrations of both bark-beaters and pigment stones. Bark-beaters were used to manufacture bark paper from the bark of the wild fig tree, and the pigments (red, black, and yellow) may have been used in painting on the paper. The residents of that patio group thus may have been part-time (or perhaps full-time) scribes, making paper and painting documents for the nobles whose palace was nearby.

Once a week – that is, every five days in the Aztec calendar – the daily pattern of household and village life was interrupted by market day (see Chapter 8). While one could usually buy a taco or some avocados in the marketplace every day, once a week the town plaza came to life with throngs of buyers and sellers. This was the time when one or more people from each household would go to buy necessities that weren't readily available locally. It was also an opportunity for the women of each household to sell small amounts of their extra food produce as well as the finished products made in the household. They would set up a small stall – perhaps just a mat on the ground and a small awning to block the sun – along with the merchants from the big city with their loads of goods (Berdan 2014; Hirth 2016).

In the evening, after the day's chores were done, people would relax and talk to their relatives and neighbors. A woman might mention that her cousin, a farmer of the highly productive raised fields near Tenochtitlan, didn't have an off-season to rest or to work on crafts. His fields were cropped continuously with several harvests a year. That led to a continuous level of hard farm work all year. But the results were good for those farmers, who enjoyed a higher level of prosperity than most. One way a terrace farmer might get ahead was to build more terraces and thereby cultivate a bigger area, but this would require more labor. Or if the baskets the family produced were particularly well-made, they might succeed in interesting one of the merchants in buying large numbers to resell.

The evening hours were also a time when curers and diviners were active. These were usually women who worked part-time, carrying out small rituals and ceremonies to help people in their little (or big) daily problems. They had knowledge of two sorts: religious knowledge such as myths and stories about gods and supernatural forces, and practical knowledge about health, healing, and curing. Both kinds of information were invoked during small private ceremonies. Patients who were ill were given cures that combined religious and medical aspects. People who wanted a prediction for the future could go to a professional priest, who would use a written (painted) calendrical record to identify times or actions that were lucky and unlucky. But a more common action was to consult with diviners, local women who cast dried maize kernels on the ground and used the patterns they formed to make their predictions. While curers and midwives likely went to the homes of their patients, perhaps the diviners worked at home, having patients come during "office hours."

Most of these activities were replicated among farmers who used other styles of cultivation, using some variation in techniques, technologies, scheduling, and the specifics of crops and local ecology. Throughout central Mexico, and especially in the warmer lowlands, farmers developed multicrop *milpas*, simultaneously cultivating several types of crops on a single plot of land. A common pattern was to plant

beans alongside maize, where the climbing vines could wrap themselves around the growing maize stalks; the broad leaves of various
species of squashes crawled along the ground, breaking the heavy
seasonal rainfall. Many other food and nonfood crops were planted
in any space available on the plot. All of these plants matured on their
own schedules, and the farmer worked year-round and had to adapt
his schedule accordingly. In the highland Basin of Mexico, farmers
built up land in the shallow lake beds, creating *chinampas*. This was a
sophisticated and durable agricultural system: farmers used crop rotation, multicropping, staggered seedbeds, and soil replenishment by
dredging water from the adjacent canals. In this way, the farmer could
plant and harvest several different crops of staple foods, vegetables,
herbs, and flowers throughout the year (Berdan 2014: 79–81). It was
a tidy and attractive system:

*Citlalin was daydreaming (again). She had just returned from a fall visit to her cousin in
Xochimilco, on the outskirts of the enormous city of Tenochtitlan. He and his family had a
nice house on a chinampa, and she secretly envied him. His chinampa seemed so lush,
compared with her husband Icnoyotl's terraced land. Parts of the chinampa already had
maturing plants, especially maize that had been planted in the summer and chiles that
were planted in September. She had watched him grunt as he scooped water and black
muck from the canal and spread it on a corner of the chinampa. And then she helped his
wife and children poke little holes (so many of them!) in the seed bed for the little tomato
seeds. She got so caught up in the painstaking work that she didn't realize how long she
had been bent over, and felt sore and stiff when she stood up. Yes, she thought, maybe she
envied her cousin, but he and his family still had to work hard. Very hard.*

LIFE CYCLE

Farmers, like everyone else in Aztec society, were expected to follow
long-standing norms of behavior and live up to traditional ideals. Everyone relied on the success of farmers for their sustenance, so it was
essential that farmers be skilled, knowledgeable, industrious, dedicated,
and willing to endure expected and unexpected hardships. Farming,
whether on highland terraces or lake-bed *chinampas* or lowland *milpas*,
required specialized knowledge and an ability to adapt to uncertain
environmental situations (even catastrophes). A fundamental job of all
farming families was to instill all of these values, attitudes, and skills into
the children who would succeed them.

Work began at a very young age for both boys and girls in farming households. At age four boys were put to work carrying water and were toting heavier loads a year later. They would help with market activities by age six. The *Codex Mendoza*, which documents this progression, shows the seven-year-old boy fishing, and we can project that in a farming family that same-aged boy would be helping his father in the fields. By age thirteen or fourteen the boy was capable of heavier, more independent work: while the document depicts a fishing livelihood, by the same age a farmer boy could be working effectively in cultivating crops. Through all these years, the father offers ceaseless instruction to the boy. Girls followed a similar path, but with different tasks. From ages four to seven the girl is instructed by her mother in the art of spinning, not an easy task to master. By age twelve she is sweeping diligently, by thirteen she has passed on to cooking and preparing the household meals, and by fourteen she is weaving with aplomb. Like the boy at that age, the girl's parent continues to instruct and correct (Figure 5.7).

All of this instruction was accompanied by very direct motivations for the child to strive for and achieve competence: punishments were severe for laziness or sloppy work, and included piercing with maguey

FIGURE 5.7. Childhood training for boys (left) and girls (right). Reproduced from Berdan and Anawalt (1992: vol. 4: f. 60r), with permission.

thorns, beating with a stick, being held over a chile fire, and (for boys), lying down on damp ground (see Figure 7.9). In short, by age fourteen both boys and girls have ideally attained the basic skills needed in adulthood, along with the values and attitudes of diligent and careful work. In the meantime, they have become practical and economic contributors to the household. In twentieth-century Tepoztlan, Nahua parents expected an elder daughter to take over much of the early morning maize-grinding duties while another daughter (from the age of seven) may help with the housework and tend younger children; boys began working with their fathers in the fields from as early as age six, and certainly by age ten (Lewis 1951: 63–72, 100).

These young years were not totally consumed with household work. Boys would attend their *calpolli* school where they learned martial arts preparing them for the eventuality of a war. There was no standing army, but men may be called up for military duty at any time, so they must be trained and ready. Further education took place at a *cuicacalli*, "house of song" (at least in the more urban areas), where both boys and girls learned the songs and dances that allowed them to participate capably in the many public ceremonies during the year, for commoners as well as nobles were required to properly venerate the gods.

It was now time for the young people to assume the responsibilities and rewards of adulthood. This occurred at around age twenty for men and fifteen for girls, when it was expected they marry, have children, and pursue their life's work. Weddings followed set rules and involved "a cast of characters that included not only the bride and groom, but also matchmakers, astrologers, and a wide array of relatives from both sides" (Berdan 2014: 205). It was a family affair that tied the two families through proper consulting (with the matchmakers and astrologers), gift-giving, feasting and drinking, and dancing. And if the young couple thought that the interminable lectures they received as children were over, they now faced the inevitable exhortations by family elders as part of the wedding ceremony. It was a relief when the knot was tied – literally, as the bride's tunic and the groom's cloak were physically tied together and the couple officially wed (Figure 5.8).

As adult farmers, men and women worked together to form hardworking and successful households (ideally). Depending on seasonal

FIGURE 5.8. Tying the knot at an Aztec wedding. The food in the center is for the feast, and four elders give advice to the newlyweds. Reproduced from Berdan and Anawalt (1992: vol. 4: f. 61r), with permission.

demands, in general when the men and boys headed off to the fields, the women and girls turned their attention to cleaning the house, preparing food, spinning and weaving cloth, caring for the younger children, tending the household garden and turkeys, and going to market, as already described under "Daily Round." This seemingly endless cycle of life could be abruptly interrupted by the greatest threats to their lives: for men, it was a summons to battle; for women, childbirth posed a comparable threat. And of course any number of illnesses or injuries could disable or end a life.

If they survived these and other dangers, Aztec men and women could live to ripe old ages. As they aged, they gained respect and certain special considerations – that is, if they had lived right and proper lives. They often played key roles in life cycle events (such as weddings) and were sought out for their lifelong knowledge and experience. With these responsibilities came a special privilege, that of being served copious quantities of *octli* (*pulque*) by their young relatives – often to the point of intoxication.


### IN AND OUT OF TROUBLE

*Icnoyotl realizes with a start that he may have expanded his terraced fields too quickly, and this could have serious consequences. His wife's talk of her well-to-do cousin who farmed the lush raised fields outside Tenochtitlan has spurred him to expand his own production as best he knew how. That meant putting a whole new hillside into production with new terrace walls. It was difficult, working long days, getting all the children to help, and even asking his best friend and neighbor Ayotochton to lend a hand for a couple of days. They had done it! Icnoyotl now had more terraces in cultivation than anyone else in the calpolli.*

*But now the reality of the situation became clear to Icnoyotl. He does not have a steady source of labor to keep up the new fields. He gave up his practice of making baskets and mats during the dry season in order to dig the new fields and move the necessary rocks into position. And the time Citlalin spent helping out was time she did not put into spinning and weaving. All of their sources of extra income had been put on hold to build the new fields. And now their landlord, a silly but powerful noble who lived in the next town, just raised the rent on everyone! He claimed it was because the king had raised taxes and he was just passing that on to the farmers to pay their share, but Icnoyotl suspected the landlord was taking the opportunity to increase his own income at the same time.*

*There was no way that Icnoyotl and his son could cultivate all the new terrace fields by themselves. That meant that they would not be able to grow enough cotton and maize to pay their rent, given the lack of extra income from crafts this year. The new terrace walls would come tumbling down in the rainy season, and he could even end up sold into slavery to cover his bills to the landlord and king! What have I done? he thinks. But Icnoyotl's visions of an avalanche of stones from the new terraces rolling down the hillside are interrupted by his son, out of breath. "Three new men just arrived in town from a large valley to the southwest where they have had droughts! They asked the calpolli head if there was any work here! Maybe one of them can help us out." Icnoyotl hurries over to the middle of town, where he quickly makes an arrangement with one of the newcomers. This new guy, with his strange accent, will live with the family and help in the fields and in other ways, to earn his keep. Icnoyotl's problem appears to be solved. So long as this guy is a good worker – reliable, strong, smart – Icnoyotl will be able to double his yields next year and pay his rent. Things don't look so bleak after all.*

Icnoyotl seems to have solved his problem, at least for the time being. But his extensive farmer's knowledge of nature and history reminded him how fickle the gods and their domains could be. He, his father, and his grandfather had lived through life-threatening droughts, famines, snowstorms, earthquakes, and vermin infestations. These were ever-present dangers to their very survival, yet generation after generation they seem to have not only survived, but thrived. There was always an array of solutions to these ever-present problems, whether it meant they grow more food, grow less food, diversify and make more crafts, weave more cloth, depend on their neighbors, migrate, or even sell themselves into servitude.

REFLECTIONS

In the year 1500, Icnoyotl had no idea what would happen to his way of life, and his livelihood, within just two decades. His customary rhythms of growing maize and cotton (albeit always rather stressful and unpredictable) will be disrupted as Spanish conquerors become new lords of the land. Along with their political control, the Spaniards also bring new crops and domesticated animals: wheat, grapes, cattle, horses, sheep, goats, chickens, and more. Some of the animals serve as draft animals, which, combined with the wheel, will transform transport from human porters to carts and carriages. Steel tools, including steel-tipped hoes, knives, scissors, and machetes, will ease his agricultural work and Citlalin's clothing production and cooking.

People will still need maize and cotton, and Icnoyotl and Ayotochton will continue to grow them. And their local markets will continue to thrive and offer them a predictable and familiar venue for exchanges of goods, ideas, and gossip. But these and other farmers will face new pressures to also grow wheat, raise a few chickens, and relinquish some of their lands to animal pasturage. In this new world they will continue to hang on to some of their traditional customs and known patterns of life. But they will also find themselves accommodating new things, beliefs, and ways of living – sometimes willingly, sometimes not.

# 6

## The Slave

*As Xilotl is shown her new room, really just a small space in a shed, she reflects on the strange turn of events that brought her from lovely Cuauhnahuac to ugly Matlatzinco, from the comfort and freedom of a farmer's wife to a slave in a household of potters. Life was normal back in the warm climate of Cuauhnahuac. She did have to put up with her worthless husband, Ce Ocelotl, who always had some get-rich scheme sure to backfire. They made ends meet by selling Xilotl's fine cotton textiles in the market. She was fast and effective with the spindle and the loom, and her products commanded good prices in the marketplace.*

*Ce Ocelotl's latest stunt once again showed him to be ixtimal ("a face of glory," all talk, no action). He was sure he had figured out an edge to betting on the patolli game, and after a few losses he bet EVERYTHING – all their possessions AND the personal freedom of the two of them – on a big game out behind the palace last month. Well, wouldn't you know, it was a losing wager! To work off the debt, Ce Ocelotl and Xilotl became the property, the slaves, of a fat noble, some distant cousin of the king of Cuauhnahuac. Then Ce Ocelotl managed to escape and run away to who knows where! The noble was really angry, and immediately sold Xilotl to the first interested buyer. This turned out to be a potter from Matlatzinco named Quauhtli, who was in Cuauhnahuac selling a load of jars. He was looking for a female slave to spin and weave and help around the house.*

*Now they had arrived in cold and gloomy Matlatzinco. This is really the sticks. A dirty and muddy city, spread all over a mountainside, with people who don't speak correctly, she grumbled to herself. Their house in Cuauhnahuac had been full of flowers, but these people hardly know what a flower is. They would go watch dances and performances at the Cuauhnahuac palace all the time, but it seems that the fool of a local king here doesn't bother to do anything for his people except collect their taxes.*

*Xilotl was worried whether they would want her to make textiles of cotton or maguey. She did NOT like spinning and weaving maguey. It was not any more difficult, but it was rough on the fingers and hands, and the result was a coarse and ugly cloth only good for bags or rope or coarse cloth. They didn't make much maguey cloth back in Cuauhnahuac, but it was known as the specialty here in Matlatzinco. Xilotl much preferred working with cotton, and was proud of the fine textiles she could make. She was also worried that her owners might want her to help with the pottery business. Xilotl had no intention of lugging clay up the mountainside, tending hot fires all night, or sitting in the market trying to sell a few bowls and jars. But she would have little choice in the matter, and it didn't help to sit around speculating about her new life.*

Xilotl's life had changed drastically and suddenly. An Aztec's life was seen as a fateful journey, and her fate had taken her to a new town, with a new family, with new duties. As a slave, she had some, but few choices in her life.

## AZTEC SLAVES

Aztec slaves were at the bottom of the social hierarchy, as one might expect (Figure 6.1). Nevertheless, the lives and conditions of slaves were radically different from the kinds of slaves that are much better known historically. In ancient Roman society, or on southern plantations in the United States before the Civil War, large gangs of slaves performed heavy and difficult economic tasks like rowing warships or picking cotton. In Aztec society, the numbers of slaves were not high; one early census reports that 1.5 percent of the people in a neighborhood of Tepoztlan were slaves (Hicks 1974: 256). Slaves tended to live with ordinary households – both commoner and noble – working at domestic tasks. While they made a modest economic contribution to

FIGURE 6.1. A rebellious king is strangled and his family is captured and enslaved. Reproduced from Berdan and Anawalt (1992: vol. 4: f. 68r), with permission.

individual households, slaves did not work in large groups and only occasionally did heavy labor.

Scholars are divided into opposing viewpoints on the position and lot of Aztec slaves in society (Shadow and Rodríguez V. 1995). One side, which we will call the *benign perspective*, focuses on the activities of slaves, and sees slaves as not all that different from dependent landless laborers (Chapter 5). Neither type of person had much say over their destiny, and both had to work for someone else to survive. There is no evidence that slaves lived in terrible conditions. Aztec slaves seem to have had a far better life than slaves in ancient Rome or the ante-bellum southern United States. These arguments suggest that slavery was not so bad among the Aztecs.

The opposing perspective – the *coercive perspective* – stresses the oppression and powerlessness of Aztec slaves. These were unfree people, who were literally the legal property of another. They were subject to the whims of their owner, and they could even be sacrificed if the owner wanted. These arguments emphasize the most negative aspects of Aztec slavery. These two opposing viewpoints have been prominent for many decades in Aztec studies. How should we view Aztec slaves and slavery? Both of these perspectives have merit. One way to proceed is to see how Aztec slavery fits with respect to other systems of slavery through history. Comparative analyses of slavery generally focus on the four key attributes of slaves (Patterson 2001; Scheidel 2008; Watson 1980):

1. **Property**: *Slaves are legal property, belonging to a person or institution.* This situation is clear in accounts of Aztec laws, which describe various ways that slaves became the property of another person (Offner 1983).
2. **Marginal status**: *Slaves have a marginal position in society.* While this seems likely for the Aztecs, in fact we have little information about just how Aztec slaves fit into society. Slaves might be cut off from their own families, but they often became integrated into the household of their owner.
3. **Labor**: *Slavery exists to provide labor for economic activities.* Most Aztec slaves did indeed provide labor for a household or an institution. Some (called "bathed slaves"), however, were destined to be sacrificed at important ceremonies and performed little economic work (female "bathed slaves" would spin fibers until their sacrifice).
4. **Coercion**: *The position of slave is not voluntary; people become and stay slaves through coercion.* This is abundantly clear for the Aztecs. Some slaves were enemies captured in battle (although most of these were soon sacrificed),

or else they became slaves through a legal proceeding often deriving from a criminal act (usually theft). However, people also became slaves from economic need and unlucky gambling (as with Xilotl's husband).

These four characteristics of slaves played out differently for the two major categories of Aztec slaves: domestic slaves and bathed slaves. The majority of slaves, like Xilotl, were of the domestic variety. They lived with families – both noble and commoner – and contributed to work around the home. Female domestic slaves relieved the women of the household from some of their time-consuming chores (such as the daily work of grinding maize), and male slaves helped farmers in the fields. But slaves also contributed to the household budget with specific economic activities. The most common of these – by far – was textile production by slave women. Because some cotton textiles served as money, this was a way for households to get ahead economically. Women who were talented spinners and weavers, like our fictional Xilotl, could command a good price in the slave market.

Aztec slaves (*tlacohtin*, sing. *tlacohtli*) were sold in the marketplace. While there were some specialized slave markets, like Azcapotzalco and Itzocan, most of the large marketplaces in Aztec Mexico offered some slaves for sale. Figure 6.2 shows lines of male (top) and female

FIGURE 6.2. Male and female slaves for purchase in Huexotzinco. Source: Códice de Huexotzinco(Hébert et al. 1995: lam. 5), modified by Michael E. Smith.

(bottom) slaves offered for sale in the marketplace in Huexotzinco (see also Figure 8.2). The slaves are indicated by their large wood collars. In the words of Friar Durán, "So that they could be identified as slaves, they wore on their necks wooden or metal collars with small rings through which passed rods about one yard long" (Durán 1971: 279). Indeed, the collar was an element used to identify individuals as slaves in pictorial manuscripts (Lesbre 1998). The female slave in Durán's images is showing off her spinning abilities to potential buyers (on the right of the Figure 8.2, below).

"Bathed slaves" (*tlaaltiltin*) are a special category of people who were purchased as slaves for the specific purpose of being sacrificed. Many or most sacrificial victims were enemy (foreign) soldiers captured in battle. Many were sacrificed in large-scale, politically motivated ceremonies, but a few may have been dressed in the outfit of a deity and sacrificed in a ceremony specifically dedicated to that god. But some sacrifices evidently required local victims instead of enemy soldiers. The sponsor of a sacrifice would purchase a special slave and carry out a ceremony of purification by "bathing" the individual. While we know few details, Spanish descriptions make it sound like the ceremony consisted of throwing some water onto the victim and not a full bathing. Even so, this transformed the slave into a proper victim for a specific sacrificial offering. Although the available historical sources focus primarily on the dealers of bathed slaves and the associated rituals, we do have some tidbits about the nature of these slaves and their lives and activities (Anderson 1982).

DAILY ROUND

Domestic slaves lived as members of the household. It was not at all unusual for Aztec families to have people boarding with them. These could be distant relatives, dependent laborers, or slaves. It is likely that daily life was not all that different for these different categories of boarder. In fact, this is the view of the benign perspective on Aztec slavery. Just as Aztec landless laborers had more rights and privileges than European serfs, and perhaps led better lives (Chapter 5), so too did Aztec slaves have an easier life than slaves in systems like ancient Rome or the antebellum southern United States. Slaves are mentioned in only one of the Nahuatl-language census documents from

Morelos, south of the Basin of Mexico, discussed in Chapter 5. But some 16 percent of commoner households had at least one unrelated commoner boarder living with the family (Carrasco 1976: 107). It is possible that the lives of these different kinds of dependent peoples (including slaves) differed little on a daily basis.

Our label for these people – domestic slaves – is important, because it reminds us that slaves lived *with* the family, in their house or perhaps in an adjacent building. Separate slave quarters and housing – as, for example, on plantations in the antebellum United States – simply did not exist in Aztec Mexico. Most Aztec houses were small, and thus all residents were packed together much of the time. Domestic slaves did not live separately; they were part of the family in many ways. It is reasonable to assume that slaves in an elite household may have been more physically separated from the noble family, spread about in a large, sprawling palace.

The main motivation for purchasing a slave like Xilotl was to increase the family's production of cloth, but female slaves almost certainly helped out with cooking and other domestic chores. Indeed, preparing meals took quite a bit of time out of a woman's day. The one and a half to five hours of grinding maize needed for a typical family's daily need was achieved more easily with an extra pair of experienced hands. The women of the house – the matriarch, her daughters, slaves, and any other residents – would be the first ones to wake in the morning. They would take the maize kernels out of the pot where they had been soaking all night, and place some on a rectangular grinding stone called *metlatl* (this is the origin of the Spanish term *metate*) (Figure 6.3). Using a two-handed grinder (*metlapilli*), called a *mano* today, the moist kernels were ground to a coarse consistency called *nixtlamal, masa* today.

While the men of the household were responsible for growing and harvesting the maize, once it was brought back home it entered the women's domain. The maize cobs were first allowed to dry out. Then the kernels were taken off the cob, a difficult task no doubt given to any female slaves in the family. In some places the dried kernels were stored in special granaries next to the house, and in others they were stored in baskets and bags inside the house, perhaps in the rafters out of the way.

Each evening, before bed, one of the women of the house would take out enough maize kernels for the next day and place them in a

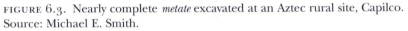

FIGURE 6.3. Nearly complete *metate* excavated at an Aztec rural site, Capilco. Source: Michael E. Smith.

big ceramic pot to soak and later boil. This softened up the kernels so that they were ready to grind in the morning. But there was another purpose to this soaking. Along with the maize and water, a small piece of limestone, or some wood ashes, would be added to the jar. These substances produce an alkaline condition in the mixture which reacts with enzymes in the maize to free up several amino acids. This process increases the nutritional value of the maize.

Soaking the maize with lime is not the only nutritionally beneficial practice in Aztec food preparation. Maize was eaten at every meal, but so were beans. The connection between maize and beans was and is fundamental to Mesoamerican cuisine. Not only do they provide a nice balance of taste and texture, but there is also a nutritional benefit. Maize is a decent source of protein, but it lacks several essential amino acids. It turns out that beans supply those specific nutrients that are not found in maize. When you eat maize and beans together, at the same meal, they form what is called a "complete protein." This means that the body gets the protein it needs from these two vegetable foods, making meat less important in the diet.

A big question is, How did the ancestors of the Aztecs figure this out? How did they know to eat beans and maize together at most meals? And why did they start adding limestone to the pot when soaking the maize? While we have no definitive answers to these questions, these practices make perfect nutritional sense, based on modern science. If you ask a traditional Mesoamerican woman today why she puts lime in with the soaking maize, she will reply that the tortillas taste better that way. She won't say anything about amino acids or nutritional value. Yet the fact that every indigenous New World society that relied on maize also processed it this way shows that somehow this practice – like that of serving maize and beans together – was taken up by societies that needed the nutritional value (Katz et al. 1974). The Aztecs added to their daily fare a long list of other plant foods, often seasonally available. These included chile peppers, squashes, tomatoes, avocados, diverse fruits, and various other vegetables and greens. Honey, salt, and vanilla boosted flavors (their frequency depending on the family's economic vitality at the moment), and chocolate added zest to a nobleman's meal.

Other foods served in Aztec households included meat from domesticated animals – turkeys and sometimes dogs. Also, wild game was hunted for food. The most common types of animal bones found at Aztec archaeological sites are the remains of meals: turkey, dog, deer, and rabbit. Chile peppers were often used to make a thick sauce called *molli* (the original version of the word *mole*), served with a small portion of meat. Tortillas were used to eat the sauce and meat, in place of spoons and forks. Besides tortillas, maize was also ground into a thin powder to make a warm gruel for breakfast (*atole*). Tamales were a special food for feast days.

Female slaves like Xilotl would spend the bulk of their time making textiles – spinning and weaving was labor-intensive and time-consuming, and was entirely women's work. All girls learned to spin and weave, regardless of their social position. As seen in Chapter 5, little girls were introduced to spinning at age four, began actually spinning at six, and were finally able to master weaving (and presumably spinning) at age fourteen (see Figure 5.7). At this point the girl was considered to have arrived at adulthood. Today, in the Sierra Norte de Puebla, little Nahua girls begin weaving small items at age five and, matching the pre-Columbian girls, complete their instruction at age fourteen.

This was entirely hand technology with easily acquired tools. For spinning the woman twirled raw fibers around a spindle (wooden shaft) with a ceramic disc (whorl) near its base. The twisted fibers collected and bulged above the whorl and around the length of the shaft (Figure 6.4a). Seeing this, the Aztecs enjoyed a riddle that asked,

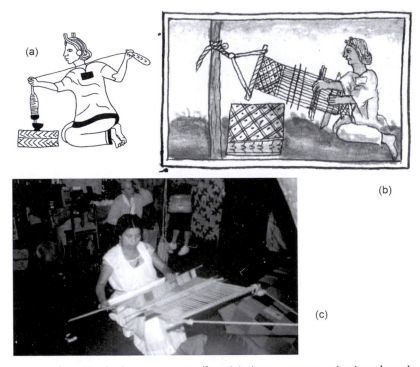

FIGURE 6.4. Producing cotton textiles. (a) Aztec woman spinning thread. Berdan and Anawalt (1992: vol. 4: f. 68r), with permission. (b) Aztec woman weaving on a backstrap loom. Sahagún (1950–1982: book 10: fig. 190). Firenze, Biblioteca Medicea Laurenziana. All rights reserved. Further reproduction in any print or digital format is forbidden. (c) Modern Nahua weaver. Source: Frances F. Berdan.

"What are those things which, at their dancing place, they give stomachs, they make pregnant? They are spindles" (Sahagún 1950–1982: book 6: 240). If spinning cotton, the woman rested the whole apparatus in a small bowl – as she twirled the spindle, it "danced" in the bowl, the "dancing place" of the riddle (Figure 6.5a, b). No such support was needed for spinning the thicker and coarser maguey fibers, although a larger whorl was required. Once the fibers were spun into nicely uniform threads (hopefully) they were stretched on a backstrap loom, which was essentially a bundle of sticks (Figures 6.4b, c, and 6.5a). A strap that was looped around the weaver's back supported one end of the loom; the other end was

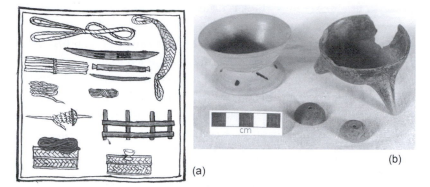

FIGURE 6.5. Spinning and weaving equipment. (a) Spinning and weaving equipment. Sahagún (1950–1982: book 8: fig. 75). Firenze, Biblioteca Medicea Laurenziana, Ms. 16, f. 31v. Su concessione del MiBAC. E' vietata ogni ulteriore riproduzione con qualsiasi mezzo. (b) Spinning bowls and spindle whorls excavated at rural Aztec sites in Morelos. Source: Michael E. Smith.

attached to a tree, pole, or other sturdy object. It took a long time to set up the warp threads (those stretched from her body to the tree), but once completed, the weaver proceeded to pass row after row after row of threads (weft) through the warp threads, yielding cloths of varying complexity and designs (Figure 6.4c; see also Figure 6.9). Indeed, some weaves were highly complex and resulted in exquisitely decorated textiles destined to adorn the bodies of noble persons and decorate the idols of revered deities. Once the cloth was completed it could be worn directly off the loom – Aztec clothing was essentially draped, not tailored.

Most cloth production was for clothing: cloaks and loincloths for men, and tunics, capes, and skirts for women. Other textiles were used for other objects such as bags, multi-use cloths, and deity adornments. A special kind of white cotton cloak (*quachtli*) served as a form of money (see Chapter 8). The finer clothing was made from cotton (brown or white) and the cheaper clothing from the coarser fibers of maguey and related plants. Commoner women would produce cloth for their own use (clothing does wear out and families tend to expand), for sale in the marketplaces in exchange for that extra load of firewood or basket of tomatoes, and for the payment of tributes and taxes to overarching lords and kings. This became magnified in quantity and presumably quality in polygynous elite settings: the larger and more opulent the household, the more weavers at work, and the more cloth woven. The upshot was that a noble household contained more wives and could afford more female slaves. Opulence bred opulence, wealth led to more wealth.

One convenience of the spinning and weaving technology was the ability to take it up and drop it at any time. Women in Aztec households had many daily chores in addition to making cloth: bearing and rearing children, preparing and cooking meals, cleaning the house and its environs, tending a kitchen garden, marketing, helping with the harvest or a domestic craft, keeping domestic peace – myriad endless duties, all labor-intensive. Xilotl would help with most of these scheduled, sporadic, and seasonal activities, so she would have been up and down a lot with her spindle and loom.

Similarly, male slaves were at the beck and call of their owners, noble or commoner, farmer, potter, or merchant. The slaves helped in the fields, aided in the production of crafts, and served as porters on the road – if Quauhtli were to acquire a male slave, he would surely help with the potting enterprise. In Sahagún's words, a slave "became someone's digging stick and tump line" (1950–1982: book 4: 5). Male slaves surely would have been assigned some of the harder tasks such as house building and repairs, tool making, and back-bending field work.

We do not know a great deal about the treatment of slaves in domestic settings, whether noble or commoner. But we do know that they could look forward to a special day in the 260-day calendar, One Death, when they would receive special treatment. Their wooden collars were removed if they were wearing them, and they were bathed and flattered and treated with great consideration and esteem; they could not be scolded or abused by their owners. This had the force of the great god Tezcatlipoca behind it, as they believed that this god would be offended by mistreatment of slaves on this day. That the slave owners needed to warn their children not to "chide, deal vainly with, nor strike the slaves" suggests that this sort of behavior indeed went on (Sahagún 1950–1982: book 4: 91).

## LIFE CYCLE

Slavery was not a hereditary status; the children of slaves were born as free individuals. As an Aztec, you believed that fate played a critical role in your future: Ce Ocelotl (One Jaguar) was not a good birth date, as it forebode that "almost all became slaves" (Sahagún 1950–1982: book 4: 5). Xilotl should have known better than to marry Ce Ocelotl! Similarly, slavery, including an end as a bathed slave, was a possible fate for those born on One House and Six Grass (Sahagún 1950–1982: book 4: 20–21, 93–95). Still, all was not lost. Although you may be born on one of these inauspicious days, you may be bathed and named on a more fortuitous day, or behave well and offset the predicted dangers of your actual birth day (Chapter 7).

If one could not be born a slave, then how did free individuals end up as slaves? As a point of clarification, enemy warriors captured on the battlefield are often called "slaves," but in reality most were rather expeditiously sacrificed by their conquerors and did not enter the social scene (González Torres 1976). But a different fate may have ensnared other conquered people: the woman and child shown in Figure 6.1 were the wife and son of a conquered ruler, who was executed on the spot. They were taken as prisoners to the court of Mexico, presumably to serve as slaves in that ruler's palace (Berdan and Anawalt 1992: vol. 4: 136–136). This probably happened more than just this one time.

We have already seen one of the pathways into slavery: one could sell oneself – and even one's whole family – into slavery to cover a gambling debt. The early Spanish friars were scandalized at the extent of Aztec gambling (even rulers gambled, but they were wealthy enough to cover their losses). The *patolli* game where Ce Ocelotl lost his and Xilotl's freedom was one of the main settings for wagering. This was a game that involved moving markers around a cross-shaped board (see Figure 1.5). It was very similar to the Indian game of Pachisi that spread around the world in the twentieth century. The other big venue for gambling was the ballgame. In a specially built ballcourt, two teams would compete for points with a bouncy rubber ball. Eager crowds would gather to watch, with an active scene of betting by both nobles and commoners.

Becoming a slave through a gambling debt illustrates a larger point about Aztec slavery – this was often an economic transaction between the slave and owner. People could enter slavery voluntarily. You would sell yourself to someone else, who became your owner. This was done in cases of extreme economic hardship. The best documented case was a widespread famine in the year One Rabbit (1454). For four years, drought wracked the highlands and farmers were unable to grow maize and other crops. Kings opened up their granaries, but it was not enough to stave off famine over large areas. The people then resorted to other desperate strategies. Some, as intact families, left their cities voluntarily, many traveling to the more luxuriant lowlands. Other Aztecs sold their children to merchants or noblemen who could support them, with the understanding that they could ransom their children later when life improved. And, as a bit of an insult, Totonac people from the Gulf coast, which was not affected by the famine, came to the cities of central Mexico "carrying great loads of maize in order to buy slaves." Families were separated in these trans- actions, children leaving parents, husbands leaving wives, siblings separated, and on and on (Durán 1994: 240).

During the famine of One Rabbit, and at other lesser periods of drought and poverty, poor farmers and others simply sold themselves – and sometimes their whole family – as slaves (Figure 6.6). What did they get in return? The owner of a slave was required to feed and clothe slaves and provide them with a place to live. This was an extreme way to avoid the famine. If slaves could accumulate funds, however, they could purchase their freedom at a later time, or ransom their children as mentioned above. How much was needed to buy oneself or one's family member out of slavery? As a possible measure, one source states that a person (of unknown social and economic status) could support himself (and perhaps his family) for one year with twenty *quachtli* (large cotton cloaks) (Motolinía 1971: 367). For a commoner, that would have been quite a lot. In some ways, slavery served as a sort of social safety net, providing living options for people in desperate straits (whether or not of their own doing).

Slaves figured prominently in Aztec law, and slavery was sometimes used as a legal punishment. Lists of Aztec law cases often indicate enslavement as punishment. For example, when two boys stole maize seeds that had already been planted, they were sold as slaves to the owner of the plants. A man could be enslaved for stealing a turkey, but not a dog (which would bring a lesser punishment). Slavery was a common punishment for the theft of low-value goods; for more expensive items, or items stolen outside the city, death could be the punishment.

FIGURE 6.6. Selling children into slavery during a famine. Sahagún (1950–1982: book 7: fig. 15). Firenze, Biblioteca Medicea Laurenziana. All rights reserved. Further reproduction in any print or digital format is forbidden.

Slaves were also sold in the marketplace. There were merchants who specialized in slaves, and certain marketplaces were known as major slave markets; in fact Diego Durán claimed that slaves could be sold in only two cities: Azcapotzalco and Itzocan (Durán 1971: 278). When brought to the market to be sold, slaves wore a wooden collar (Figures 6.1 and 6.2). If a slave managed to escape the marketplace and flee to the house of a local official, his freedom would be granted (although anyone impeding his escape could be enslaved in his place). We don't know how often this may have happened. Another way slaves could gain their freedom was to pay back their owners for the full price due to them. And if a person had been unjustly enslaved, he or she could be absolved on the day One Dog, which appeared once every 260 days (Sahagún 1950–1982: book 4: 91). Although

FIGURE 6.7. Arraying a bathed slave for sacrifice. Sahagún (1950–1982: book 9: fig. 36). Firenze, Biblioteca Medicea Laurenziana.

most slaves lived a hard life of labor, they were legally free to marry, to acquire property, and even to maintain their own household. These considerations show that the line between slaves and dependent laborers was not as sharp as one might imagine.

We have been talking about the lives and conditions of domestic slaves. Life for the bathed slaves was quite different. Because they were destined to be sacrificed, their relationship with their owner was probably different as well. Sacrificial victims were treated well in the weeks or months prior to their killing. After their symbolic "bathing," these slaves were dressed in special costumes for their sacrifice (Figure 6.7). These slaves were locked into their fate; they could not hope to marry, to own property, or to purchase their freedom. Their fate lay with the priests and the gods.

We know the most about "bathed slaves" offered by merchants during the month of Panquetzaliztli, when wealthy merchants would purchase healthy and attractive slaves, men or women, who were also fine singers and dancers. We have discussed the merchant's role and perspective in Chapter 4. But what about these activities from the slave's perspective? A particularly ambitious merchant may buy more than one slave for this purpose. The slaves were confined in wooden jails (more like cages) overnight in their new owner's homes. In the morning they were released: a woman was given cotton to spin while a man was given no particular duty or activity. The merchant would construct more houses so his slave(s) could "always" go dancing on the rooftops – this may have occupied much of their time between their purchase and their sacrifice. This may have gone on for some time, as now the merchant traveled far south to Tochtepec for requisite rituals with other merchants, returning to perform still more rituals and feasts. Finally, the bathed slaves were put on display: they were dressed in fine clothing and adornments, and given flowers to smell and tobacco tubes to smoke. The slaves sat on mats in front of the merchant's house as others admired them. This display continued for three days, after which the slaves were put in the care of a priest, escorts, and female "face-washers." A complexity of rituals followed, including special drinking, eating, a mock battle, and ultimately sacrifice atop the temple of Huitzilopochtli in front of a large audience (Sahagún 1950–1982: book 9: 45–61). So, a bathed slave knew his or her fate for some time before being ritually sacrificed. While we expect that a woman continued to spin and spin and spin, we do not know if male or female slaves made other domestic contributions or, if more than one slave was bought, if they were allowed or expected to interact with one another.

## IN AND OUT OF TROUBLE

If you are a slave, you are already in trouble. But things could get worse:

*Xilotl had almost grown accustomed to her new life as a domestic slave in the potting family in the city of Matlatzinco (Figure 6.8). Her initial worries about having to help in the family business were not borne out. While she occasionally had to pitch in at key moments – carrying firewood or arranging the unfired pots to dry – she was able to avoid lugging clay around or painting the boring and repetitive design on serving bowls. Most of her time was spent making textiles and helping with the maize grinding and other tasks in the kitchen. But she really disliked the family, all except Tototontli, the oldest daughter, who was learning to weave from Xilotl. Tototontli was eager to learn and was doing a good job. She was the closest thing Xilotl had to a friend in her new home.*

*Xilotl didn't pay much attention to the sacrifices and ceremonies that took place at the major temples in the city. These did not concern her. But, one evening, she was stunned to overhear a hushed conversation between Quauhtli and his wife Cihuacomitl. They were talking about an upcoming sacrifice that required an adult woman from the community to be sacrificed, not an outsider. Evidently, the head priest was looking for someone to sponsor the sacrifice and provide the victim, and rumor had it that the*

FIGURE 6.8. The archaeological site of Calixtlahuaca, which is the remains of the Aztec-period city of Matlatzinco. Source: Michael E. Smith.

*sponsor might receive some benefits from the king. Xilotl could not believe her ears when Quauhtli suggested, "Why not offer Xilotl?"*

*What Xilotl had interpreted as a simple lack of close and friendly interactions with the family was taken by Quauhtli and Cihuacomitl as an aloofness, even a sense of hostility on the part of the slave. She must have a chip on her shoulder, they thought. Cihuacomitl had initially been eager to have another adult woman around the house, both for the work and for companionship. But Xilotl never wanted to relax or socialize with Cihuacomitl; she just did her work and kept to herself. Xilotl had been pleased when they had originally negotiated an arrangement that let her keep every fourth cloth she wove. The others belonged to the family. This seemed like a great arrangement. But it had become increasingly obvious that Xilotl would weave three hasty and sloppy cloths for her slave obligations, and then one fine and intricate cloth for herself (Figure 6.9).*

*All of these things came into play in Quauhtli and Cihuacomitl's conversation that evening, and after overhearing it, Xilotl was suddenly fearful of her life for the first time. Would they really think of sacrificing me? What can I do? Just then, Tototontli dropped in and sat down. Xilotl repeated the conversation to her and started crying. Tototontli awkwardly tried to comfort Xilotl, and then said she had heard her parents complaining about Xilotl for weeks. She hadn't realized their complaints were serious, though. Tototontli was devastated. Xilotl was like an older sister, one of her few friends.*

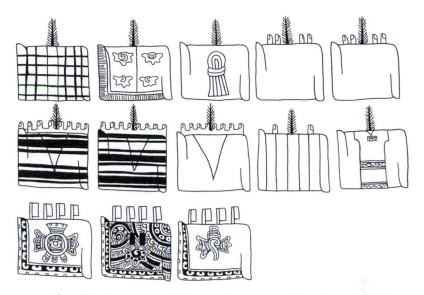

FIGURE 6.9. Finely woven and decorated cotton textiles. Reproduced from Berdan and Anawalt (1992: vol. 4: f. 52r), with permission.

*Tototontli immediately confronted her parents. "You can't sacrifice Xilotl! She is part of the family! She is my only friend! I am learning so much from her! How else will I learn to spin and weave properly?" Taken aback, Cihuacomitl responded, "Don't I know how to weave? I was your teacher before Xilotl showed up, and I can teach you again. I'm sick of getting low-quality cloths from her, cloths that don't command much of a price in the market." "Obviously, she can do much better," Quauhtli continued. Tototontli pleaded with her parents, and eventually won them over. Xilotl could stay, but only if ALL of her cloths were of a high quality.*

*Xilotl stayed with Quauhtli, Cihuacomitl, and Tototontli. They never talked about the sacrifice; a rich merchant found a suitable victim in the market, and was rewarded with favors from the palace. The quality of Xilotl's cloths were more uniformly high, and now she made more of an effort to be pleasant with Quauhtli and Cihuacomitl. Tototontli developed into a competent spinner and weaver. Xilotl would occasionally wonder whether they had been serious about the sacrifice, or was their conversation simply a ruse to rein her in?*

Xilotl made adjustments to make her life in this household more secure. Perhaps, over time, she may be able to buy her freedom from the sales of her personal weavings. She had already seen that life could take many twists and turns – hadn't she been taught that the earth is slippery?

REFLECTIONS

We have seen that slavery among the Aztecs was a quite different affair from the large-scale economic institution of slavery in imperial Rome or the antebellum United States. Most slaves belonged to the domestic category. They lived with a family and helped out with household chores and whatever economic activity the family was engaged in. Most male domestic slaves helped in the fields, with all aspects of the agricultural round. Most female slaves produced cloth, in addition to kitchen duties.

Both perspectives on Aztec slavery – benign and coercive – are apt in describing aspects of the lives and conditions of individual slaves. On the benign side, Xilotl's life was not rough and her duties were not onerous. She lived with a family and was well fed and cared for. She was even able to produce income for herself in the form of some of the cloths she produced. But on the coercive side, Xilotl was not free. Her choices were limited. If a problem arose, as in the vignette above, she was the one who had to yield. She was obligated to provide labor for a household of nonrelatives. Overall, her position in society was marginal. Although she could accumulate wealth, it would probably take many years to build up enough cloths for her to buy her freedom.

As for the bathed slaves, we know less about these people. They could have lived in a household only in a temporary and very special capacity. Their fate was to be sacrificed to the gods. While some authors claim that sacrifice was a great honor, to the point where victims went willingly to their death, one should not lose track of the fact that, once purchased for that purpose, these victims had a fixed destiny and their participation was based on coercion.

There was a certain fluidity in Aztec social life. A person could rise on the social ladder, but also descend to dismal depths. In that tumble, slavery served as a kind of social safety net, losing status but assuring at least temporary survival. For the slave it was an opportunity to pay off a debt, a chance to be redeemed from theft, or the prospect of overcoming extreme poverty; for the slave owner, it meant household and field labor that could be directed to whatever tasks he or she needed. Still, it was not a particularly rosy situation for the slave: slavery was not without its risks, the greatest of which was possible sacrifice atop a lofty temple.

# Part II

## Intersecting Lives

How did the many Aztec people, from different individual backgrounds, from different walks of life, and with different personal goals, wend their way through the intricacies of the vibrant and uncertain Aztec world? To broach this question we take a look at the Aztec persons from Part I (along with some of their friends and enemies) within the everyday web and extraordinary highlights of their daily lives. All Aztec persons experienced their own and others' life-cycle events (in this case, a birth and naming ceremony), went to the market, may have faced a judgment at the royal palace (or at least heard about someone else's tribulation), and gone to war (or, again, certainly knew someone who did and prayed or mourned for him).

An Aztec person's life was a tapestry of these and other ordinary and signal events, some happening daily, some weekly or monthly, some occasionally, and some infrequently and unpredictably. Some overlapped, since people then, as today, multitasked. The four events we have chosen encapsulate and reveal a great many fundamental features of Aztec life – developing a family, exchanging goods and services in marketplaces, dealing with crimes and facing justice, and engaging with warfare as a frequently recurring activity that saturated Aztec culture. Other events, such as public and private ceremonies, the pomp of a royal funeral, travel to distant lands, and even daily meals, are interspersed throughout all of this book's chapters.

# 7

## A Child Is Born

*Chilpapalotl kept playing the words through her head: thank the gods, offer incense, work hard at household tasks, eat and drink well, don't chew chicle, don't get angered or frightened, don't look at anything red, don't eat earth or chalk, don't lift heavy things, don't overdo the sweat bath (but what a temptation!). Her parents, her grandparents, everyone, had been repeating these words to her for months. And more recently, the midwife. She knew it was well-intended and that they loved her, but enough is enough! By now she knew all of this by heart.*

*Can't they see how exhausted she is, with her precious jewel getting bigger and bigger and more active day by day? Her belly was so big now that she could no longer bend over the metate to grind the morning maize, and weaving was a bit of a stretch. She found herself going less and less to market, and got out of breath just walking around the house. And the heartburn! She could still spin thread, though – that was almost therapeutic. But she couldn't sit still for long, especially for those lectures.*

*She looked forward to the visits from her midwife Cuicatototl, because that meant that she could retreat into the temazcalli, the sweat bath, which was so relaxing. Cuicatototl got the sweat bath temperature just right and massaged her belly, which made her feel so much better! Soon, if all went well, her precious jewel, her precious feather would become the newest member of the family. Soon.*

Even though Chilpapalotl quietly complained, remembering all of the lectures and admonishments of her elders by heart was, in fact, the point. Even though Chilpapalotl was supremely uncomfortable, with only about one Aztec month (twenty days) to go, she managed to discipline herself and sit through the endless talking. It was all part of the necessary and scripted narrative that preceded the birth of an Aztec child.

ANTICIPATIONS

Children were highly valued in Aztec society, so it comes as no surprise that great care and precautions were taken to ensure full-term pregnancies and successful births. Established procedures were followed to assure the health of both the mother and the baby, along with the favor of the gods. These procedures hit high points at four major moments: when the pregnancy first became known, during the seventh or eighth month, at the time of birth, and four days following the birth.

There is need for one small caveat here: most of our information on these procedures comes from the Franciscan friar Bernardino de Sahagún, who compiled his accounts some fifty years after the Spanish conquest. Although his *Historia* was written in Nahuatl and illustrated by native scribes, much Spanish ideology and culture crept into the account. In this case, which calendar is being followed? The Christian calendar contained twelve months, the Aztec calendar was composed of eighteen. So was the seventh or eighth month in the third trimester (in the Christian count), or less than halfway there (in the Aztec calendar)? Our guess is that the Christian calendar is the referent here, given the activities of the midwife at this stage. Similarly, the details of the bathing of the newborn child should be looked at as perhaps infiltrated by motions and narratives associated with Christian baptism.

When a pregnancy became known, there was great rejoicing and the relatives of the parents-to-be assembled to celebrate *in cozcatl, in quetzalli* ("the precious necklace, the precious feather," i.e., the baby). Feasting and lectures were highlighted. Feasting at this early rally would have differed in abundance and sumptuousness from household to household, depending on the householders' economic wherewithal. Food and drink were prepared, if possible augmented with flowers and tobacco tubes. Eloquent speeches were first presented by the older relatives, "the white-haired ones, the white-headed ones" (*in tzoniztaque, in quaiztaque*; Sahagún 1950–1982: book 6: 135), who opened the orations with exhortations about the importance of the moment and the need for prayer and reverence to the omnipotent gods who have given this precious gift to the woman. There was quite a bit of talk about all the things that could go wrong, and the possibility that the gods who had generously given this life can as readily take it away – much of this perhaps comes across as rather dismal and depressing to a modern reader, but it probably was well-taken by an Aztec listener who deeply believed in the power of the gods and the omniscience of fate.

Following the eloquent words spoken by an older relative, the father-to-be's parents addressed their daughter-in-law, reminding her that the gods have favored her, exhorting her to thank them, admonishing her to not become proud, and advising her to take special care to not abort this tender gift from the gods. At this point, apparently it was fine for the pregnant woman to still be "diligent in the sweeping, the cleaning, the arranging of things, the cutting (of wood), the fanning (of the fire), and the offering of incense" but she should not lift heavy objects, view anything frightening, or overdo sweat bath sessions (Sahagún 1950–1982: book 6: 141–143; Figure 7.1a, b). At the same time, her husband was admonished to limit his romantic advances, as these may cause the baby to be born weak and lame, or even be stuck in the womb. The old men and women then took over the monologue with loving and caring words. This was all quite lengthy and repetitive, but it was not over yet. Another relative took up the artfully crafted narrative, followed by eloquent words of the pregnant woman's parents, and finally a humble response by the pregnant woman herself. This was a signal life-cycle event, and it appears that several important relatives in attendance were allowed to speak, offer advice and moral support, and respond to others. They all, repeatedly, underscored the primacy of the gods and the fragility of life, tossing in bits of practical advice here and there. It is possible that the in-laws were a bit "on stage" vis-à-vis one another at this event.

It was convenient that, as the woman's pregnancy progressed and her belly grew, she had no real need of special maternity fashions. The traditional female attire of tunic or cape and skirt were conveniently constructed to fit women at whatever stage of life – the tunic and cape were loose and draped in any event, and the skirt was worn by gathering up the material around the waist and could be expanded or contracted as needed.

A second feast rallied the relatives again and took place when the pregnancy was around seven to eight months along. At this time there

FIGURE 7.1. Sweat baths, ancient and modern. (a) An Aztec sweat bath. *Codex Magliabechiano* (1903: f. 77r). (b) A present-day Nahua sweat bath. Source: Frances F. Berdan.

was more eating and drinking and eloquent speaking, and also discussion as to the selection of an appropriate midwife. A recurring theme of these and the earlier speeches was the new baby as the "thorn, the maguey" (*inhuitz, inmeuh*) of the great-grandfathers that is now metaphorically sprouting (Sahagún 1950–1982: book 6: 142). That is, the lectures emphasized, again and again, that the pregnant woman and her baby were carrying on the bloodline and the traditions (*in tzontli, in iztitl*: the hair, the fingernail) of the revered ancestors from a distant but continuous past – a daunting social responsibility. These speeches also reiterated the supremacy and benevolence of the gods and the tenuousness of life.

On that same occasion, or perhaps shortly after, the midwife was selected. Once chosen by the assembled relatives, the midwife took center stage – the pregnant woman was now placed in the hands of this skilled practitioner.

## THE MIDWIFE (*TICITL, TEMIXIUITIANI*)

Midwives were female medical specialists who assisted women in pregnancy, childbirth, and postpartum situations. They shared the name *ticitl* with male and female physicians who performed services such as setting broken bones, lancing and stitching wounds, and treating eye and other ailments (Sahagún 1950–1982: book 10: 30, 53). The seventeenth-century Spanish priest Hernando Ruiz de Alarcón mentions, with some Spanish editorializing, that the name *ticitl* is "accepted among the natives as meaning sage, doctor, seer, and sorcerer, or, perhaps, one who has a pact with the Devil'" (Andrews and Hassig 1984: 157). He adds that midwives were also called *tepalehuiani* ("helper") and *temixiuitiani* ("midwife"; also in Molina 1970: 97v). Like other physicians, midwives called on supernatural intervention as well as natural aids and remedies.

A midwife had weighty duties and responsibilities before, during, and after a birth. A skilled midwife was experienced in the practical side of facilitating successful pregnancies and childbirths. This included emphasizing many important dos and don'ts for the expectant mother. As an advisor, the midwife was equipped with a vast armory of practical advice, each rule coupled with its own scary consequence. For instance, a nap during the day would result in a child with "abnormally large eyelids"; chewing chicle resulted in a child with abnormal lips and therefore unable to suckle; eating earth or chalk meant a sickly child would be born; lolling in a too-hot sweat bath caused the baby to roast and be stuck; and if the mother fasted, the child would starve (Sahagún 1950–1982: book 6: 156–157). If the mother did not take precautions during a lunar eclipse by placing an obsidian knife in her mouth or near her breast, her child would be turned into a mouse or born without lips or a nose, cross-eyed, or otherwise imperfect (Sahagún 1950–1982: book 7: 8–9). The midwife was well aware of the expectant mother's uncomfortable condition and she recognized the pressure on her charge's lower back, her need to change positions, her difficulties in getting up and down, and her overall discomfort. So some of her advice was more positive: the

FIGURE 7.2. Midwife massaging an expectant mother's belly. Sahagún (1950–1982: book 6: fig. 24). Firenze, Biblioteca Medicea Laurenziana.

expectant mother was admonished to eat well, to take on only light household tasks, and to avoid being startled or frightened. All of this was heard by the mother's immediate relatives, and the advice was certainly aimed as much at them as at her.

The midwife's practical work also included proper use (and temperature) of the sweat bath and positioning the fetus by aggressively massaging the mother's belly (Figure 7.2). The midwife also commanded specialized knowledge of herbal and other medical aids, especially the herb *cihuapatli* ("woman's medicine") and the careful and strategic use of pulverized opossum tail – both helpful in alleviating difficult births. She was expected to be capable, knowledgeable, and effective in facilitating births, managing postpartum procedures, and introducing the baby to its new world. She also must be adept in handling stressful childbirth emergencies that may crop up.

On another plane, it was also necessary that the midwife be well-versed in the roles and efficacy of the goddesses that could help or harm her work and her charges. Particularly important were

Yohualticitl, grandmother of the sweat bath; Quilaztli, a warrior version of the mother goddess Cihuacoatl ("Woman Serpent," and, along with a related goddess Toci, a patroness of the midwives); and Chalchiuhtlicue ("Jade Her Skirt," a water deity called on during a baby's bathing ceremony) (Berdan 2014: 232). In scripted dialogues with the midwife, the expectant mother's elderly female relatives recognized that the midwife was "the skilled one, the artisan of our lord," but that her duty was to "Aid our lord; help him." They charged her to "Take up thy charge ... Aid Ciuapilli, Quilaztli" (Sahagún 1950–1982: book 6: 152, 155). The midwife was a helper, of both the pregnant mother and the gods.

Failure, resulting in the death of mother or child or both, was a very real and recognized possibility. Midwifery had its share of risks and dangers, which even worked their way into metaphoric speech: "of a midwife, when she would cure [the child], if it just died in her care, it was said: 'Thou hast shattered it; thou hast broken it'" (Sahagún 1950–1982: book 6: 249). Still, whether she succeeds or fails is not entirely hers to determine – it is in the hands of the gods. Much familial and midwifery dialogue stresses, over and over again, that the gods may not will this child to live or the mother to survive her ordeal. Still, midwives were practical, active players and not just instruments of the gods: they associated with one another and surely must have talked about difficult or unusual cases.

In addition to information sharing, they may have taken some comfort in mutual camaraderie. They shared a patron deity and celebrated annual ceremonies as a group; notably, during the month of Ochpaniztli they were major celebrants in highly scripted dances and other roles – all requiring a good deal of group practice and coordination. In specific cases, noble women could expect to have more than one midwife at their service, the "head midwife" assisted by others (who were perhaps neophytes still undergoing their training). We do not know what midwives charged for their services, but it would be expected that wealthier families could afford more experienced and extensive care. This may also have resulted in higher survivability of both mother and child among the elite, although we also do not know this for sure.

Back at the house of the mother-to-be, the chosen midwife was asked to join in a feast and dialogues with the relatives of both anticipating parents. Elderly kin spoke in turn, entreating the midwife to take the pregnant woman into her wise and capable care. The midwife responded in self-deprecating tones, elaborating on her responsibilities and expectations as a midwife, and proceeding to take over the process. At this time, admonitions and actions were both ideological and practical. After reiterating her reliance on the gods, the midwife fired up the sweat bath or *temazcalli*, called *xochicaltzin* ("revered flower house") in this context. Within this toasty environment, the midwife massaged the woman's extended belly, positioning the baby for birth. She apparently continued the sweat bath and massage treatments until birth was imminent.

## THE BIRTH AND FOUR DAYS AFTER

### The Baby's Arrival

As the time for giving birth approached, the pregnant woman's family summoned the midwife so she was on hand for the highly anticipated (and in some ways highly dreaded) event. If the family was noble or wealthy, the midwife might arrive at the household four or five days early; poorer families probably could only afford to call on the midwife at the onset of labor pains. In either event, the mother was bathed in the sweat bath and given a drink prepared with the *cihuapatli* herb, a known expellant. If that failed to hasten the birth, an infusion of ground-up opossum tail (with water) was given to the woman to drink (Sahagún 1950–1982: book 6: 159). The usual birthing position was squatting, with gravity assisting. But if the baby was stubborn, the midwife would help gravity along; she "suspended the woman (by the head); she proceeded to shake her, to kick her in the back" all the while entreating the woman to "exert thyself" (Sahagún 1950–1982: book 6: 160).

These aids and strategies to speed up the birth were standard in Aztec life. The herb *cihuapatli*, "woman's medicine," is described in the Badianus herbal as one of several concoctions used to ease parturition (Gates 2000: 106; Figure 7.3). Sahagún mentions it as a drink, but the Badianus herbal also suggests that its leaves could be ground up with tomato root and opossum tail, used to wet the womb. This herbal of 1552 also mentions other remedies: one is a

FIGURE 7.3. *Cihuapatli* plant, "women's medicine" (middle plant), in the Badianus herbal. Source: De la Cruz and Gates (2000: 106). Image is in the public domain.

drink from the bark of the *quauhalahuac* tree. Another was an anointing concoction of animal hairs, bones, gall (of cock and hare), deerskins, eagle wings, and onions all burned together, to which was added salt, pulque, and prickly pear cactus fruit. A greenstone and a "bright green pearl" could be "bound on her back" (Gates 2000: 106). Some of the ingredients of these remedies, such as the greenstone, pearl, and eagle's wing, might only be within the purview of wealthy nobles. Others were probably more widely available, but still seem to have involved something of a treasure hunt. Among these was the most intense expellant, the tail of an opossum. This was so powerful it was used only in the most dire circumstances.

*Chilpapalotl was exhausted. She remembered, remembered well (!) the labor pains that engulfed her very being, over and over again. She vaguely recalled the midwife leading her to the sweat bath and giving her something to drink. After she drank it, the contractions came faster and harder, and it wasn't long (or so she thought, she really had no sense of time) before the baby emerged. Through all of that, the soothing and sonorous words of the midwife helped calm her down. Her parents had insisted on this midwife – her name, Cuicatototl, meaning "Singing Bird," said it all. Through all the pain, Chilpapalotl somehow felt as though she was in a room full of birds! Still, she had just wanted out of that room and onto her familiar petate (mat). Then suddenly she had heard the bold, unbelievably loud war cries from Singing Bird's mouth. Yes! She knew that soon she would be holding her baby, her precious jewel, her brilliant quetzal feather. She had won her battle, just as everyone had hoped. Still, she knew she must thank the gods who held the fates of everyone, including her new one, a little boy, in their hands.*

Chilpapalotl's drink was surely *cihuapatli* leaves (most likely *Montanoa tomentosa*) mixed with water. It was a well-known and widely used herbal relief, sometimes used in difficult births to induce and/or shorten labor (Ortiz de Montellano 1990: 185; Pomar 1964: 215; Santamaría 1978: 242). There apparently were several species of this useful plant – Francisco Hernández, traveling in New Spain in the 1570s, describes twenty-three different plants called *cihuapatli*, many of them named after their location, which could be lowlands, highlands, or household gardens (1959, vol. 1: 293–299). So it was widely available. He reinforces the accepted wisdom that these plants aided women in childbirth and other womanly medical matters, hence their name (*cihua* = woman). The midwife may also have rubbed Chilpapalotl's stomach with crushed tobacco, and added aromatics such as copal incense and *yauhtli* (a marigold) flowers to the sweat bath (Andrews and Hassig 1984: 159). All of this helped to relax her, along with Cuicatototl's calming voice.

The midwife's war cries signaled that the baby had been successfully born and that the mother "had fought a good battle, had become a brave warrior, had taken a captive, had captured a baby." The midwife continued honoring the fatigued woman, calling her an eagle warrior, a jaguar warrior, a warrior who has returned "exhausted from battle" – all putting her on an equal plane to her male warrior counterparts (Sahagún 1950–1982: book 6: 167, 179). But then the midwife changed her tone, warning the woman to not be proud, presumptuous, or a braggart, for the baby was considered the property and creation of the gods and they could still take away her precious little jewel. As the woman rested, her older relatives and the midwife engaged in rather lengthy and apparently scripted dialogues, in every speech being humble, deferential, and grateful to the gods who could will either good or evil to this newborn child. They reminded one another of the omniscience of the gods and the tenuousness of life here on earth.

Upon birth, the baby was welcomed into this world with lengthy, prepared (memorized) lectures, spoken by the midwife (lectures began early in this culture!). Whether boy or girl, the midwife warned the baby that he or she had arrived in a world of fatigue, torment, misery, and travail, but perhaps gaining some merit by the favor of the gods. The midwife introduced the infant to its grandparents (and certainly other relatives). After additional (less than cheerful) words to the child and its relatives, the midwife removed the afterbirth and buried it in a corner of the house (it is not known if the afterbirths of subsequent children were buried in the same or different corners). She then cut the umbilical cord.

The cutting and disposing of the umbilical cord was no small thing. If the baby was a boy, the cord was dried, attached to a small shield with four little arrows, this assemblage later given to distinguished warriors to bury on a battlefield (Sahagún 1950–1982: book 4: 3). If the baby was a girl, the cord was buried in the home by the hearth and grinding stone. In both cases, these acts presaged the futures of adult Aztec men and women: men would become warriors and women would work in the home. Like all the prior activities, this occasion was highly ritualized and again the midwife addressed the infant in what resembles a care-fully crafted performance. If a boy, the baby was dedicated to a life of war; if a girl, she was expected to live her life in the home, at the hearth. The boy will become an eagle, a jaguar, a roseate spoonbill who will leave his nest; the girl will stay at home preparing food and drink, grinding maize, spinning, and weaving. To ritually assure these comple-mentary futures, the boy's umbilical cord ended up on a field of battle (symbolically drawing him outward, to war), the girl's was buried by the hearth by the midwife, cementing her life at home. At this time, and in the next few days, the child was placed in the care (and at the whims) of the gods and dedicated to his or her future. Important stuff.

## What If . . .?

Everything did not always go according to plan. No matter how skilled or clever the midwife, and how careful and diligent the mother, things could go awry. If the baby died in the womb, the skilled midwife dismembered and removed it with an obsidian knife, thereby saving the mother.

Women died in childbirth, although we do not know how frequently. These women, called *mocihuaquetzque*, were highly revered
and honored. They had fought a fierce and exhausting battle, but lost.
Like their male counterparts who died in battle or were sacrificed,
these women were granted exceptional afterlives. The souls of men
who died on the battlefield accompanied the sun on its journey from
its rising in the east to the zenith. There, the souls of women who died
in childbirth, armed as for war, took up that burden (honor, actually),
carrying the sun on a litter of glorious quetzal feathers on its after-
noon journey to its setting in the west. At that point, on certain days
(or perhaps all of them) these rather testy women (as *cihuateteo*,
"women goddesses") hopped off and roamed about the earth, often
causing grief to whatever humans they might encounter (Figure 7.4).

FIGURE 7.4. Female deities, the *cihuateteo*, descending to earth. Sahagún
(1950–1982: book 4: fig. 38). Firenze, Biblioteca Medicea Laurenziana. All
rights reserved. Further reproduction in any print or digital format is
forbidden.

A woman's transformation into a *cihuateotl* "elevated the deceased woman's spirit to godly status" (Dodds Pennock 2017: 395). The days One House, One Monkey, One Rain, One Deer, and One Eagle were considered particularly ominous (Miller and Taube 1993: 62), and on One House at least, midwives made offerings in their own homes to these goddesses. The *cihuateteo* were greatly feared by everyone, and a very good reason to not wander about at night.

But what about the woman herself, she who had fought such a valiant battle but lost in the end? Such a woman, in death, carried a great deal of reverence and, indeed, magical qualities. Her body was bathed and dressed in new clothing. There was great weeping at her death, but also rejoicing that she would be with the sun. Her husband carried her on his back to her burial place; it is worth noting that she was buried, not cremated (Sullivan 1966: 87–89). Midwives accompanied this emotional retinue – "They bore their shields; they went shouting, howling, yelling. It is said they went crying, they gave war cries" (Sahagún 1950–1982: book 6: 161). Along the way they skirmished with youths who tried to seize the deceased woman. While this might appear as a mock battle, Sahagún's informants insist that they fought in earnest. This behavior is grounded in Aztec beliefs, for if a warrior could cut off a finger or a lock of hair from a woman who died in childbirth, he would insert these relics in his shield: it was believed that these relics "furnished spirit; it was said they paralyzed the feet of their foes" (Sahagún 1950–1982: book 6: 162). Such a belief would have emboldened the warrior in deadly hand-to-hand encounters on the battlefield.

Not just warriors, but also thieves greatly desired to get ahold of the *mocihuaquetzqui*. Their target was the woman's left forearm, which they believed embodied the magical ability to stun and incapacitate people. Thieves (notably those born on the day One Wind) would carry this appendage with them on their nefarious outings, banging it on a house's courtyard, doorway, lintel, and hearth, thereby stupefying the householders into a deep sleep and deftly relieving them of all their belongings (Sahagún 1950–1982: book 4: 101–102). It is easy to see why the *mocihuaquetzqui* was diligently protected from theft by family and midwives, before and after burial, for four nights (perhaps the efficacy of her body parts waned after that time). Clearly the midwife's duties continued even if the mother died in childbirth.

Her obligations also extended with successful births, notably with bathing and naming ceremonies.

## The Bathing Ceremony

The midwife was responsible for ceremonially bathing the baby, calling on the goddess Chalchiuhtlicue, a water deity (Figure 7.5). According to the *Codex Mendoza*, this ritual bathing took place four days following birth, although Durán (1971: 264) claims that newborn babies were washed four days in a row (current wisdom suggests delaying bathing of newborns for up to two days). Whatever the

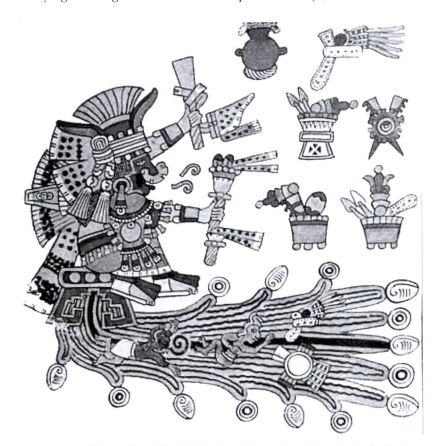

FIGURE 7.5. The goddess Chalchiuhtlicue. Reproduced from *Codex Borbonicus*, reprinted in Nowotny and Durand-Forest 1974, with permission.

bathing habits, the most significant day, ritually, was the fourth. Early in the morning the midwife ritually cleansed the baby from any inherited badness by touching the baby's mouth, chest, and head with water, placing it in the care of this powerful goddess. She then more comprehensively bathed the infant and swaddled it. The midwife spoke constantly through all of this; she modulated her voice from a whisper to a shout in addressing both the baby and the newly delivered mother. It must have been a captivating performance.

The bathing ceremony required specialized objects and actors. The *Codex Mendoza* (Berdan and Anawalt 1992: vol. 4: f. 57r) clearly depicts and identifies the ritual props: a reed mat with a large earthen basin atop and tiny implements representing the infant's anticipated life path. If a boy was to be bathed, he was accompanied by a wee object symbolizing his father's profession: the *Codex Mendoza* illustrates tools of a carpenter, featherworker, scribe, and goldsmith, but there were certainly others. The ubiquitous shield with arrows is also present. If the baby was a girl, she was given a tiny distaff with its spindle and attached cotton, a reed basket for holding her spinning and weaving equipment, and a broom – all symbols of her lifelong work around the house. As with so many things, nobles could be quite extravagant, in this case with basins made specifically for this ceremony, while those less wealthy and fortunate merely bathed their infants in springs or streams (Durán 1971: 264).

The principal actors in the bathing ceremony were the midwife, the baby, and young boys who were offered a meal of toasted maize with beans. Their primary duty came at the end of the ceremony, when the infant's name was made known by the midwife: the boys ran off to shout this name, officially announcing the identity of the new little person to one and all. The parents and other relatives were apparently quiet observers to all this. But more was to come: for the next ten or twenty days they would receive visitors who would formally greet the baby, its mother, and its family. If the baby was of royal or noble lineage, it was particularly important that nobles and representatives of other rulers pay their respects and verbally recognize the continuation of a legitimate rule or noble lineage. This was accentuated in their lengthy and respectful greetings and back-and-forth formal dialogues between the visitors and the baby's family. Gifts of fine clothing were also offered by the visitors. If the child was from a commoner family, visitors admired the child and addressed the baby and its mother, elderly relatives, and finally the baby's father, but less elaborately since no great political relations were at stake. Gifts were less costly and consisted of food and drink, including pulque. Whether wealthy or poor household, one imagines a bit of a party (Figure 7.6).

FIGURE 7.6. Visiting and feasting in honor of a new birth. Sahagún (1950–1982: book 4: fig. 86). Firenze, Biblioteca Medicea Laurenziana.

## What's in a Name?

Preliminary to the bathing ritual, a name was determined for the infant. Ideally, the parents consulted a *tonalpouhque,* or reader of the book of days, the *tonalamatl* (Figure 7.7). This soothsayer was an expert in reading and interpreting the days of the Aztec's divinatory calendar. The calendar consisted of 260 unique days (twenty day names multiplied by the numbers 1–13), each day embodying good, bad, and neutral qualities. Now, summoned to a house at a fairly high price – they fed him well and sent him on his way with turkeys and a load of food – the job of the soothsayer was to identify the day on which the child was born and to assess its meaning for the child's fated future. Suppose the child was born on the day One Flint Knife. If a boy, he would be "valiant, a chieftain; he would gain honor and riches." If a girl, she likewise would be "of merit, gifted, and deserving."

On the other hand, suppose the child, male or female, had the misfortune to be born on the day Two Rabbit: they were destined to be hopeless drunkards (Sahagún 1950–1982: book 4: 11, 79). The day Two Deer foretold a future of cowardice and timidity to its bearer,

FIGURE 7.7. Divination: a mother consults the *tonalpouhqui,* or reader of the book of days. Sahagún (1950–1982: book 6: fig. 28). Firenze, Biblioteca Medicea Laurenziana.

that of One Rain carried with it a life of sorcery and misery, the days
Five Monkey and One Flower anticipated an entertaining and
amusing person, and so on for each of the 260 days. Technically,
the child would be named for the day of its birth, good or bad,
yielding names such as Yey Ehecatl (Three Wind), Macuilli Cuetzpalin
(Five Lizard), or Ce Atl (One Water). But what if the day portended
nothing but misfortune and sorrow? All was not lost if the baby was
born on such an unfortunate day – the surrounding days might mute
its potentially calamitous effect and open the door for a positive life.
But even more importantly, the soothsayer could look ahead in his
manual and find another, more propitious day to name the child. This
new day name would foretell a more fortunate future for the child.
Such was the power of the soothsayer.

   Sahagún (1950–1982: book 4: 113) suggests that poorer families
may not have been able to afford the services of these learned specialists, and therefore saddled their children with ill-omened day names,
and hence ill-fated futures. More wealthy nobles, however, had the
luxury of consulting soothsayers and naming their children on auspicious days. In the very significant Aztec perception of the impact of
fate, class played a part. Apparently, noble babies enjoyed exaggerated
opportunities here as well as in the practicalities of inherited wealth
and position.

   While it appears that any person, regardless of social standing, was
associated with the day of his or her birth, another name (or names)
may also be given. These names might be martial, poetic, physically
descriptive, or even degrading: Yaotl (War) was popular for men,
Miauaxihuitl (Turquoise Maize Flower) or Tonallaxochiatl (Flowery
Water of Summer) were sonorous choices for a woman, Huitzilcoatl
(Hummingbird Serpent) was a fairly poetic name for a man, Tzonen
(Hairy) described a man with particular physical characteristics, and
Tomiquia (The Death of Us) was perhaps acquired through knowing
this woman over time. A man might earn a name such as Tequani
(Fierce Beast) or Ocelopan (Jaguar Banner) through his personal
exploits, especially on the battlefield. It was said that the ruler Motecuhzoma Xocoyotzin (Our Angry Lord the Younger) was given that
name since he scowled at his naming ceremony. We might surmise
that Cuicatototl (Singing Bird), although fictional, acquired her name
from her particularly melodious and calming voice. Some such names

may have been acquired early in life, some later; whichever, it is not known how many names a person might carry simultaneously.

With its name bestowed, the infant entered the world of Aztec life, which was more than often characterized as a life of torment, of misery, of suffering; but if care was taken, the gods were honored, and fate was on your side, there could be hope for a life well lived.

## LOOKING BACK, LOOKING AHEAD

*As Chilpapalotl watched him, she also secretly worried about him. All the time. His name was Yaotl, a popular name for boys because it meant "War," and what boy didn't want to go to war? But she worried because she knew she had given birth to him seven years ago on the day Eight Reed. Although he had been bathed and named on a later, more auspicious day (Ten Eagle), she still couldn't forget that Eight Reed carried with it great misery and bad fortune. Even though Ten Eagle declared him to be courageous and fearless, perhaps if he went to war he wouldn't return. Surely he would go, for it seemed that the wars were more and more frequent. There was no escaping it. At least she also now had her little daughter Centzonxihuitl, who would stay here at home until she married. And now she was pregnant again, and only the gods knew what this little gift would be. She had lost one child to a fever, at only three months old – the gods had not willed it to live, and she hoped they would look favorably on this one. She would burn incense tonight and pray for the beneficence of the gods. There was so much to do – her husband Coyochimalli was off somewhere, in some faraway land fighting for their new king Motecuhzoma. She would burn incense for Coyochimalli tonight too. But now she must tend to her hearth, making sure that her food doesn't stick to her cooking pot – otherwise his arrows would miss their mark.*

The Aztecs viewed life as a gift from the gods, and the gods were omniscient and could be unpredictable, even capricious. Recognizing that life was tenuous, and in the hands of divine fate, people did what they could to improve their children's life chances. The sixteenth-century Spanish judge Alonso de Zorita emphasized that "Lords, principales, and commoners alike showed much vigilance and zeal in rearing, instructing, and punishing their children" (1994: 135). In painfully long (and seemingly tedious) lectures parents exhorted their children to be hard-working, honest, obedient, respectful, humble before the gods, and moderate in all things. They must be diligent and engage in careful and conscientious work. Following this advice would probably have helped keep the child out of trouble as he or she grew into adulthood. Early instruction, in both morals and

FIGURE 7.8. Children receiving instruction, ages five and six. Reproduced from Berdan and Anawalt (1992: vol. 4: f. 58r), with permission.

practical matters, took place in the home with fathers teaching sons and mothers teaching girls (Figure 7.8), responsibilities and expectations increasing with age. Punishments likewise were meted out by parents (Figure 7.9). Instruction and enforcement were not subtle among the Aztecs.

Yaotl, at age seven, was becoming adept at his future work, still being instructed by his father or other adult male, and perhaps beginning out-of-home education. At the same age, Spartan boys left their homes and began military training, and noble boys in Medieval England likewise left their natal homes and were sent to work and learn in another elite household. Whether among the Aztecs or other historic cultures, age seven may have signaled a moment when boys (and possibly girls) began to take on more independent responsibilities and when expectations were more keenly enforced; it is perhaps notable that beginning at age eight, the *Codex Mendoza* shifts its life cycle story from learning to punishments.

At variably recorded ages (ranging from five to fifteen), at least part of the education of boys and girls was transferred to more formal and community institutions (Berdan 2014: 203, 307). Noble boys typically now attended a *calmecac*, or school run by priests – the curriculum

FIGURE 7.9. Children being punished, ages ten and eleven. The eleven-year-olds are held over a fire of chili peppers until they cry. Reproduced from Berdan and Anawalt (1992: vol. 4: ff. 59r, 60r), with permission.

here revolved around esoteric topics such as history, philosophy, calendrics, writing, orations, and songs as well as military training – boys exposed to this education were expected to pursue occupations especially in government or the priesthood (see Chapter 2). Other boys, commoners, received military training in a *telpochcalli* school, a fixture in each *calpolli*. Boys attending both schools were given some direct military experience, being taken to a war under the care of established warriors in a sort of internship: "they taught him well and made him see how he might take a captive" (Sahagún 1950–1982: book 8: 72). Girls received less formal education, but some could be dedicated as infants to religious service at a temple where they served for a limited time later on, probably in their early teen years, then leaving the temple to marry and raise families.

Both boys and girls between the ages of twelve and fifteen attended a local *cuicacalli*, or "house of song," where they learned the songs and dances needed for proper participation in the endlessly cycling religious ceremonies. While learning to dance, sing, and play musical instruments they also assimilated the myths, lore, beliefs, and philosophies embedded in these arts. This included such weighty matters as sorting out and praising the many gods; recounting creation stories of people, nature, and the very universe; and understanding the meaning and cycles of life and death. All of this training was extremely important to the successful performance of every ceremony, as these individuals participated in the perpetual round of public and household rituals throughout their lives.

Children and youths themselves frequently took center stage in public ceremonies. During one monthly ceremony, Atl Caualo, children were ritually sacrificed to the rain god Tlaloc to ensure rain, this at a time immediately preceding the highly anticipated rainy season. Children were also sacrificed during four other monthly ceremonies. And there was more: young girls played prominent roles in processions during the month of Huey Toçoztli, while small children, young boys, and youths suffered knife cuts on their arms, stomachs, and chests during Toxcatl. Children were especially featured during the final month of the year, Izcalli. At that time, small children were essentially initiated into Aztec ritual life by having their earlobes pierced and their necks stretched to stimulate their growth; they were also held over a fire and offered tiny sips of pulque in tiny drinking vessels – all the while their parents and other adults enjoyed boisterous eating, drinking, singing, and dancing (Sahagún 1950–1982: book 10: 61–65, 76, 165–166).

Responsible child care also included protecting children from diseases, illnesses, and other dangers. Infants, whether nobles or commoners, may have been breast-fed for up to four years (Zorita 1994: 135). Mothers, while nursing, could keep their infants healthy by avoiding eating avocados. While four years may have been an acceptable nursing tenure, there were pressures to shorten that time as it was believed that stammering and lisping in children could be avoided by early weaning. Illnesses most commonly threatening the lives of children were dysentery and diarrhea, either of which could be treated with an *atole* drink made with chia, or a drink with a specific herb or the bark of a "white tree" mixed with chocolate. That was said to do the trick (but we do not advise trying this at home) (Sahagún 1950–1982: book 10: 158). Some children also seem to have suffered from iron-deficiency anemia caused by intestinal parasites or dietary deficiencies (perhaps as a result of diarrhea). Malnutrition and infections also led to dental pathologies (Berdan 2014: 250–251; Ortiz de Montellano 2001; Roman Berrelleza 2008; Sahagún 1950–1982: book 10). The Aztecs countered these infirmities and maladies with a selection of natural remedies, appeals to sorcerers, and rituals appeasing the gods. Perhaps a friend or neighbor could recommend a good doctor or sorcerer. Or the ailing child's parent could head to the marketplace and consult with a knowledgeable herbalist.

# 8

## Market Day in Tlatelolco

*Xochitl's head was spinning as she hurried to the market plaza. Thoughts of the broken pot she needed to replace were cast aside as her mind reeled with the vague gossip floating around her calpolli: Were they about to go to war – again? Would her brothers have to go? She hoped Huilotl would be at the market today; she knew everything. She would go around to where people sold baskets; her friend would be there. A lot of people sold baskets, but Huilotl's father sold the best, and always gave her a good deal. She was sure they would be there because today was a major market day, one that comes only once every five days. It will be busy. And noisy. And crowded. That's what she loved about it!*

As the daughter of a featherworker, Xochitl lived near the great Tlatelolco marketplace and was intimately familiar with it. She went there often, yet every time she approached the bustling marketplace, her senses were exhilarated by the sounds, smells, sights, and textures ahead of her. Even from a distance her ears caught the low and irregular rumble of thousands of cheerful, convivial, argumentative, and frustrated voices. As she hurried along inside the plaza she could almost taste the savory tamales, sizzling grasshoppers, and chile sauces as their irresistible aromas wafted from the many vendors of street food. Her eyes took in a bewildering, many-hued mosaic in motion – a haughty noblemen in a red-bordered cape examined green jewels displayed by a wealthy merchant; a woman in a plain tunic and skirt hawked her many varieties of beans, neatly arranged on a woven mat (Figure 8.1); a husband and wife, with a squirming infant beside them in a basket, displayed polished gourd bowls brightly decorated in reds and yellows. She passed the cotton cloth sellers and was tempted to

FIGURE 8.1. A bean seller in the Tlatelolco marketplace. Sahagún (1950–1982: book 10: fig. 123). Firenze, Biblioteca Medicea Laurenziana. All rights reserved. Further reproduction in any print or digital format is forbidden.

run her fingers along the soft fabric – but a stern look from the merchant held her back. Xochitl knew where everything was in the marketplace, and she hurried past these insistent and protective vendors and headed to the corner of the plaza displaying baskets.

Hers was a purposeful trip – she needed to replace the pot she clumsily broke. But she was cheered by the opportunity to socialize and catch up on the latest gossip. Or, perhaps, she might catch a view of someone of special interest. After all, at fifteen, Xochitl should be married by now, or soon.

As Xochitl knew, the marketplace was not just a place to trade and exchange goods; it was also the community's primary destination for the latest news and rumor – local, regional, and remotely exotic. It is no wonder that the Tenochtitlan ruler sent merchant-spies (*nahualoz-tomeca*) disguised as locals to distant markets to take the pulse of the region: were there rumblings of a rebellion or was it ripe for conquest? Markets also provided a periodic venue for establishing, renewing, and reinforcing social relations – chatting with your favorite aunt who married a man from another *calpolli*, meeting the new artisan in town, trying to again catch the eye of someone encountered in last week's market. Much of the social life of the community was played out in the marketplaces: some of it revolved around idle gossip, some entailed information-gathering (such as keeping up with the latest styles or whispers of incipient wars or rebellions), and some focused on more purposeful concerns such as testing the waters for initiating a courtship. The marketplace brought its participants both traditional comfort and invigorating novelty in its mélange of material offerings and social encounters.

## *TIANQUIZTLI*, THE MARKETPLACE

The central Mexican marketplace, or *tianquiztli*, was a favorite meeting spot. It had almost everything: you could supply and renew your practical household needs, upgrade your clothing, replenish your craft supplies, purchase a slave for an upcoming ceremony, and pick up a little snack along the way. You can keep up with the most recent gossip, styles, and politics. Here converged people from all walks of life, from austere government officials strutting about the expensive merchant stalls to the humble farmer bartering for turkey eggs with his few cacao beans. Vendors, both men and women, displayed and hawked virtually every kind of good and service available locally and from distant lands. In short, the *tianquiztli* was both a location and a multifaceted activity, an essential setting for people to establish, facilitate, reinforce, or contest their economic, social, political, and ceremonial relations. It was one of the most central, predictable, and integrating institutions in the Aztec world.

Markets were held in large, open, centrally located spaces, or plazas. These market plazas were essential features of virtually all cities and towns throughout central Mexico, lying adjacent to or near the city's primary temple(s) and palace(s). In other words, this essential economic and social venue shared "downtown" with the community's major ceremonial and political edifices. At the end of a lively market day the plaza was swept clean, erasing all or almost all evidence that a market had taken place there at all. Between markets held every five, eight, nine, thirteen, or twenty days were days when nothing in particular happened, and the plaza was just a plaza, an open space with no scheduled activity. Or on other days multitudes of people crowded the plaza to celebrate scheduled religious ceremonies.

The Tlatelolco marketplace was the grandest in the land, and convened every day. Even though it held a daily market, everyone knew that a bigger market was scheduled there every five days (an Aztec week). The conquistador called the Anonymous Conqueror (this is the best name we have for this shadowy but very reliable figure) toured this pre-conquest marketplace and states that its daily population of 20,000–25,000 people swelled to a whopping 40,000–50,000 on its every-fifth-day big market. His captain, Hernando Cortés, was also on the tour but reports that the market handled more than 60,000 buyers and sellers daily (The Chronicle of the Anonymous Conqueror 1963: 178–179; Cortés 1928: 87). Unfortunately, we do not know exactly how these men arrived at these figures, or why they differ so dramatically. But whatever their reasons or circumstances or differences, all of these numbers are impressive.

How were so many people accommodated at this venue, whether on a daily or weekly basis? First of all, holding a daily market, the Tlatelolco marketplace developed a certain permanence, an infrastructure capable of handling large crowds. Hernando Cortés tells us that the plaza was completely surrounded by arcades, and he also mentions "houses … of apothecaries," shops where barbers washed and cut patrons' hair, and other shops for prepared food and drink. He furthermore mentions a "very fine building in the great square" where ten to twelve judges sat and passed summary judgment on any wrongdoers (Cortés 1928: 87–89). His colleague Bernal Díaz del Castillo, on the same market tour, recalls cochineal for sale under the arcades, and speaks of three, not ten to twelve, judges (1963: 233). A conquest-era plan of a Tenochtitlan marketplace places a sizable structure in one corner – the judges' station may have been in such a place (Durand-Forest 1971).

Furthermore, marketplaces (and most surely this one) were graced by a prominent stone sculpture, or *momoztli*, that served as a marketplace shrine. Diego Durán (1971: 275–276) mentions that this shrine housed the "idol of the market" who received offerings of all kinds of foods (and perhaps other goods) sold in the market. He admits he does not know for sure if the foods were appropriated by the priests or simply left to rot. Such a structure, complete with side platforms for offerings, may have been present at Xochicalco a few centuries earlier; it is roughly square and its size of approximately 3.5 meters on a side and 80 centimeters high offers us some idea of the shrine's scale – a somewhat diminutive but distinctive statement of the strong connections between religion and commerce. Food remains would not be expected from this site, but six ceramic effigy figures were associated with this offertory, suggesting that more than food may have been offered (Hirth 2009: 93).

The conquest-era plan of the Tenochtitlan marketplace mentioned above depicts a six-sided shrine in the center of the marketplace (Durand-Forest 1971), while Durán's image reveals a circular, decorated object (see Figure 8.2). With all of this, it is safe to conclude that

FIGURE 8.2. Marketplace with slaves and other goods. Based on Durán (1971: plate 29). Source: Michael E. Smith.

there was permanent urban investment in the Tlatelolco marketplace with its encompassing arcades, various shops, *momoztli*, and fine judges' building. We might envision that the shops were strung out under the arcades, and while only barbers, apothecaries, and cochineal vendors are mentioned, surely there were others that attracted daily patrons or buyers. Location in an arcade shop may have been something of a luxury – they were sheltered from sun, rain, and wind and perhaps could allow for long-term storage (although we do not know if or how they could be secured). Also, as vendors were taxed for their individual selling spaces (and/or merchandise), one might guess that an arcade location was relatively costly.

A second way that the Tlatelolco plaza was able to accommodate so many people was that it was a dedicated market space, a rarity among Aztec cities. In most communities, market day shared the single plaza with a series of social, political, and religious activities. The Tlatelolco market was held in a dedicated space that did not have to accommodate other uses each week. Public religious ceremonies, which would share the plaza in other cities, were held directly next door, in and around Tlatelolco's major temple complex.

And third: location, location, location – and access. The great Tlatelolco marketplace had several commercial advantages in gaining its stature as the grandest trading venue in the Aztec known world. It was located adjacent to the largest city in that world, teeming with a multitude of buyers and sellers. But this was not all. The Basin of Mexico as a whole may have had as many as a million people, all in need of one thing or another – some extra beans and a few tomatoes for the day's meal, charcoal for the home hearth, a replacement broken pot or glue to repair the old one, medicine for that nasty cough, a new loincloth to replace that threadbare one (if you're a commoner) or a fancy decorated loincloth (if you're a noble on-the-rise), an assortment of fine feathers and stones for the mosaicist, or a slave to offer in your once-in-a-lifetime ceremony. If your load is particularly heavy or bulky, or you as a noble would not deign to carry your own purchases, porters were available for hire in the marketplace for a fee. All of these, and much more, were available in that renowned marketplace. In fact, Cortés tells us that "There is nothing to be found in all the land which is not sold in these markets" (1928: 89), and we can almost see Bernal Díaz del Castillo throw up his arms

FIGURE 8.3. Paddling a canoe. Reproduced from Berdan and Anawalt (1992: vol. 4: f. 6or), with permission.

in surrender when he writes, "If I describe everything in detail I shall never be done" (1963: 233).

Everyone needed to provision their households, but in addition, the market was a destination for an unusual number of elite consumers, craft specialists, and non-farming households. Aside from access to a large and demanding population, the Tlatelolco marketplace also benefited from its strategic location. Situated on the northern portion of the Tenochtitlan/Tlatelolco island (see Map 2), it could be readily reached from the larger Tenochtitlan by foot or canal and from anywhere on the mainland across the lake by canoe or causeway. Canoe traffic on the lake was brisk and crowded – López de Gómara (deriving most of his information from Cortés' recollections) speaks of 200,000 canoes plying the lake waters, with the lake especially crowded on market days (1966: 159) (Figure 8.3). Even if that is an exaggeration, just half that number would be quite astonishing.

To make access even more efficient, three broad causeways connected Tlatelolco with the mainland to the north and west, two of them leading directly from Tlatelolco's ceremonial precinct and a third passing close by the eastern side of the marketplace. Streets, causeways, and canoes all provided ready access to the Tlatelolco marketplace and would have thronged with people on market day. And of course its reputation only added to its business – everyone knew they could buy and sell anything there, count on friends being around, and find out the latest talk of the town.

It is only fair to look at the Tlatelolco market in context. It did have some competition from nearby Texcoco's daily market and other markets on the island and mainland. A market was held beside the Tenochtitlan ruler's palace, but it paled in comparison to the gatherings at Tlatelolco and may have primarily served as a food and utilitarian market, operating rather like today's convenience stores or serving the palace's immediate needs. Plazas in other Tenochtitlan districts probably held similar small markets. Some markets on the mainland, however, specialized in certain popular commodities and perhaps were worth the trip. We have already seen that Quetzalhua enlisted his relatives to go with him to the market at Azcapotzalco to obtain a slave – that market (and one further afield at Itzocan) was well known as a slave market, and the selection would have been exceptional.

Some other markets also had developed specialized reputations: Texcoco for ceramics, cloth, and fine gourds; Otompan and Tepepulco for turkeys; and Acolman for dogs. A knowledgeable consumer could also find an especially nice selection of pottery at Cuauhtitlan and wood products in Coyoacan. These specialties would have augmented the usual market offerings of foods, utilitarian goods, and luxury objects. If you lived on the island, was it worth the trip to these other cities for an enhanced selection of cloth, turkeys, or slaves? Perhaps. And especially perhaps on days preceding important ceremonies (public or private) when you desired a higher quality cloak, or turkey, or slave to properly celebrate the obligatory ritual. Regardless, the main purpose of the marketplace was to provide a venue for buyers and sellers to meet and arrive at agreed-upon exchanges.

## BUYERS AND SELLERS, AND THEIR WARES

The marketplace was a colorful, noisy, boisterous place. It appeared quite bewildering to the Spanish conquistadores who visited it on the eve of the conquest and marveled that they would never be able to itemize (let alone recognize) everything available for sale. Any stranger might feel the same, but the locals were intimately familiar with the offerings, the patterns, and the rules. They knew what they wanted, where to go, who to see, and how to get the best deal. And they had a great many choices.

Who were these sellers, and their customers? Many different types of traders displayed their wares in the lively Tlatelolco marketplace. There were the haughty professional merchants (*pochteca*) who traveled great distances to obtain their shimmering tropical feathers, precious stones, golden lip plugs, jaguar pelts, fine decorated textiles, and other luxurious goods (see Figure 4.2). Needless to say, these wares were expensive and their customers consisted of the upper crust of Aztec society – those who could afford such luxuries, and who were the only people normally permitted to openly wear or display these status-linked fineries. Also expensive were slaves, and some merchants specialized in selling them. The slaves wore cumbersome wooden yokes which constrained their movements and ability to escape (although occasional attempts were made). Slave sellers would dress their slaves to the best advantage (the clothing was removed when the slave was sold), and when a customer wished to purchase a slave who could dance well, the slave was ordered to do so. Such bursts of activity must have added to the energy and vibrancy of the marketplace.

Other full-time traders brought other valued goods to the Tlatelolco marketplace from afar, especially cacao beans, fine salt, and cotton. To obtain these goods, merchants trekked from lowlands to highlands and back again, carrying these lowland products in exchange for highland goods such as obsidian tools and rabbit fur (Sahagún 1950–1982: book 9: 17–18). The wares they carried from the lowlands were bulky and heavy, but not as expensive as luxuries such as feathers, precious stones, and golden objects. These traveling traders gained economically through their service as middlemen, buying cheap and selling dear – but investing in long treks, porters, and market taxes. Their customers would have been a more varied lot, although their goods (with the possible exception of some types of cacao beans) were more expensive than the usual farmer or potter could typically afford.

While glittering luxuries, salt that shone like diamonds, and downcast slaves captured the eye, most marketplace vendors sat on a mat or at a stall selling relatively small lots of their own surplus production: a

FIGURE 8.4. The tamale seller. Sahagún (1950–1982: book 10: fig. 127). Firenze, Biblioteca Medicea Laurenziana.

few extra chiles, tomatoes, or medicinal herbs from a farmer's household garden; fish and fish eggs from the fisherfolk; firewood from a collector in the *monte*; or baskets from a lakeside dweller. Potters sold their pottery; straw broom makers hawked their wares; color sellers attractively arranged their pigments; others sold bricks, stone, or wood for construction; still others offered dogs, or turkeys, or birds, gourd seeds, or local salt. Those who sold obsidian blades sat in the marketplace fashioning blades on the spot, on order. Sandals, flower arrangements, and herbal remedies, at least, also could be made to order in the marketplace. And clothing. All women in Aztec society learned to spin thread and weave cloth, and could market whatever exceeded their family's needs. Maize was sold in grains but also as creatively prepared tortillas and tamales: as a small sample, tortillas made with honey or served with turkey eggs, and frog or rabbit tamales were on offer (Figure 8.4).

Marketplace vendors were well aware that marketgoers spent much of the day in the market and became hungry – prepared foods and drinks were offered from household cooks, and the aromas from that section of the market must have been particularly enticing. Services were also available: barbers have already been mentioned, and there were also porters, prostitutes, and perhaps others who may have wandered about the marketplace in search of customers. And on and on. Most, if not all, of these vendors also produced the goods they offered for sale. Their products appealed to everyone, at one time or another. Nobles and commoners needed to eat, replace worn mats or chipped knives, repair houses, relieve a cough or a stomachache, and basically obtain goods they did not themselves produce. These various vendors appeared in the marketplace on a regular or more sporadic basis when the ups and downs of their individual livelihoods made it possible or profitable for them to do so. They appealed to customers based on the quality of their wares, availability, competitive prices, reputations, and prior relationships. After all, your aunt would be insulted if you purchased your chiles from anyone else.

Each type of commodity was displayed and sold in its own designated location in the marketplace. It was supremely predictable and orderly: "Each kind of merchandise is sold in its own particular street and no other kind may be sold there: this rule is very well enforced" (Cortés 1928: 89). Conquest-period documents identify the locations of many of the commodities, from cotton and clothing to foods and feathers. The central shrine in a market was encircled by vendors of cloth-production materials and clothing (such as thread and rabbit fur), while other areas focused on goods such as paper, tobacco, ceramics, sandals, baskets, woven mats, foodstuffs, and prepared foods. While each marketplace may have arranged these commodities differently, each consistently allocated specific areas for specific goods. Furthermore, making a living from selling, or just augmenting your usual production, required a sensitivity to your potential or regular consumers. So displays were attractively and artfully arranged to catch the eye. At the Tlatelolco marketplace, heavy and bulky goods such as lumber, stone, lime, bricks, and other construction materials were sold at the market's periphery, possibly near or at a canal (López de Gómara 1966: 160). The same may have been the case for the sale of water, which was done from canoes. These arrangements made solid transportation sense where goods moved only on human backs or in canoes.

Xochitl knew right where to go to find a new cooking pot. They were always in the same place, almost always sold by the same vendors. In fact, the marketplace was easy to navigate with everything always in its appointed place. Still, she, like others in the plaza, enjoyed admiring the other goods on display: the plump fruits brought in from the lowlands and invitingly framed by bright flowers, the glittering gold adornments, and especially the screeching, variegated birds preening their finery or protesting their captivity. It was easy to get distracted in the *tianquiztli.*

## MARKETPLACE BUSINESS, MONEY, AND JUSTICE

Tempting as it was to casually browse about the colorful and some-times exotic displays, the marketplace was still fundamentally a serious place of business. And those business activities conformed to well-understood rules and norms. We have already seen the rules for orderly selling – one could not offer up one's goods just anywhere. But there were also rules for arriving at an acceptable price, rules for fair and proper measures, and rules for selling through paying a tax. To violate these norms brought immediate justice, since lofty judges (probably high-ranking *pochteca*) sat in state in a corner of the plaza, aided by their many inspectors who strolled about with keen eyes open to any violation of established market rules.

### Arriving at a Price

In the *tianquiztli,* bargaining was the order of the day. Imagine a clamorous place with innumerable verbal transactions constantly in play. No wonder that Bernal Díaz del Castillo was prompted to write that "the mere murmur of their voices talking was loud enough to be heard more than three miles away" (1963: 235). What might a bar-gaining scenario look like?

*Tlatlapalli perked up when she saw them coming. The turquoise mosaic-workers, father and son, Ce Mazatl and Ozomaton. She critically glanced at her neatly arranged piles of copal resin (used for incense and glues) on the corner of her mat. Along with her bright pigments, she had several different types of copal and other resins, and she knew they would want the ones that worked best as glues. Yes! They stopped and examined her wares. She tried to steer them to her finest resins, those that cost the most. But this was no problem, for she knew them and had done business with them before. Still, each encounter was new. After a few pleasantries, the time for serious bargaining arrived:*

*Ce Mazatl: Hmmm, what do you think, Ozomaton? Are these balls a bit "off" today?*

*Tlatlapalli: Oh, not at all. Perhaps you do not see how solid and plump they are. Look at these over here! Like golden balls! I can offer them to you for six cacao beans per measure.*

FIGURE 8.5. Copal incense for sale today in the Tepoztlan market. Source: Frances F. Berdan.

*Ozomaton: Six?! As I recall, Father, didn't we buy the same kind last time for only two?*

*Tlatlapalli: Two?! You're dreaming, or perhaps you bought from my neighbor who only collects her resin from old and worn out trees?*

*Ce Mazatl: I'll give you three cacao beans for each measure.*

*Tlatlapalli: Five.*

*Ce Mazatl: Four, and I'll take five measures.*

*Tlatlapalli: Agreed.*

Although this scenario is rather abbreviated, it nonetheless makes clear that the idea was (and is today) to arrive at a price acceptable to both buyer and seller. At the end of a successful exchange, the seller tries to ensure that the customer will return and the buyer hopes for a dependable supply of the best merchandise (Figure 8.5). In this fictional case, Tlatlapalli selects each copal ball carefully and generously piles them up in each measure, and Ce Mazatl and Ozomaton will surely return to her next time, guaranteeing her of their business (and cacao beans). Ce Mazatl enjoys the little extra he receives and knows that Tlatlapalli will reserve the best copal for him. They are both satisfied, and both enjoy the verbal exchange, which can become quite creative and lively indeed. Among those who enjoy the banter, one might interject snippets such as "Swallow-mouthed!" (Such a chatterer!), "Have you become a wild bee?" (So uppity!), "Where is the sorcerer?" (Are you trying to stiff me?), or "Is it your real nose?" (Honestly?). Bargaining reinforced the fundamental goals and norms of the marketplace: profitable business (for both buyer and seller), convenience, efficiency, competition, respect, honesty, and the prominent cultural values of harmony and balance.


## Barter and Money

Bargaining was the road to agreed-upon prices. But how did buyers pay for their purchases, and what did vendors accept as payment?

Most marketplace exchanges took the form of barter – the exchange of goods/services for goods/services. A buyer may carry a few extra tomatoes to market from her household garden, hoping to trade them for the firewood and chiles she needs. But what if the firewood vendor or chile seller do not need her tomatoes, or she didn't bring enough? There was always an element of uncertainty with barter, and the practical possibility that the trade simply may not work out. Still, barter was used even for the most expensive goods: Durán tells us that merchants bartered "cloth for jewels, jewels for feathers, feathers for stones, and stones for slaves" (1971: 138). So whether humble tomatoes for chiles or costly jewels for feathers, barter must have worked pretty well since it was the prominent means of realizing exchanges in marketplaces throughout central Mexico and beyond.

But at some point, prior to Aztec ascendency, commodity monies arrived on the scene. The use of cacao beans, large cotton capes (*quachtli*), thin copper axes, and possibly copper bells, stone and shell beads, and quills filled with gold dust as universally accepted media of exchange relieved some of the uncertainty associated with barter (Figures 8.6 and 8.7). With a few cacao beans in hand, it did not matter if a vendor wanted or needed a farmer's chiles or a potter's pot: cacao beans would be accepted regardless of whatever the buyer or seller needed. As an example, in 1545 a Spanish royal judge established price caps for specified subsistence goods, all valued in cacao beans: a turkey hen or a hare cost one hundred cacao beans; a

FIGURE 8.6.  Cacao beans. Source: Michael E. Smith.

small rabbit cost thirty; a turkey egg, newly picked avocado, or fish wrapped in maize husks cost three; and one cacao bean would buy two fully ripe prickly pear cactus fruits, one large tomato, twenty small tomatoes, or a tamale (Anderson et al. 1976: 208–213). This was in early colonial times; we suspect that prices in pre-Spanish Mexico were more flexible.

Commodity monies such as cacao beans carried their own baggage: a certain amount of vagueness, indeterminacy, and variance. In the first place, most of these monies also served as commodities: the most important of these were cacao (also a prized drink) and large cotton capes (also perhaps worn as male attire). Copper bells and stone and shell beads served as gifts, godly adornments, and burial offerings. On the other hand, the thin and fragile copper axes may not have had a separate practical use; there were several types of cacao beans (not all may have served as money); and it is not entirely clear that *quachtli*, specifically, were worn as clothing. Second, the commodity monies themselves varied in quality – an early colonial-period document recorded the cost of market goods in terms of either 200 full cacao beans or 230 shrunken cacao beans (Anderson et al. 1976: 208–213). Trade values of *quachtli* also varied depending on their quality, equal to sixty-five, eighty, or one hundred cacao beans (of what quality we do not know) (Sahagún 1950–1982: book 9: 48). Bargaining may have ironed out the wrinkles in these rather fluid valuations. It also appears that barter and money could be combined in individual transactions: What if, at the close of a lively market day, a local farmer's wife finds herself short of enough chiles to exchange for her final purchase, a couple of strips of pine bark for kindling?

FIGURE 8.7. A sample of clothing paid to the Aztec rulers. The two items on the right are large white cotton cloaks, or *quachtli*, a form of money. Reproduced from Berdan and Anawalt (1992: vol. 4: f. 28r), with permission.

Fortunately she is carrying a few cacao beans, and two of them along with her last two chiles will do the trick.

## Market Administration, Law, and Order

Alongside its spatial orderliness, the Tlatelolco marketplace also exhibited an administrative orderliness. Judges and inspectors were prominent fixtures and maintained conformity and order by their mere presence and by their aggressive actions against wrongdoers. In an overall sense, they (or perhaps other officials) assured that each vendor paid a market tax to the local ruler. This was an in-kind assessment, a set fee based on the type of good to be sold, probably collected at the market entrances (Anderson et al. 1976: 138–149). Additionally, marketplace food vendors had a role to play when war was imminent: they would find themselves obligated to provide provisions for the army preparing to march to battle. Economy and politics were not far separated.

Everyone knew the marketplace rules, but not all abided by them. Among delicts, cheating and theft topped the list. Vendors might taint their consumables: the "bad" bean seller mixed spoiled and infested beans with the good ones; the "bad" maize seller arranged good grains atop fetid and mouse-gnawed ones; the "bad" turkey seller offered old, sick birds. Vendors of cacao beans might counterfeit them by removing the chocolate from the bean and inserting sand or ground avocado pits – he or she would then mix these counterfeit beans with the good ones to deceive the customer. And measures could be falsified: goods were sold by number and measure (but not weight), and if a marketplace inspector spied a vendor cheating in his dealings, he destroyed his or her false measures (as witnessed by Cortés in his stroll through the Tlatelolco marketplace). Thieves were summarily tried and faced possible execution or slavery. Even an inattentive or unschooled marketgoer could become an unwitting accomplice to a crime: if a slave attempted an escape by racing through the market to reach sanctuary beyond the market bounds, and a bystander impeded his escape, the slave would be freed and the bystander would become the slave (Durán 1971: 285–286). It was indeed imperative that one knew the rules of the marketplace, for there were no excuses and justice was swift and public, whether by inspectors or judges. Even with such known deterrents, the marketplace offered a particularly opportune setting for criminal action with its tempting and open array of merchandise, its elbowing crowds, and its focused buyers and sellers (see Chapter 9).

RHYTHMS

You could measure the pulse of everyday life by heading to the marketplace. There were rhythms to marketing activities, responding to daily, weekly, monthly, and annual schedules. People knew these schedules, and planned their trips accordingly. They also had choices of marketplaces – much as you may choose a particular grocery store because of its offerings or perhaps its convenience.

On market days, plazas pulsated with activity. They responded to rhythms in production (especially in the agricultural cycle), rhythmic patterns in consumer demand, and predictable and unpredictable supplies because of the vagaries of distribution.

Production obviously dictated availability of marketplace goods. Some products such as basic foodstuffs, turkeys, salt, fish, clothing, and myriad other products could be found year-round in the Tlatelolco marketplace. Yet some of these reflected seasonal production cycles: while maize could be found in marketplaces year round (maize kernels stored well), the seductive aromas of cooked *xilotl* or *elotes* (fresh corn on the cob) wafting through the marketplace would be inhaled only in the fall at harvest time. In the Basin of Mexico, the big maize harvests occurred from September through November, although the local *chinampa* fields yielded maize and many other crops at other times throughout the year (Sanders et al. 1979). Agriculture fully occupied farmers' time from spring through fall, but wintertime allowed farmers to turn their attention to other activities, including the production of crafts such as pottery, reed mats, and stone tools (as in Chapter 5). These activities supplemented the farmers' income, and one would expect to see such newly crafted objects displayed in the marketplaces during the winter and spring months.

In addition to the known cycles of basic staples such as maize and beans, the market reflected other seasonal availabilities. Netters of migratory birds (including ducks) would have swelled the basin marketplaces in the winter as the birds descended in hordes on the lakes at that time. The hunters of wild animals (especially deer and rabbits) would have appeared in greater numbers in the fall as their hunting activities increased. And an Aztec's favorite fruits ripened and flowers bloomed at known seasons and could be found in profusion in the markets at those times. These were cyclical but known and predictable. More unpredictable (and dreaded) events included the droughts, famines, and pestilences that plagued the land fairly often and had severe impacts on household and market supplies of the most basic products.

There is comfort in the predictable, but excitement in the novel, the unexpected, the surprise. Aztec marketplaces offered both. Among the less predictable were the exotic luxuries transported from the lowlands of the empire and beyond. The return of a large merchant caravan with its string of exhausted porters most certainly drew the interested and curious to the next market day: no one wanted to miss stroking the soft jaguar skins and seeing the new shimmering multicolored feathers, rich green stones, impressive red sea shells, tortoise shell cups, glamorous decorated clothing, and much more. All of this was on offer from these adventurous and wealthy traders. This would be a somewhat unpredictable, although much heralded event.

The market responded not only to the seasonal rhythms of crops and other foods; it also responded to demands of ritual and social cycles – that is, consumption as well as production influenced marketplace offerings. The endless cycles of public and private ceremonies meant that periodically unusual quantities of specific goods and materials needed to be available to ritual participants – and the marketplace was the most reliable venue for this. Most of these materials, from foodstuffs for feasting to utilitarian and luxury goods for displays and offerings, were available in the Tlatelolco marketplace and certainly other surrounding marketplaces as well.

Each ceremony had its own specific requirements and marketplace vendors were certainly attuned to the scheduling of these events. For instance, they would make copious quantities of amaranth seed tamales and flower bouquets during the festivities of Toçoztontli, display paper and rubber during Ochpaniztli, and offer small red feathers to be pasted on the arms and legs of dancers during the month of Toxcatl (Berdan 2017). Festivities during Huey Toçoztli required obtaining copious quantities of food, flowers, and decorative materials (Figure 8.8). Marketplace merchandise ebbed and flowed with these scheduled demands. Consider dogs at the renowned Acolman dog market: on a day when Diego Durán visited this market, he was astounded at the enormous number he saw (more than 400 dogs), but was assured that today there was "a tremendous shortage of them!" (1971: 278).

Many events were well known and predictable. However, some events would have occurred almost continuously, when distributed among the estimated 200,000 residents of Tenochtitlan (and as many as 1 million in the Basin of Mexico as a whole). Many goods needed to be available in the markets on a regular basis to supply everyday feasts celebrated at life-cycle rituals (as in Chapter 7) and, less commonly, if a merchant such as Quetzalhua wished to overwhelm his guests by purchasing a slave and an abundance of feasting foods. Supply and demand structured market activity.

Not all market goods were local. Many were imported. Some were brought to the Tlatelolco marketplace by producers who were willing to trek (or paddle) relatively long distances to gain a better price for their merchandise. More notably, though, regional and long-distance merchants, acting as middle-men, carried non-local and sometimes exotic wares to the market for sale. These included widely demanded goods such as cotton and cacao, and luxuries such as colorful feathers, fine worked stones, perfect sea shells, and golden ornaments, all from distant lands. Merchants of these goods appear to have been constant fixtures of the largest marketplaces and repeated visitors to

FIGURE 8.8. Offerings during the ceremonies of Huey Toçoztli. Sahagún (1950–1982: book 2: fig. 13). Firenze, Biblioteca Medicea Laurenziana. All rights reserved. Further reproduction in any print or digital format is forbidden.

marketplaces of all kinds. Still, any one merchant may not appear in the Tlatelolco marketplace for months, being on the road; he may perhaps never return, being attacked and robbed along the way (see Chapter 4). The murder of merchants is one way that marketplace supplies could become rather suddenly unavailable; others include a war interrupting supplies or diverting merchant itineraries, or a flood impeding canoe traffic (as must have happened during the disastrous flood of 1500).

Thinking more broadly, some marketplaces were transformed over time, perhaps experiencing unexpected fates (in Aztec terms). For instance, Azcapotzalco's marketplace was denuded and planted with maguey after a military defeat (but later became an important slave market), and Tepeacac's marketplace was revitalized by imperial requirements to sell luxury goods after its conquest by the Aztecs. A marketplace's fabric could be recast or even traumatically interrupted, perhaps by war and conquest, perhaps by official edict, or perhaps by a realignment of trade routes. Interestingly, though, the Tlatelolco marketplace did not seem to undergo any particular trauma after Tlatelolco's conquest by neighboring Tenochtitlan in 1473. Still, it and other marketplaces in the realm experienced some alterations (but not fundamental changes) after the Spanish conquest with the introduction of new merchandise such as wheat, iron/steel tools (like hoes and scissors), candles, wool, tailored clothing, and chickens (Figure 8.9).

FIGURE 8.9. The tailor. Sahagún (1950–1982: book 10: fig. 55). Firenze, Biblioteca Medicea Laurenziana. All rights reserved. Further reproduction in any print or digital format is forbidden.

## RETROSPECT AND PROSPECT

*As she headed toward the basketmakers, Xochitl was so focused on her destination that she passed by, without even noticing, the featherworker friends Centzon and Chimal-chiuhqui as they ambled along, chatting amiably. Xochitl got the news that she so eagerly sought as she hurried to the tianquiztli earlier. The war was but a rumor – this time. But Centzon and Chimalchiuhqui stumbled upon some unexpected news: they had talked with merchants who had recently arrived from the eastern coast and learned that the region was in an upheaval and the roads were too dangerous for travel.*

The merchants had many options and would find other sources for their precious wares. They were used to the anxiety of wars, the uncertainties of life, and the harshness of deprivations on the road. But they had no idea of the difficulties to come:

*The widow Malinalli headed to the market plaza: my knees are bothering me again, she griped. But she hobbled along with a determined face, anxious to hear more about the new rumors of unrest. People were bent over, whispering to one another. They glanced about furtively as she walked past. She picked up, a bit here and a bit there, that this time the rumors were right. But the foe was not a known enemy; no, this time "they" were rather odd strangers advancing on her treasured city – here! Can you imagine, here?*

The strangers came from across the eastern sea, and they brought with them things and ideas that she never even remotely imagined.

# 9

## Judgment Day

*A nervous Xoxoacatl arrived early for the hearing at the Yautepec royal palace. Although he was familiar enough with the marketplace and temple in Yautepec, his visits to the palace had so far been limited to low-level dealings with tax collectors and labor supervisors. Now he was part of a lawsuit and would have to give testimony in a trial before a judge. What if he wasn't believed? What if he got scared and couldn't talk? Some guy from downriver had stolen some maize ears from Xoxoacatl's irrigated field. He was seen by a merchant, who brought the accusation to the palace. A hearing had been scheduled, and Xoxoacatl would have to testify that his fields had indeed been vandalized.*

*Xoxoacatl noticed lots of people arriving at the same side entrance to the palace, where he had come in. This area had several rooms where the judges held court. After an initial irrational worry that they were coming to watch his own case, he saw that everyone was trying to squeeze into the courtroom next to his. He recognized his cousin, a servant who supervised the household of a noble, and asked what was going on. It turns out that a high-ranking nobleman was accused of falsifying some painted land records in order to steal fields from a nearby calpolli. The penalty could be death! "I'd rather watch that trial then testify about a few ears of maize," thought Xoxoacatl. But now there was another disturbance, and the crowds of people – including a knot of nobles by the door – parted to let a very distinguished-looking foreign noble pass into the crowded courtroom. Xoxoacatl's cousin smiled. "So, it's true! Rumor had it that the king asked to have one of the judges from the Tenochtitlan high court come down to Yautepec to help on this case, but no one knew whether he would come or not. I guess he did!" Just then Xoxoacatl heard a scribe calling the relevant parties to the commoners' courtroom. As he entered, he realized that he was no longer quite so nervous. With all the big crowds and excitement over corruption by a high noble, his little case did not seem so dramatic anymore.*

This vignette – set in the city-state capital of Yautepec, near modern Cuernavaca – illustrates several features of the Aztec legal system.

Trials, presided over by a judge or a group of judges, were held at the royal palace. Nobles and commoners were tried in separate courts, and witnesses were called to testify. Serious crimes, particularly by a noble, were punishable by death. And additional judges could be called in to help in particularly difficult cases.

## CRIME AND PUNISHMENT

We have seen that Aztec children were raised according to strict cultural codes and that they faced severe discipline for any infraction, no matter how small. However, these exacting teachings and harsh punishments did not always "take." There was deviance and crime in Aztec society. To deal with these eventualities, there were well-established institutions and procedures to handle any malfeasance, from theft to murder to impersonating a nobleman.

In order to understand crime and its enforcement, it is first necessary to reiterate the essential principles that guided an Aztec's life, and how these principles were codified into laws. The principles centered on moral propriety, orderly conduct (especially in household and community settings), proper performance of expected duties, respect of others' personal rights and property (including land), maintenance of social status rights and boundaries, and diligent propitiation of the gods (Berdan 2014: 214). Violations of these rules can be boiled down to crimes in four general arenas: persons and property, social status, the state, and the gods. Beyond actual crimes, sometimes people came into conflict with one another, each side perhaps feeling that right was on his or her side. These were frequently domestic disputes.

Crimes against persons and property included homicide and other personal violence, theft, selling stolen goods, counterfeiting cacao beans, overpricing and undermeasuring marketplace goods, and adultery. Adulterers typically faced the death penalty. Punishments frequently matched the crime, as when the murderer of a woman's husband may be required to perform the dead husband's work and support the surviving wife and children.

A closer look at one of these offenses, theft, is particularly instructive. Theft (Figure 9.1) was thought of as a particularly reproachable crime and was often punished with death. But there were degrees of

FIGURE 9.1. A thief. Reproduced from Berdan and Anawalt (1992: vol. 4: f. 70r), with permission.

seriousness of the crime and its punishment, based on the value of the stolen item(s), the quantities stolen, who it was stolen from, the location of the theft, the number of prior offenses, and the response of the thief to his crime. These criteria emerge when looking at the punishment meted out to the offender, although the rules and penalties varied to some degree from city-state to city-state and circumstance to circumstance.

Strangulation or stoning were popular punishments for theft, or thieves may be sentenced to serve their victims by working off the amount of the theft. In one account a thief who broke into a house was strangled, while in another version he was enslaved for his first offense and then strangled for his second. In any case, a thief who made away with objects of great value or quantity from a house could expect strangulation. Theft in a marketplace, heavily sanctioned perhaps because of the breadth of opportunity, was met with strangulation. The marketplace in particular provided fertile ground for all kinds of wrongdoing. It perhaps comes as no surprise that "punishments were most severe if crimes occurred in the marketplace. Such public flaunting of disorderly behavior could, certainly, not be tolerated, and it so happened that the laws were strictest where the opportunity was greatest" (Berdan 1999: 263). These malfeasances especially included counterfeiting money (cacao beans), cheating on prices and measurements, theft, and passing stolen goods.

Context was also important in thefts from agricultural fields: a thief who stole maize from the first row of the field next to a road may not have been prosecuted; if he stole maize from elsewhere in a field or in quantity, he was strangled for the offense. But there were still nuances: if he stole maize from temple lands he was less severely punished than if he pilfered them from the fields of commoner farmers, the idea being that the farmer depended more heavily on each plant than did the temple priests. And still more nuances: at least in Teotihuacan, a crop thief was fined one cotton cloak (*quachtli*) per plant stolen; if he could not pay he was stoned to death. If he showed remorse for his actions and returned the stolen goods, he was merely enslaved (bad enough, but at least he was still alive) (Offner 1983: 271–279).

Offenses against social status rules focused on commoners' infringements on the exclusive rights of nobles and improper use of the symbols of nobility. Motecuhzoma Ilhuicamina (r. 1440–1468) promulgated a set of laws of which eleven of the sixteen statutes concerned protection of the nobility, their rights, and symbols of their status (sumptuary laws). For instance, this august ruler decreed that only the ruler and his second-in-command were allowed to wear sandals in the palace, although other great noblemen could wear sandals in the city at large. The types, materials, and lengths of men's cloaks were legally defined: nobles wore cotton, commoners wore maguey fiber; noble cloaks were decorated, commoner cloaks were plain and simple; noble cloaks could reach the ankle, commoner cloaks must just cover the knee (unless the wearer had suffered leg wounds in battle: "Since that leg did not flee from the sword, it is just that it be rewarded and honored") (Durán 1994: 208–210).

Only great nobles and honored warriors could build houses of two stories (Durán probably means houses raised on platforms), and adornments (such as gold for nobles and bones or nondescript stones for commoners) were regulated by status. These laws, codified by this early imperial ruler, were designed to visibly maintain the exceptional status of hereditary nobles and highly achieved warriors (as quasi-nobles). His successors zealously enforced these laws, although it appears that among them, Ahuitzotl was rather lax and egalitarian in his approach to status (Berdan and Anawalt 1992: vol. 3: ff. 9v–15r).

The state could be violated by spying and treason, by assassinating political officials or merchants on the road, by judges embezzling and taking bribes, and by tax/tribute collectors skimming off a little extra for themselves. Some punishments for these offenses were meted out on a grand scale: the assassination of political officials or professional merchants resulted in swift reprisals as armed forces furiously set upon the offenders' communities. The slaves in Figure 6.1 represent the wife (or wives) and children of a distant lord who had rebelled in such a manner from his Aztec overlords. The lord himself was strangled for his misdeed (and miscalculation) (Berdan and Anawalt 1992: vol. 3: f. 66r). Traitors were particularly offensive to the state, and they were dismembered for their crime. Extortionate tribute collectors were executed.

Neglecting or improperly observing the gods were supernatural affronts and therefore received supernatural sanctions; they were crimes but were handled beyond the thrall of mortal jurisdictions. The gods were particularly offended if their mortal worshippers failed to properly worship them. The Aztecs believed that their afterlives were determined by how they died rather than how they lived their lives. Therefore, threats of an unpleasant afterlife were meaningless to them – they needed to be sanctioned in their lifetimes. And they were, with disagreeable and visible diseases or deformities such as boils, trembling feet, or misshapen limbs (Berdan 2014: 212). If you displayed these afflictions, fellow Aztecs would be likely to pass judgment on you for your lax observance of religious rituals.

In addition to all of these, drunkenness and sorcery were highly disapproved, but, at least in the case of drunkenness, considered more of a means to crimes than crimes themselves. Thus, in the *Codex Mendoza* (Berdan and Anawalt 1992: vol. 4: f. 70r; Figure 9.2), a couple is pictured sitting beside a pilfered chest while imbibing cups of pulque. Sorcerers were nefarious individuals who went about engaging in antisocial and malevolent acts. Some of the most dangerous of these, called *tlacatecolotl* ("man-owl"), could transform themselves into powerful creatures and thereby cause soul loss or the embedding of a foreign object into their victims; these attacks could lead to illness and even death. Similarly, some sorcerers sought out the forearm of a woman who died in childbirth, using that talisman to do ill (see Chapter 7). These powerful forces were countered by other

FIGURE 9.2. Drunkards. Reproduced from Berdan and Anawalt (1992: vol. 4: f. 70r), with permission.

magical specialists; we do not know of judicial responses to these socially malicious activities.

All of these occurrences, whether crimes or disputes, led to responses by society and the state to determine rights and wrongs and to either punish the offenders or guide them back into conformity, thus ideally restoring social order. It is worth reiterating that punishments were especially attuned to class and context. Judgments appear harsher on nobles than on commoners in matters of drunkenness, but easier on the elite for adultery (in this society where noble polygyny was the rule, it may have been a bit difficult to identify adultery). Even so, adultery along with theft were usually met with strangulation or stoning (Figures 9.3 and 9.4). Judges who accepted bribes were warned for their first offense and had their heads shaven and were removed from office if the practice continued (Berdan 2014: 213). This seems relatively mild in a culture where theft and adultery could result in stoning and strangulation. Context was always important: crimes committed in the palace were particularly reprehensible; entering a house with the intent to steal was almost as bad; and the marketplace was tightly policed since it provided fertile ground for all kinds of wrongdoing. On the whole, punishments were severe and were meted out swiftly.

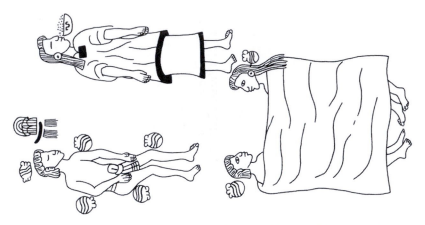

FIGURE 9.3. Stoning an adulterous couple as punishment. Reproduced from Berdan and Anawalt (1992: vol. 4: f. 71r), with permission.

## COURTS AND JUDGES

Each city-state had its own legal institutions. The best documented were those of Texcoco, which was the recognized legal center of the imperial realm (Offner 1983). Even though we know most about legal institutions and judicial proceedings from that city-state, it appears that other city-states in highland central Mexico established similar legal structures and procedures (Zorita 1994: 124).

Most crimes and disputes were brought to a court for adjudication. There was a hierarchy of courts – the *Codex Mendoza* (ff. 67v–69r; Figure 9.5) shows two levels. The lower level includes four judges, all with different but exalted titles, hearing and determining a case brought to them by three men and three women (perhaps a domestic dispute?). That case was apparently appealed to a higher court located in Motecuhzoma's palace; four judges also presided there. Sahagún (1950–1982: book 8: 55) basically verifies this arrangement, mentioning procedures whereby cases heard in a lower court were sent to a higher court, and Diego Durán (1994: 192–193, 210) specifies several levels of "tribunals" where cases were heard until they reached the "supreme council." That highest court, according to Alonso de Zorita (1994: 128–130), consisted of twelve judges, but different city-states may have constituted their courts differently. At this highest level at least, the judges were assisted by scribes who recorded every detail and

FIGURE 9.4. Strangling and beating as punishments. Sahagún (1950–1982: book 8: fig. 66). Firenze, Biblioteca Medicea Laurenziana.

by constables who did the judges' bidding in collecting evidence or arresting offenders. Apparently, the judges of the lower courts could apprehend delinquents and criminals, collecting and assembling initial information on their cases. They left the final decisions and sentences to higher courts. The most dire or perhaps controversial cases were referred to the ruler, whose decision was final.

Separate courts, each with its own judges, were designated for nobles and commoners. Judges for the noble courts were righteous and experienced nobles, and those for commoner courts were "those of sound and righteous upbringing, who had been reared in war:

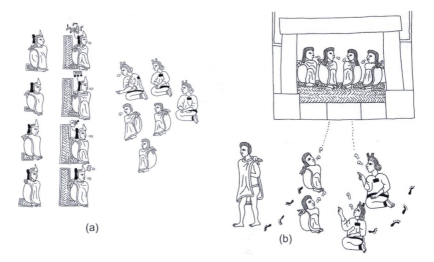

(a)

(b)

FIGURE 9.5. Levels of Aztec courts. (a) A high court. (b) The highest court, located in the palace of Motecuhzoma Xocoyotzin (see Figure 1.3). Each court shows judges sitting on reed mats, with groups of supplicants. Reproduced from Berdan and Anawalt (1992: vol. 4: ff. 67v–69r), with permission.

brave warriors and men" (Sahagún 1950–1982: book 8: 54). It is not clear if this noble/commoner court segregation was maintained throughout the entire juridical hierarchy, but we might assume that it was. We also assume that the cases heard in noble and commoner courts, while overlapping in some instances, were unique in others. A crime such as homicide or theft could be committed by noble or commoner, but bribery and extortion tended to be elite crimes, and it would be hard to think of a nobleperson counterfeiting cacao beans or, as in the vignette above, pilfering maize ears from a farmer's field.

Additional sets of judges oversaw the marketplaces (see Chapter 8). In Tlatelolco at least, these judges were drawn from the ranks of the most important professional merchants. They sat impressively in a special corner of the market plaza, providing buyers, sellers, and potential malefactors a visual reminder of the costs of any crimes they might be considering. But crimes there were, and the judges were assisted by a cadre of inspectors or constables who roamed about the marketplace with keen eyes to cheating, pilfering, counterfeiting, or any other improper or illegal behavior. Justice was swift and the inspectors had the prerogative to mete out immediate penalties, for example, smashing deceitful measures on the spot.

The Aztecs took their legal procedures very seriously. Judges, chosen by the ruler, ideally were wise and capable, honest and honorable, and were men who thought and spoke deliberately. Written sources agree that judges maintained the highest level of moral rectitude and honesty. In the words of Sahagún (1950–1982: book 10: 15–16), the magistrate or judge was

Dignified, fearless, courageous, reserved, stern-visaged. The good magistrate (is) just: a hearer of both sides, an examiner of both sides, a listener to all factions, a passer of just sentences, a settler of quarrels, a shower of no favor. He fears no one; he passes just sentences; he intercedes in quarrels; he shows no bias.

Still, the judges were beholden to their ruler and supported by the palace. The ruler provided lands with tenants for judges, as well as various gifts and services (Offner 1983: 251). Judges were not allowed to receive gifts or favors from anyone but the ruler, and those who violated this rule were punished severely. Judges had several types of assistants. Scribes recorded the details of each case. For example, a hearing over land ownership would probably include a painted list of farmers who occupied or used various fields in or near the plot in question. Bailiffs or constables did the judges' bidding in collecting evidence, arresting offenders, and organizing witnesses. The existence of a Nahuatl term for attorney, *tepantlato*, a person who "solicits, appeals, accuses, and offers rebuttals" (Hirth 2016: 143), suggests that the parties in a case were represented by specialists, although we have little information about these occupations.

Judges probed deeply into the evidence of each case: after hearing the complaint, they deliberated upon the case by carefully examining the facts and questioning witnesses, and then recording everything in paintings that set down "who were the parties to suit, what it concerned, and the various claims, witnesses, and the finding or sentence" (Zorita 1994: 128). Zorita (1994: 126–128) expands on this:

The Indian judges of whom I spoke would seat themselves at daybreak on their mat dais, and immediately begin to hear pleas. The judges' meals were brought to them at an early hour from the royal palace. After eating, they rested for a while, then returned to hear the remaining suitors, staying until two hours before sundown.... Every twelve days the ruler held a council or conference with all the judges to discuss difficult cases or important criminal cases. Every case that the ruler had to consider was first carefully examined and the facts ascertained. Witnesses told the truth not only from respect for the oath they swore but from fear of the judges, who were very skillful in getting at the facts and displaying much wisdom in their questioning and cross-examination. They punished very severely one who did not tell the truth.

The intensity and meticulousness with which the Aztecs performed their legal activities, as described by Zorita, suggests a high degree of legalism in this society: judges paid tight attention to the letter of the law (Offner 1983). A legalistic stance resulted in laws being unstintingly upheld regardless of complicating and confounding matters such as social status. It also tended to standardize laws and legal systems across ethnic groups and therefore lead to more social homogeneity (Offner 1983: 82). But this was in theory; what about real life, and death, on the ground? Let's take a look.

## TWO EXTRAORDINARY BUT REVEALING CASES

Where criminality and wrongdoing were involved, we know a good deal about laws, courts, and procedures in a general sense, but much less about specific cases. We know that justice was swift and severe, that judges were held to the highest standards, and that the ruler, judges, and constables wielded extraordinary power. But how to recreate a case such as that of Xoxoacatl? We have precious little in the documentary record, and the archaeological record is silent on this. Specific stories? Detailed proceedings? Personal names? Only a very few. The following are two particularly interesting ones.

The first of these involves Tetzauhpiltzintli, a highly touted son of the Texcocan ruler Nezahualcoyotl. This case has a little bit of everything: palace intrigue, sibling rivalry, deception, desperation, a sense of justice, and an extraordinary climax. According to the most detailed account (Alva Ixtlilxochitl 1965: vol. 2: 219–222), this son of the ruler and his primary wife grew up to become admired and accomplished in every way: in philosophy, poetry, the mechanical arts, and the martial arts. He was an illustrious prince, trained and poised to take up the throne on the death of his father. One of Tetzauhpiltzintli's half-siblings, the son of the ruler and a concubine, stirred up discord within the family by spreading a falsehood about his half-brother and making their father suspect that his legitimate son and heir was planning a revolt. Nezahualcoyotl sent a servant on a fact-finding mission; the servant returned with the news that Tetzauhpiltzintli had a room full of military arms. This was highly suspicious. Apparently not willing to remand this emotionally charged case to the established courts, Nezahualcoyotl called on his two imperial co-rulers (from Tenochtitlan and Tlacopan) to reprimand his allegedly rebellious son. It turned out that his trust was ill-placed, for these two rulers arrived with officers who summarily and deceitfully strangled the young man, a form of execution. Nezahualcoyotl loved his son dearly, but he also held true to his own standards of justice – he wept bitterly at the harshness of his kingly colleagues, but did not take any action against them.

The second case involves Nezahualcoyotl's successor, Nezahualpilli, who stepped in as heir in Texcoco following the death of Tetzauhpiltzintli. Mirroring the prior case, Nezahualpilli's eldest son Huexotzincatzin, a notable poet and philosopher, fell victim to the intricacies and intimacies of palace life. He and his father's favorite concubine came under scrutiny when it was discovered that they were enjoying lively poetic exchanges. Suspected of engaging in more than just poetry, this fine prince was brought before the court and found to be guilty of treason against the king, his own father. According to the laws the son was executed, even though his father loved him beyond measure (Alva Ixtlilxochitl 1965: vol. 2: 294).

These are fairly long stories, but they were notorious and entered the histories because of the prominence of their main characters and their moral lessons. These were kings and princes, the most powerful in the land. Yet the law still applied to them. No one was above the law. Furthermore, laws and their enforcement transcended family relations and emotions. And if kings and princes were subject to the law and its stern demands, then surely a farmer or merchant, indeed anyone, had good reason to fear the law and its enforcers.

## PALACES AND COURTS

Apart from the hearings held in the Tlatelolco market by market judges, most courtrooms were attached to royal palaces. The high court for nobles shown in Figure 9.5, for example, was held within the royal palace of Tenochtitlan. Aztec royal palaces, like this one, were large compounds where many activities of government were concentrated (Rojas 2012). In addition to serving as living quarters for the king and his extensive family, palaces were the settings for meetings of legal courts and military councils, and for the storage of weapons, food, and other goods. Stewards, singers, and perhaps war captives were housed at the palace. In addition, palaces had vast courtyards where meetings and gatherings were held, and where people came to pay their taxes and tributes, and line up for their periodic labor service (see Chapter 1).

The palace at Tenochtitlan at least contained a jail – in essence, claustrophobic wooden cages – to detain serious offenders (Figure 9.6). These detainees were noble wrongdoers, those accused

FIGURE 9.6. An Aztec jail. Sahagún (1950–1982: book 8: fig. 67). Firenze, Biblioteca Medicea Laurenziana. All rights reserved. Further reproduction in any print or digital format is forbidden.

of drunkenness or concubinage or of exacting extra tributes on a subject town. In these cramped quarters they awaited their fate, most likely strangling, stoning, or beating with wooden cudgels (Sahagún 1950–1982: book 8: 43–44). Non-noble criminals were also detained in wooden cages, but we are not sure if they were housed in the palace jail or elsewhere.

An idealized picture of a royal palace was painted in the Mapa Quinatzin (see Figure 1.4). The basic architectural features are a large central courtyard with a single exterior entrance, an elevated dais opposite the entrance, and a series of rooms elevated on platforms that enclose the courtyard. These same features are found in the royal palaces excavated by archaeologists. For example, the royal palace at Calixtlahuaca (Figure 9.7) is laid out around a large rectangular courtyard with a single entrance on the west side. Opposite the entrance is a tall platform reached by three parallel stairways. To the north of the courtyard are some platforms, and an opposite area on the south contains a warren of rooms and passages.

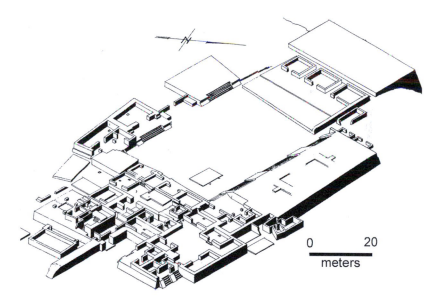

FIGURE 9.7. The Calixtlahuaca royal palace. Source: Michael E. Smith, based on drawings by José García Payón.

We do not know which of the rooms in these palaces may have been used as courtrooms. The number and size of courtrooms, and the number of judges, must have varied with the size and power of the local polity. José Luis de Rojas (2012: 145) has estimated that Tenochtitlan – a city with more than 200,000 residents that ruled an empire with several million subjects – had an estimated thirty-six judges, although the number may have been higher. On the other hand, provincial city-states such as Yautepec (the setting for the vignettes in this chapter) or Calixtlahuaca (Figure 9.7) probably had fewer judges, and some smaller communities may have had only a single courtroom for both nobles and commoners. Speaking generally, the placement of courtrooms and jails within palaces, and the supplying of judges with meals from the palace kitchens, assured that legal activities took place within the city-state's political nerve center and were under the watchful eye of the ruler and his officials.

### RETROSPECT AND PROSPECT

*"I'm too old for this," thought an elderly Xoxoacatl. "What am I doing here, anyway?" He stood at the entrance to the town's cabildo, or council building. Today it served as a courtroom. His mind wandered back to his other courtroom experience, thirty-eight years ago. It was over some ears of maize that a man had stolen from his field – the man was found guilty (there was a witness), and he paid Xoxoacatl five cotton cloaks (quachtli) that he borrowed from his brother, one cloak for each ear stolen. The man had taken the maize from a row close to the road; still, he was lucky. Everyone knew that he could have been strangled for stealing.*

*And now he stood in confrontation again. But this was a new building. The Nahua judges, from his own town, had new and different titles. But much else felt familiar to Xocoacatl. He had been told that he would see the same procedures and attention to detail in this new setting: formalities were observed, the case was identified, witnesses were called, oaths were sworn, testaments were made, everything was written down, and a judgment was made.*

*Everything was based on facts and adherence to truth. He was okay with that. He and his two friends had clearly seen the man from a neighboring town move their town's boundary marker. They had reported it, and the town was in an uproar. The accused man had denied the charge, and now here they are: Xoxoacatl and his two farmer friends must swear as witnesses in court in front of important men. At least they were Nahua, like himself. But he had heard that a Spanish official would be there as well, and that made him a bit uneasy. Maybe it was just him – he was uneasy and uncertain about a lot of things these days.*

*His thoughts were interrupted as the door opened and they were ushered inside.*

In the nearly two decades since the Spaniards arrived, Xoxoacatl had had only fairly limited contact with them – mostly in the market, the church, and when the tax collector came around. This was his first time in a dispute in this new setting, but he knew that the native council members acted as judges although a Spanish official was often present on court days. The formal judicial proceedings were legalistic and similar to those practiced in pre-Spanish times – based on facts and designed to determine the truth of the matter, as Xoxoacatl's thoughts reflect. However, local courts may have been somewhat less formal and more casual, but no less rigorous than the Spanish courts (Boyer 2000).

Xoxoacatl and his friends were living in a new age. Since their arrival, the new lords of the land had imposed their religion, technology, styles of clothing, legal system, crops and domesticated animals, and things in general (such as metal hoes and scissors) upon their native subjects. For a while and in most towns, native conflicts were adjudicated by native judges as in the scenario above. But particularly serious conflicts and disputes with Spaniards were typically handled by Spanish courts (Sousa 1997).

While Spanish legal procedures were not initially particularly new to most native lives, some types of conflict were. Spanish-introduced livestock invaded native fields and destroyed their crops; some unscrupulous Spaniards tried to unlawfully acquire native lands by whatever means they could; Spanish officers were often accused of violating tribute-collection rules (this may not have been particularly novel); thieves stole Spanish money, clothing, and animals; scandalous behavior was charged between Spaniards and natives; women were arrested for selling wine in the marketplace; one litigant complained of being trampled by a horse in the market (Haskett 1991; Sousa 1997; Spores 1984). New and different people and things created new details in conflict and litigation. But much that was familiar to the native peoples persisted.

# 10

# A Battle Far Afield

He awoke to a cacophony of bird songs. *Sweeooo, pwu-pwu, turrit-turrit-turrit, wef-wef-wef, trrreeh, deedeedee.* He listened intently, his eyes still closed. No, he didn't recognize any of them. Disoriented, he quickly sat up. He rubbed his eyes – where was he? He stared at the rising sun: Tonatiuh, hefted by valiant warriors from the underworld to warm and brighten the day. It shone through tall, unfamiliar trees as he looked around him in the hazy dawn.

Now he remembered. The long, dusty marches. Day after day, skirting the volcano Popocatepetl and stepping fretfully past the lands of the enemy Tlaxcallans to Tulan-cinco. And then the unexpected drop from his familiar plateau into a hot, green, mountainous land. Strange, dropping down into mountains! But they had, and followed a well-trod road through friendly Xicotepec and Cuauhchinanco, and now they were close to Papantla, their destination.

Coyochimalli had been to war before, to the south of his home of Tenochtitlan. Those lands were also mountainous, but drier. These were hot and humid, even though it was the cooler time of the year. He was tired, but energized. Men were warriors. This was what he lived for, was trained for, looked forward to, and it was not his first time. It was his destiny, whatever happened on the battlefield. Last time he had captured an enemy warrior and offered him to the gods on his return home. Perhaps the gods would look on him favorably again. He prayed to them before he assembled his gear for one more day's march, to Papantla and to battle.

Farther back in the lines, in a separate contingent, marched Tecolotl. In his day job, he was a farmer in a small village near Texcoco. The Texcoco ruler had also called up troops to fight in this war. Actually, from what he had heard, his ruler controlled more lands here to the east than the Tenochtitlan ruler – apparently it was a point of unpleasantness between the two rulers. But that was not his business. Like all other men of his town, he was obligated to serve his ruler in times of war, and this was one such time. His first. As he marched steadily to the east, he thought of taking a captive, maybe some loot, and then back home to his family and farm.

FIGURE 10.1. Totonacs from the eastern part of the Aztec Empire. Sahagún (1950–1982: book 10: fig. 195). Firenze, Biblioteca Medicea Laurenziana. All rights reserved. Further reproduction in any print or digital format is forbidden.

Coyochimalli and Tecolotl were headed to war. We do not know precisely what provoked Motecuhzoma Xocoyotzin's war against Papantla. We do know that Papantla was rich in resources greatly valued by the highland Aztec elite: cotton, cacao, vanilla, sweetgum (*Liquidambar*), and agricultural staples such as maize, beans, and chiles. We also know that Papantla was an important Totonac center. The Totonacs were known (or at least stereotyped) by the Aztecs as quite "civilized." In their estimation, Totonac men and women were beautiful and tall, adept in singing and dancing, and the women were expert embroiderers. As a result, the Totonac were known as elegant dressers, and they attended fastidiously to their appearance, from hairdos to adornments (Figure 10.1). And they apparently ate well, their hallmark dishes being meat tamales and tortillas dipped in chiles. Still, they spoke a "barbarous tongue" – no language was quite up to the standard of the Aztec's Nahuatl (Sahagún 1950–1982: book 10: 184–185). Despite these accolades, the Aztecs had a certain animosity toward the Totonacs: back in the year One Rabbit (1454), while the Basin of Mexico people were suffering a devastating famine, Totonacs came from the lowlands with loads of maize to buy individuals as slaves, often separating families. They took their new slaves to Totonacapan, the land of the Totonacs. This was during the reign of the first Motecuhzoma, the current Motecuhzoma's great-grandfather, and it was a great insult. Perhaps, now, revenge will be sweet.

The collective allied forces of the Basin of Mexico city-states had gone to war frequently over the past seven decades or so, and they had become a well-organized military machine. They were fully prepared, they relied on allies along the route, they gathered intelligence, they used multiple fighting strategies, they were well-equipped with armor and weapons, and, perhaps most important, there were a great many of them. They usually overwhelmed, in numbers, any enemy force they faced. On this expedition, Coyochimalli of Tenochtitlan could see contingents from Texcoco and Tlacopan, and there were perhaps others that were beyond his vision. Tecolotl, as well, looked around him at the endless lines of warriors and porters. Although the armies on occasion returned home depressed and defeated, both these warriors were confident that they would be victorious, and that they would return home with enemy captives.

## WAR AS A WAY OF LIFE

Warfare was a way of life among the Aztecs and their neighbors. From the moment they stepped foot in the highly contentious Basin of Mexico in the thirteenth century, the migratory Mexica were embroiled in the internecine wars among competing city-states. They became attached to established polities as mercenaries, quickly demonstrating their value as fierce and relentless warriors. As they gained victories, they also gained renown, reputation, and resources. And they never stopped. By 1430 they had established a political-military alliance with the two largest polities in the Basin, Texcoco and Tlacopan, this triumvirate grasping control of most of that Basin within a brief generation of rulers. It did not take long for the Mexica to achieve military preeminence in the alliance and set forth on an insistent agenda of conquest and subjugation of most of their known world. By 1519, when the Spaniards arrived, they had conquered much of central Mesoamerica. They were, however, perennially frustrated by powerful polities that withstood their military power, notably

FIGURE 10.2. Human sacrifice. *Codex Magliabechiano* (1903: f. 70r). Reproduced from Michael E. Smith.

the Tarascans to their west and the pesky Tlaxcallans to the east. They showed relatively little interest in moving very far north, and access to desirable resources beyond the southern borders of their empire was largely attained by diplomacy and trade.

With war such a prominent theme in Aztec culture, it comes as no surprise that an ideology of warfare penetrated every aspect of Aztec life. We have already seen that newborn boys were handed tiny shields with miniscule arrows as symbols of their later lives. Midwives shouted war cries at a birth, bringing the delivering woman into the realm of war, as she won her battle by being a brave warrior in capturing her baby (see Chapter 7). A god of war (Huitzilopochtli) shared the apex of the great temple of Tenochtitlan with the rain deity, Tlaloc. This and other temples were the scenes of flamboyant theatrical ceremonies, sometimes involving ritual sacrifices of battlefield captives (Figure 10.2). Rulers, prior to their coronations, were required to personally go to war and bring home captives for sacrifice to the gods (see Chapter 1). A primary avenue for social advancement was through military achievement, and successful warriors were publicly rewarded and honored. Tributes collected from conquests reinforced the subservience of the subjugated peoples and financed future imperial campaigns as well as the extravagant lifestyles of rulers in their opulent palaces. And myths recounted gripping conflicts and ferocious battles deep into the supernatural past. Even just looking at the rising sun, as did Coyochimalli, prompted thoughts of valiant warriors.

Schools providing military training for noble and commoner boys were found throughout the cities of the Basin (and probably beyond). Both *calmecac* schools (for noble boys) and *telpochcalli* schools (for commoner boys) trained students for military service. This training began by at least age fifteen, and perhaps as early as five or ten (Berdan 2014: 203, 307). In addition to military education in the school sites themselves, these boys were actually taken to wars for some supervised battlefield training: "And they taught him well how to guard himself with a shield; how one fought; how a spear was fended off with a shield. And when a battle was joined . . . they taught him well and made him see how he might take a captive" (Sahagún 1950–1982: book 8: 72). This on-the-job training was certainly useful, especially since battles were typically loud, violent, confusing melees, and prior exposure to these struggles would undoubtedly help avert the initial shock of the chaos of battlefield clashes and help instill courage and confidence in the warrior's heart and order and purpose in his actions.

While all boys were trained to perform as warriors, there was no standing army. The rank and file of the Aztec fighting force perhaps more closely resembled a militia, fighters who could be called up when needed, and were obligated to serve. While militias (historically) are often mustered for defense of their own territory, these warriors were primarily called on to join offensive forces, sometimes very far afield. Tenochtitlan itself seemed almost immune to attack, although the ruler was charged with constant vigilance, just in case. That case happened only once, when their long-term enemies the Huexotzincos notoriously burned the temple of the goddess Toci ("Our Grandmother") on the fringes of the city. The Mexica were outraged and immediately pursued revenge (Durán 1994: 456–459). The penetration of the Spaniards and their indigenous allies into the seemingly impregnable island city in 1521 was unprecedented. So, prior to the Spanish siege of Tenochtitlan, the Mexica and their allied warriors fought in other lands, some very far away.

The lack of a standing army did not mean there were no professional military men. There were. Success on the battlefield allowed the warrior to climb a military hierarchy, based on the number of enemy warriors captured in battle. These had to be single captures – a capture made with the help of another warrior simply did not count. And so a valiant man climbed the military hierarchy: one captive earned the captor a cape with a flower design; with two captives, the warrior was awarded an orange cape and a Huaxtec-style warrior costume; with three, a "jewel of Ehecatl" cape and a butterfly back device; and with four, a diagonally striped cape and a jaguar costume (Berdan and Anawalt 1992: vol. 3: f. 64r; Figure 10.3).

Similarly, priests who went to war could also gain renown and the right to wear and display specific cloaks and warrior devices (Berdan and Anawalt 1992: vol. 3: f. 65r; Figures 10.3 and 2.8). Four was a magic number here: with that many captures (which may have

FIGURE 10.3. Warriors capture enemies and win rewards. Reproduced from Berdan and Anawalt (1992: vol. 4: f. 64r), with permission.

required several military engagements), the courageous and seasoned warrior could participate in the war councils. Beyond these if a warrior was able to capture five or six enemies in battle, he was awarded with a "claw" back device that identified him as an Otomí warrior, a powerful adversary indeed. Still more prestigious was a Quachic warrior, whose many captures included warriors from the perennial enemy Huexotzincos. He too was awarded a distinctive device, this of a "banner" style. The capes could be worn (or, more to the point, flaunted) about town; the feathered warrior costumes were meant to be worn in battle. These sometimes-frightful costumes would have presented a formidable sight, intimidating an enemy who perhaps shivered in fear, knowing that their bearers were not only skilled and well-armed but also completely fearless in combat.

Especially notable were the eagle and jaguar warriors, likened by modern scholars to warrior knights (Figure 10.4). These valiant, tested warriors had proven themselves in battle and were the army's most reliable contingent, often leading the force into battle. Like the Otomí and Quachic warriors, they were expected to race aggressively and eagerly into battle, and never retreat. The eagle warriors, at least, enjoyed their own large meeting chamber, right beside the Great

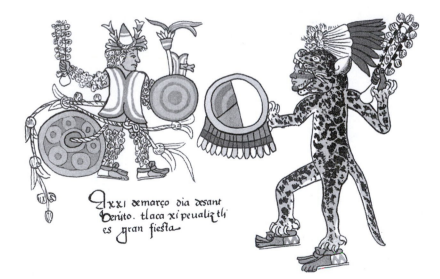

FIGURE 10.4. Jaguar warrior in ceremonial combat. Reproduced from *Codex Magliabechiano* (1903: f. 30r).

FIGURE 10.5. Titled warriors. Reproduced from Berdan and Anawalt (1992: vol. 4: f. 65r), with permission.

Temple in downtown Tenochtitlan. But the real leaders and strategists were the "generals," who organized and commanded the wars – but always at the behest of the ruler (Figure 10.5).

## GOALS AND PROVOCATIONS

The Mexica and their allies went to war for many reasons. Some of their goals were based on traditional practices handed down from generation to generation well before the Mexica arrived in the Basin of Mexico. They went to war, "since time immemorial," because "people always went to war." But, as with so many other things, there was more to it than just past practice.

Wars were pursued for political and economic reasons. The political climate of thirteenth- to sixteenth-century central Mexico was one of political and military volatility; almost constant warfare among one or another polities was the rule. To not engage in these conflicts was a sign of weakness and therefore invited conquest and subjugation, or rebellion of one's current subjects. As part of this climate, rulers of the profusion of city-states depended on ostentatious displays of wealth to advertise their power – they did this through lavish feasts designed to impress and intimidate friend and foe alike. The massive quantities and qualities of goods displayed at these extravaganzas were obtained from a ruler's own lands and those he controlled through conquest. The rulers needed many subjects to supply this wealth (largely through imposed tribute); the display of wealth advertised and flaunted the ruler's control over those many subjects; if a ruler failed to successfully participate, it was a sign of weakness and vulnerability.

Conquest and subsequent tribute supplied many material needs of rulers, although those needs seem to have grown over time and never been quite satisfactorily satisfied: cities grew in size, feasts increased in flamboyance, and wars became more and more expansive. All of these needed constant provisions of subsistence and luxury goods. The gods also demanded their share. For Tenochtitlan alone, subjects supplied materials and labor for the building of massive temples, and sent myriad goods for ritual displays and sacred offerings – from greenstone beads, turquoise masks, and copper bells to seashells and rubber (Berdan 2014: 156). And as with the rulers' living standards, the material needs of the priests and their hungry gods also appear to have increased as the empire grew.

Among the most persistent demands of the gods were human sacrifices. Some of these individuals were obtained locally, but others were warriors captured on nearby or distant battlefields. Almost every major ceremony required one or a few human sacrifices, but more rarely sacrificial ceremonies involved perhaps thousands of captured enemy warriors. These events were always ritual, as offerings to one or another deity, but they were also political. The best known of these surrounded the 1487 dedication ceremony of the Mexica's Great Temple in Tenochtitlan: recorded numbers of sacrificed warriors at this drama vary wildly from 20,000 to 80,400 (Berdan 2014: 241). Allied and enemy kings were invited to view this event, the allies glad to be friends of the Mexica, the enemies thinking twice about opposing them.

Aztec (and other) warriors were highly motivated to obtain captives for sacrifice. As already mentioned, Mexica warriors were granted specific rewards – designed capes and heraldic devices – for each captive they secured and offered to the gods. In a melee of largely hand-to-hand combat, this was strong incentive to fight bravely and fearlessly. Collectively, it could make the difference between "taking the field" or not.

There appears to have been an unwritten rule: polities did not go to war without provocation. Assuredly, it was not difficult to find acceptable reasons for aggression against another polity. One was some perceived affront: a particularly good example of this came when Moquihuix, ruler of Tlatelolco, overtly maltreated his wife, who was also the sister of the neighboring Tenochtitlan ruler Axayacatl. This was in 1473: Tenochtitlan attacked Tlatelolco, Moquihuix was killed, and Axayacatl came to control the greatest market in all of central Mexico (a rather nice side benefit, if not the underlying motivation for the conflict). Other insults were more subtle: a ruler may decline an invitation to a feast offered by another ruler, or may refuse to comply with requests for "favors" – either was sufficient cause for aggressive military action. More directly, ambassadors, tribute collectors, and *pochteca* merchants were quite frequently assaulted on the road (Figure 10.6). These affronts were met with prompt and fierce military responses. Similarly, if an already-conquered domain rebelled from its overlords (a rather frequent occurrence), the Aztec army, often with its allies, was immediately on the march. If reconquered, reprisals were severe – in addition to the toll of battle casualties and captures, rebellious city-states were now subject to a doubling of tribute payments. It usually did not pay to defy the greatest army of their known world.

Although this was a violent, aggressive political climate, there were rules. Wars needed to be legitimized with some provocation as a reason or excuse. This was so important that the Mexica ruler Ahuitzotl mentions, at the end of a distant campaign, that "he did not wish to go farther, in part *because those people had not offended him in any way* and in part because his men were exhausted and their ranks depleted" (Durán 1994: 380; emphasis ours). Whether in this case or others, legitimation was important in order to rally allies for military support – perhaps the most significant advantage the Aztecs had in the military arena was the sheer numbers they could muster in their wars.

FIGURE 10.6. Merchants assaulted on the road. Reproduced from Berdan and Anawalt (1992: vol. 4: f. 66r), with permission.

## PREPARING FOR WAR

Assembling allies was only one of the many preparations for a military campaign. It was pursued and achieved early on in the process. Especially in the later years of the empire, Triple Alliance wars were organized under the direction of the Mexica ruler, who would send envoys to the Texcocan and Tlacopan kings, soliciting their participation. If more troops were needed, envoys were sent to the kings of other Basin of Mexico city-states, such as Xochimilco, Chalco, Coyoacan, and Cuitlahuac, who invariably agreed to join the expedition. In some cases, conquered city-states from farther afield were called up. The choice of allies for each war was often based on the nature of the affront – for instance, in a war directed against the eastern Huaxtecs, the Mexica ruler called upon Texcoco, Tlacopan, Chalco, and Xochimilco to join him, since merchants from these specific cities had been killed by the Huaxtecs, and this was a war of retaliation (Durán 1994: 160–161). Furthermore, the Mexica ruler would assess the scale of the impending war and summon forces superior in numbers to those he anticipated to meet on the battle-field. The mustering of a vast collective force was the first step in assuring success on the battlefield, plundering the conquered cities, and securing sustained tribute from the vanquished populations. Once alerted, the allied cities provided military men for the exped-ition, having prepared them for a long, tedious march and a furious, violent encounter.

Next was the matter of gathering intelligence. The ruler sent experienced military men to the realm of the enemy, to carefully study their city – its layout, its landscape, its roads, any rivers or other obstacles, and the type and strength of its defenses. A good deal of information on the enemy realm may have already been supplied by traveling merchants (see Chapter 4). With this intelligence in hand, the ruler consulted with his generals and devised a specific strategy, since the Aztecs "had always been crafty and ... used a thousand cunning tricks in war" (Durán 1994: 316; Figure 10.7).

Organizational matters were also high on the list. There was inten-tional order in the march to war: at the head of the Tenochtitlan army

FIGURE 10.7. Aztec warriors surround an enemy city. Reproduced from Berdan and Anawalt (1992: vol. 4: f. 67r), with permission.

went the priests, who gave spiritual validation to the enterprise and heart to the men. Marching one day behind them were the commanding generals and accomplished warriors, and one day behind them trudged the mass of warriors. If the overall army was made up of allied cities, each force met at an agreed-upon rendezvous point before marching in order to the target city.

Behind the Tenochtitlan army came the warriors from Tlatelolco, and then, arranged in order, warrior contingents from other participating allies. Each city-state army marched separately, set up separate camps, was deployed separately on the battlefield, and fought as an integral unit. Since the men marched perhaps twelve to twenty miles per day, and thousands of men were involved, the armies would have stretched for miles, and their collective arrival at their destination would have taken days; contingents from different allied city-states may have marched, as a general rule, a day apart (Hassig 1988: 66–70). All of this needed to be orchestrated and coordinated beforehand (Sahagún 1950–1982: book 8: 52).

Meanwhile, warriors and others attended to practical matters, particularly provision of field rations, weapons, and armor. Army food was reportedly supplied at least in part by those vendors in the Tlatelolco marketplace who dealt in relatively nonperishable foods: "biscuits, and finely ground, dried maize and chia seeds, and dried maize dough, and dried, lime-treated maize dough" (Sahagún 1950–1982: book 8: 69). For one campaign, warriors carried toasted maize kernels and maize flour, bean flour, toasted tortillas, sun-baked tamales, chiles, and ground cacao – from the rulers' storehouses and from their own homes (Durán 1994: 350). These supplies may not have been sufficient, especially on long marches, and the troops also relied on foods provided by city-states through which they passed on their expedition; the Aztecs felt it their right to demand food and other supplies from these communities, and the people in the path of a marching army expected their crops and food stores to be devoured. In some cases this must have been devastating to the local people, since thousands, sometimes hundreds of thousands, of warriors would have marched in a major military expedition.

The Mexica and their allies also had another recorded source for trail food, notably Motecuhzoma Xocoyotzin's tributes from conquered Tlatelolco, which consisted of "many sacks of ground cacao, of toasted maize, maize flour, bean meal, loads of maize breads [tortillas], loads of chiles and of pumpkin seeds." In addition to these relatively well-preserved foods, the Tlatelolcans also paid up sandals, cloaks, shields, arrows, swords, and slings. All of this was a prelude to Motecuhzoma's heading out on a major military campaign; we do not know if these demands were invoked for subsequent expeditions (Durán 1994: 411–412). However it was obtained, trail food was both durable and nourishing, if a little uninteresting. It perhaps reminds one a bit of "hardtack" as a staple of armies of the United States' Civil War – not particularly tasty but it kept one going.

The Aztecs, their allies, and their enemies all had roughly the same arsenal of armor and weaponry. Armor consisted of quilted cotton garments which covered the torso and wooden shields that offered flexible protection against the weapons-of-the-day. The armor of an officer or seasoned warrior would be more elaborate than that of the common warrior: depending on his status, the accomplished warrior would lead the battle decked out in specially designed feather costumes and back devices, and carrying equally embellished feather shields (see Figures 10.3 and 2.8). The sight of a great many of these dazzling and frightful warriors in the army's front lines was intended to make the enemy pause and tremble (and perhaps reflect on their mortality).

Weapons consisted of projectiles (spears, bows and arrows, atlatl darts, and slings with their stone shot) that provided deadly offensive from a considerable distance, perhaps as far as 180 feet for an atlatl and even farther for a slingshot (Hassig 1988: 79–80). All of these projectiles had the ability to pierce an enemy's cotton armor. A fighting force meeting a hail of spears, arrows, darts, and shot from slings was in trouble before even tangling with the enemy head-on. When the armies were physically engaged, shock weapons (spears, swords, and clubs) came into play that could "cut, crush, and puncture in hand-to-hand combat" (Hassig 1988: 81). Most notable among these was the *macquauitl*, an obsidian-studded club made of strong oak and about a meter long. Wielded by an experienced and determined (or desperate) warrior, it was a feared and deadly weapon. Some of these arms and armor were supplied from the ruler's ample storehouses, most of them surely assigned to the capable hands of elite warriors. Other warriors may have been more personally responsible for the manufacture and provision of their own weaponry, as well as their repairs (Durán 1994: 167).

Porters were enlisted to tote these victuals, arms, and supplies, each porter carrying around fifty pounds. One porter for every two warriors is mentioned for one war (Hassig 1988: 64), seemingly a pretty rich ratio. Perhaps what is meant is one porter for every two accomplished or seasoned warriors, who were accorded greater respect and therefore supplied with elaborate materials and devices and more food. Durán (1994: 350) tells us that all warriors (probably commoners) carried their victuals, along with their shields, swords, and other weapons in packs on their own backs. We do not know if the porters were slaves, or if they were paid for their services – we do know that porters generally did make themselves available in the Tlatelolco, and probably other marketplaces. If they were hired, it may have been through individual transactions with wealthier warriors who were able to pay them.

Now everything was ready to go: the dramatic priests, the commanders and seasoned warriors with their proud banners and awe-inspiring costumes and devices, the contingents of non-elite warriors lined up and armed, porters heavily laden, families weeping. It was a colorful but poignant scene.

Each ruler was responsible for his own military forces: he recruited his own men; managed supplies of food, arms, and weaponry; and saw to the orderly deployment of his troops on the march and in battle. Rulers frequently accompanied their armies into battle; they or their proxies were expected to deliver inspirational speeches before the actual engagements, spurring their troops to acts of extraordinary bravery with exhortations such as "Go now, run, attack! Show that you are brave, spirited men.... Sell your lives dearly ... do not take one step backward" (Durán 1994: 266–267, 378). Having arrived on the enemy's doorstep, they were primed, armed, and eager for battle.

## THE BATTLE

The Aztecs, as a collective imperial military force, won some wars and lost others during their ninety-year history of empire building. On balance, they won more than they lost, but some of their conquered subjects were also prone to later rebel when opportunities presented themselves. These opportunities arose at times of perceived imperial vulnerability such as a change in rulership or a serious defeat elsewhere. But whether taking up a new conquest or suppressing a rebellion, each war presented its own special demands, challenges, and opportunities.

*Coyochimalli looked around him at the assembled forces. The sun was just rising through the mist, and he could barely see that the Aztec generals had deployed warriors on long and deep lines facing Papantla. In front of him, and to each side, he admired the colorful military banners that identified each force – he would keep an eye on his, to make sure he moved in concert with his fellow warriors. He knew that the generals had carefully worked out a battle plan, and each part must work along with each other part. He also suspected that they had sent some forces around the other side of the city, to close off any retreat. Spies had already reported on Papantla's weak spots.*

*Sometimes the enemies would come out of their cities to fight in the open, sometimes they lay in wait behind their walls – Coyochimalli waited impatiently to see what they would do. Attack was imminent – they liked to attack at dawn. Hopefully the battle would be over before sunset, so they would not have to fight another day. His mind wandered and he drank in the overwhelming aroma of vanilla – he loved vanilla and would take some home with him when this was over. But now he needed to concentrate: in his mind, he replayed his general's inspirational words: "Think of no other things except that you must conquer or die . . . try to understand your shield and your sword" [Durán 1994: 267]. He steadied himself and looked ahead at his banner. He was ready.*

*It was midday. The sun had risen high in the sky, bringing its heat – too much heat, Tecolotl thought irreverently. The Totonacs had come out to meet them, and he felt like he had fought for hours (he had). His armor stuck annoyingly to his skin. His wooden shield was in tatters. The obsidian blades on his club were all but shattered, and he swung the heavy weapon with whatever strength he had left. And then all was quiet. He looked around, and saw that his side had taken the field, and the few remaining Totonacs were either captured, in retreat, or standing humbly with their arms crossed, asking for mercy. He had taken a captive, as had some of his fellow warriors. As he took stock of himself, he observed some bruises and cuts, one still bleeding, and a throbbing headache. But he was alive. He thanked the gods for allowing him to survive and return home.*

We know next to nothing about the details of the battle for Papantla, so this is a fictional but realistic scenario. But we do have detailed accounts of several other Aztec wars. To gain a flavor of the Aztec style of war (and that of their adversaries), we present here a small selection of well-recorded wars that they fought against the Huaxtecs in the northeast, the Tarascans to the west, and Quetzaltepec to the south, chronologically arranged. The Aztecs also fought several wars against their perpetual enemies to the east, the Tlaxcallans, Huexotzincos, and Cholulans, and those "flower wars" had their own goals, styles, and consequences.

## The Pesky Huaxtecs

Eleven years into the reign of the first Motecuhzoma (r. 1440–1468), Huaxtec people from the northern Gulf coast cities of Tochpan, Tzicoac, and Tamapachco offended the Aztecs by killing merchants from Tenochtitlan, Texcoco, Tlacopan, and other Basin of Mexico cities. This was tantamount to a declaration of war, and Motecuhzoma assembled his allies and forthwith marched to war. The march was similar to that experienced by our fictional Coyochimalli and Teco-lotl, although once in the lowlands they headed north; they were welcomed and their supplies replenished all along the way by friendly allies. After they had set up their massive camp, within sight of the enemy, they were exhorted to great deeds by an eminent captain: "be angry … be aggravated … if you are not inflamed … you will not show spirit and valor, you will do nothing" (Durán 1994: 163). Such words, in long speeches, inspired individual effort and valor in a war that was largely hand-to-hand combat.

All that said, the Aztecs deployed their forces: each allied contingent was arranged under its own visible banner, and an additional 2,000 experienced, armed men were concealed in a strategic location behind the lines. The bulk of the army moved forward to the enemy, both sides taunting one another with caustic insults and biting provocations. And so the battle was engaged. The Huaxtecs ferociously threw themselves into battle, with their clanging rattles, hair-raising howls, frightful feathered costumes, and terrifying face paint. They presented an alarming sight, and the Aztec warriors feigned a retreat, leading the Huaxtecs into the hands of the 2,000 hidden warriors – the trap was sprung and the enemy was completely surrounded, with a great many captives taken. All of this took place in the open, but once the field was taken, the Aztecs and their allies entered the cities, burned the temples, and sacked and looted until restrained by their leaders. The remaining Huaxtec leaders then appeared with arms crossed in front of them and implored the Aztecs to be merciful, promising "perpetual subjection and servitude, as well as rich tribute" (Durán 1994: 165). This was what the Aztecs wanted to hear: great quantities of gifts were immediately lavished on the Aztec leaders, a hefty tribute was negotiated, and the conquerors headed home with booty and captives in hand (Durán 1994: 160–165).

## The Mighty Tarascans

During the rule of Axayacatl (r. 1468–1481), grandson of the first Motecuhzoma, war was declared against the powerful Tarascans, a bulwark on the western border of the growing Triple Alliance empire (Durán 1994: 278–282). Axayacatl's rationale for declaring this war was to acquire sacrificial victims for the dedication of a monumental stone in Tenochtitlan. The response from his allies was enthusiastic, and, as was usual, all of the allied states participating in this war provided their own men with provisions and weapons. Axayacatl ended up commanding a total of 24,000 warriors. Axayacatl himself accompanied his army on this expedition, of course much more splendidly adorned and equipped than his men-of-the-line.

These allied forces gathered together at a locale three-days' march from the Basin of Mexico. As the army moved, spies were sent ahead to assess enemy numbers, weaponry, and fighting plans and styles. They returned with the distressing news that the Tarascans had amassed 40,000 well-armed warriors for this encounter. Axayacatl was visibly dismayed at this report, recognizing his error in judgment. But he followed his captains' advice in forging ahead anyway. To back away from battle was to lose face, and hence invite rebellions through-out the Aztec domain. As in the Huaxtec battle, inspirational speeches were delivered and military order was meticulously followed, with the most experienced warriors leading the army, especially the stalwart Quachic and Otomí warriors who vowed never to retreat.

Just before engaging, a delegation of Tarascans approached Axaya-catl, orally berating him, or perhaps trying to intimidate him. Axaya-catl refused to be ruffled, and the Tarascans mounted a furious attack. Seeing his army weakening, the Aztec ruler called up reinforcements, and the ferocious battle went on and on until sunset. Taking stock, the Aztec forces found themselves severely diminished, with a great many of their most valiant warriors wounded or dead from the Tarascan onslaught of clubs, arrows, spears, and shot from slings. The following day, reinforced with additional men and weapons, the Aztecs attacked again but were repulsed; so many warriors fell into enemy hands that it was "like flies that fall into the water" (Durán 1994: 281). Contrary to their training, the Aztecs retreated broken-spirited and in disarray. The losses were so great that, in the end, the allied Aztec forces lost more than 20,000 men, including most of the Quachic and Otomí warriors and a close relative of Axayacatl himself. The journey home was certainly dismal and depressing, and when the ragged survivors entered Tenochtitlan, "The entire city was filled with sorrow and lamentations, mourning, and tears" (Durán 1994: 282). The Tarascans handed the Aztec allies their greatest single defeat, in just two days.

## Obstreperous Quetzaltepec and Tototepec

When Motecuhzoma Xocoyotzin (r. 1502–1521) "requested" special stone-working abrasives from two distant cities, he was rebuffed. This was sufficient insult ("excuse") to mount a massive campaign into these southern lands. As usual, this ruler called on his allies for support, amassing a recorded (and perhaps exaggerated) 400,000 fighting men, fully equipped and ready to march in three days. In the meantime, knowing that a great force was approaching, Quetzaltepec and its neighbor Tototepec threw up massive defenses. They encircled their cities with five strong walls of earth, stone, and wood, four to six *brazas* (about 7–11 meters) high. Armed guards were placed along the walls. Furthermore, they blocked the roads with rocks, thorns, and trees. Motecuhzoma sent out the usual spies, who discovered these impediments. Tototepec was additionally protected by a raging river, but the Aztec troops constructed reed bridges in the dead of night, crossing the swollen river, surprising the overconfident city, and swarming through holes they made in the walls. They overwhelmed the defenders and residents, burning their temple and palace, and looting at will.

Their next target was the people of Quetzaltepec, who had their own spies: they had learned the fate of their neighbor, and also saw that Motecuhzoma was building ladders to scale their walls. In response, the defenders piled stones and wood atop the walls and

FIGURE 10.8. A burning temple (at the city of Huehuetlan), symbol and reality of military conquest. Reproduced from Berdan and Anawalt (1992: vol. 4: f. 13v), with permission.

placed armed warriors around its perimeter, shouting insults all night at the assembled Aztecs. In the morning, during the customary inspirational speech by the Aztec ruler, the Quetzaltepec army formed outside their city walls to confront their enemy. As usual, the Aztec army was well-ordered: only some of the contingents were sent into the initial fray, while others were held in reserve, who in their turn relieved the original fighters. Warriors from each city fought as a unit, proudly yelling its name ("Tenochtitlan!" "Texcoco!") as they forged ahead. The battle was inconclusive for six days, until the Aztecs finally managed to scale and dig through the walls, allowing them to take the city and burn its temple (Figure 10.8). As the first Motecuhzoma did with the Huaxtecs, this Motecuhzoma arranged terms of subjugation with these southern cities, including the provision of valuable gifts and tribute (Durán 1994: 417–424). This was a relatively long battle in Aztec terms, involving back-and-forth flows of defense, offense, defense, offense. It reminds us that the Aztec's enemies were not without their own spies, strategies, resources, and courageous fighting men. Which brings us to some of the prickliest military adversaries faced by the Aztecs: the Tlaxcallans, Huexotzincos, and Cholulans.

## A "FLOWER WAR"

The Aztec Triple Alliance was never able to conquer these three steadfast city-states, who frequently joined together in battle with a few of their friendly neighbors. These wars were ostensibly for two purposes: to provide warriors with battlefield experience without having to travel too far afield, and to capture enemy warriors for sacrifice to the gods. These scheduled wars were given a special name, *yaoxochitl,* "flower war." However, it has become clear that these battles were fought in earnest, and that defeat and conquest were the underlying goals (Berdan 2014: 158). In one such engagement, under the second Motecuhzoma, reportedly 100,000 Aztec allies faced off against an unrecorded number of enemy Huexotzincos. The battle was furious, one side gaining a little ground, the other sending in reinforcements; these fresh troops were engaged by new opposing troops, and so it went, back and forth, late into the day. It was described as "a great slaughter" and "a most cruel battle." The Aztec commander, a brother of Motecuhzoma, was vanquished after a physical effort of mythic proportions, as were two of Motecuhzoma's other brothers and a great many nobles and lords from Tenochtitlan, Texcoco, and Tlacopan. In the end, it was a glorious victory for the Huexotzincos and a humiliating and sorrowful defeat for the Aztec allies, leaving Motecuhzoma "sunk in despair" (Durán 1994: 426–427).

These brief examples portray Aztecs as masters of the art of war. For ninety years they went to war with basically the same arsenal of weapons, armor, spies, showmanship, and types of fighting men, but they also astutely adapted the size of their forces, the deployment of their warriors, and their battlefield tactics to local conditions and the nature and strategies of the enemy. Much of their war-making was customary and standard: calling on allies; keeping each city-state army separate on the march, in camp, and in battle; exhorting the troops with grand speeches; parleying with enemy rulers prior to actual engagement; using banners to maintain order on the battlefield; trying to out-grandstand the enemy to instill awe and fear, who did this in turn; and leading the battle with the most experienced and courageous warriors. There was a great deal of yelling, taunting, and insulting.

If the king himself went to war, he was spectacularly dressed and adorned, and an inspirational sight to behold. Both sides made furious attempts to capture each other, although in large battles casualties were enormous. In the heat of battle, feathers from shields and costumes flew about everywhere, and obsidian shards from clubs shattered wildly about, unexpectedly blinding an eye or slicing an arm. If the Aztecs won, they burned the enemy city's temple to seal the victory, tried to limit wholesale destruction and looting, and negotiated terms to end the conflict. In the wars they lost, they often left in some disorder, fleeing, since they were always fighting on someone else's turf.

## MEANWHILE, BACK HOME . . .

With the families' warriors off to war – seeking renown and booty – those left at home assumed weighty responsibilities to assure a successful outcome on the battlefield. These duties were carried on within the confines of their houses, no matter how humble. They were highly ritualized and taken very seriously. For example, a warrior's wife did not wash her face or hair during the entire span of her husband's absence at war. She must attend to her cooking, being careful to not let food stick to the pot (see Chapter 7). She also took great care to build a fire at midnight, step outside and sweep, and wash her body (all but her head and face); she then made offerings to the idols in her household shrine: tiny tortillas and other foods, incense, and prayers for her husband's victory and safe return (Durán 1994: 161–162, 350–351). The accounts suggest that the wife repeated these rituals at dawn, midday, and sunset – making it sound like a continuous and consuming part of her daily round. Even if she did not perform these rituals to this extent, she would have done them sufficiently often to remind her of her husband's precarious situation and offer him moral support at a distance. Her well-scripted prayers and sincere offerings cast the strength of the gods behind her husband's mortal efforts. Warfare embraced the lives of everyone, on the battlefield and off.

## THE AFTERMATH

And now the warriors returned home. If victorious, the glad news had already been broadcast days ahead: flutes and conch shells were blown and drums beaten, and the cities rejoiced. The triumphal procession was led by the king (when he went to battle) and followed by his commanding generals, elite warriors, and then the remainder of the army. The prisoners of war, bound and restrained with neck yokes, dragged despondently behind (or sometimes in front), loudly lamenting their fate. If instead defeat had fallen on the warriors, upon hearing the sad news the Aztec city was silent and the people wept bitterly. Although the returning procession was a miserable sight – the city's nobles and elders met them bravely, all in fine dress, with the priests offering incense – there was still some of the customary pomp and circumstance, and a "stiff upper lip" attitude (Durán 1994: 282, 301). Victorious or not, battlefield captives were delivered to the temple of Huitzilopochtli by their captors, and these brave warriors then went to the ruler's palace where they were ceremoniously feasted. Those who did not return were not forgotten: elders went to each widow, offering them gifts and presenting lengthy speeches of sincere condolences. The surviving warriors returned to their homes to greet their families and resume their everyday lives.

*Coyochimalli arrived home to his welcoming wife and children. He had a small claim to nobility, being the youngest son of the youngest son of a high noble (tecuhtli). He resided in that lord's extended household, but was not wealthy and needed to struggle to earn all the rights and recognition he had. So he had taken a warrior's path. And now he had taken a prisoner, his second, and he would be richly rewarded by his king. He was happy that the gods had favored him, and he hoped his noble overlord would also grant him approval and perhaps gifts as well. His wife was just relieved. Not so their neighbor, who had lost her husband in the war. They would console her tonight.*

There were always battlefield casualties, on both sides. If the battle took place close to home, the warriors' bodies were returned to their home cities where nobles were cremated (with their honorable insignia) and other less distinguished persons were either cremated or buried (Hassig 1988: 118). However, if the Aztecs lost men on a distant battlefield, their bodies were left there (perhaps to be cremated), but their memories were honored in household ceremonies and their families compensated with gifts. Images were made of a resinous wood to represent them in place of their bodies, and dressed with clothing and adorned with feathers. These images were ritually honored and collectively burned. This was only one aspect of five intense days of mourning and ceremonies that involved cycles of condolence speeches, public weeping by widows and family, singing by professional singers, more weeping, music, ritual dancing, more speeches, and yet more weeping.

After the images were set aflame, the women went into eighty days (four Aztec months) of mourning during which they did not wash their faces – special "ministers" dropped by to scrape the dirt and tears from their faces, collecting them in papers and delivering them to priests (Durán 1994: 283–286). In a sense, they were casting off their sorrow and placing it in the hands of the gods. In the case of Motecuhzoma Xocoyotzin's loss of his three brothers in the Huexotzinco war, the customary statues were made, complete with clothing, fine adornments, and painted faces. Because of the prominence of the deceased, the burning of their statues was accompanied with sacrifices of slaves, whose bodies were also burned for the occasion (Durán 1994: 427–428).

During and after this period of mourning, life went on. Captured warriors were detained and sacrificed at an appropriate ceremony (see Chapter 2). Captors were rewarded by the king himself with cloaks and regalia that publicly advertised their valiant achievements. The kings themselves had some important decisions to make. Would the conquered city behave and pay its tribute as agreed? Or should the city be watched for restlessness and rebelliousness in the region? Perhaps the king should install a governor, or a garrison, as his predecessors had done elsewhere. The rank-and-file men of the Aztec armies returned to their usual work, whether farming, fishing, a craft, or a profession. Many of them were recovering from their battlefield wounds: the Aztecs had an impressive medical arsenal that was directed toward treating and healing cuts, punctures, slashes, bashes, and bruises. Business was brisk for physicians and herbalists when the troops returned from war.

*Tecolotl bent over, holding his head. It hurt. The cut alongside his ear had been delivered by the club of a strong adversary, but Tecolotl had dodged the brunt of it. It was still open and didn't feel right, so he had summoned the physician. She had just left, having washed his wound with urine (he didn't ask whose) and rubbed it with hot maguey leaf sap. It was still sore, but she had assured him that it would heal cleanly. He reflected. He was lucky. He thanked the gods that all the wars were elsewhere, and his comfortable village and beautiful nearby Texcoco and Tenochtitlan were not ravaged like their kings ravaged other cities. The thought gave him comfort. Even so, he would burn incense tonight to safeguard his family and village.*

Little did Tecolotl know what was coming. Not in his wildest dreams could he imagine that in a few short years his entire world would be turned upside down.

# Epilogue

It must have come as an incredible shock. Despite the forebodings of Tenochtitlan's supreme ruler, Motecuhzoma Xocoyotzin, the strange-looking people with their odd and intimidating animals and unusual, powerful weapons marched along the causeway and into their sacred and impregnable city. Not only that, throngs of enemy Tlaxcallans marched right in too! Something was terribly wrong.

This was November 8, 1519. Nearly two years later, on August 13, 1521, the Spaniards captured the current Mexica ruler Cuauhtemoc, ending the exhausting conflict and ushering in a new order. The fighting had been fierce, the casualties high, and the devastation to cities and landscapes severe. The fighting left Tenochtitlan in shambles. Aztec temples, palaces, and other structures were dismantled; those that remained relatively intact were raided for their stones to construct new buildings for Spanish overlords in Spanish styles. And even before Tenochtitlan fell, native people (whether enemies or allies of the Spaniards) began dying in horrific numbers from catastrophic, introduced diseases (see Berdan 2014: 277–293; Restall 2018; Thomas 1993).

Ollin, Xochitl, Icnoyotl, Chilpapalotl, indeed everyone within the pre-Spanish Aztec thrall was caught up in the dizzying events of the conquest and its immediate aftermath. This war of the worlds had wreaked havoc on their cities and homes, on their very persons, and on their familiar way of life. This was now a new universe for them, and for their conquerors. In this world turned upside-down, what happened to the people in our story? They are fictional here, but they represent very real people who lived through these turbulent and unsettled times.

At the time Tenochtitlan fell to the combined forces of Spaniards and their innumerable native allies, the ruler was Cuauhtemoc, a son of Ahuitzotl. Ahuitzotl died in 1502 (a decade after Columbus had landed in the Caribbean) and was succeeded by his nephew Motecuhzoma Xocoyotzin. This ruler welcomed the Spaniards into Tenochtitlan and died violently in 1520 under mysterious circumstances during a conflict between enraged locals and intrusive Spaniards. Motecuhzoma's brother Cuitlahuac succeeded him, but died of smallpox even while the battle for Tenochtitlan raged. Cuauhtemoc himself was held prisoner by Cortés but hanged in 1525. All of this did not put an end to the native aristocracy, at least not right away. For the first decades following the conquest, surviving *altepetl* rulers (*tlatoque*) frequently became *gobernadores* of their communities in the colonial political order. They often retained traditional lands and control over subservient communities, but now they were under the colonial institution of *encomienda*, a royal grant of labor and tribute paid by the native population. A daughter of Motecuhzoma controlled the largest *encomienda* in the Basin of Mexico in 1526. These were boons from the Spanish government. The native elite also assimilated into their new world by substituting old symbols of status and authority for new ones: some now had rights to "carry swords or firearms, to wear Spanish clothing, to ride horses or mules with saddles and bridles" (Gibson 1964: 155). Some nobles took on other Spanish trappings such as chairs, tables, serving spoons, Spanish-style ceramics, and Christian images. Their privileged status, however, was in serious decline by a century after the conquest.

We see a great deal less of the native priests following the conquest. These elevated positions and essential occupations under the Aztec regime had no place in the newly introduced religion. These were turbulent religious times in Spain – the Inquisition was in full throttle, and religious personnel traveling to New Spain (most of colonial central Mexico) encountered people believing in a multitude of gods, worshiping idols, and practicing human sacrifice. The process of conversion to Christianity was pursued with energy by regular and secular clergy: churches rose on the sites of demolished temples; icons of Jesus,

Mary, and the saints replaced the native godly idols; the Christian calendar defined time and ordered religious festivals; and Christian-themed plays captivated the imagination. With their temples demolished and their godly idols smashed, the priests attached to the state religion had no discernible purpose or livelihood. However, priests attending smaller temples at the *calpolli/tlaxilacalli* level seemed more able to protect their local godly idols, albeit only for a short time.

Many native religious beliefs and practices persisted, especially private rituals at the household level (Tavárez 2011). The Aztecs and their neighbors did not take their religion lightly, and they preserved aspects of their beliefs by identifying saints' feasts with native ones at the same times of year and by assimilating their gods with Christian saints (most emphatically, the Virgin Mary and the Aztec mother goddess Tonantzin merged to create the Virgin de Guadalupe). At a more personal level native religious specialists variously called "diviners, witches, enchanters, and healers" filled important niches in colonial New Spain (Klor de Alva 1982: 362). In Aztec Mexico household rituals focused on life-cycle events, curing, and fertility, and individual householders would call on these specialists. Midwives and curers so essential in the pre-Spanish world still enjoy popularity to the present day in some communities.

Featherworkers were less vulnerable in the colonial setting. The fancy feathered headdresses, banners, warrior costumes, textiles, and mosaic shields were no longer needed under the colonial regime. But the featherworkers were not out of a job. Instead, their finely honed skills were redirected to other objects and motifs – they were put to work fashioning truly exquisite Christian objects from feathers, ranging from decorative panels to "paintings" to miters. The Spaniards were impressed, even astonished, with the native featherworking skills and appropriated those talents to the glorification of their churches and the adoration of their god. Whereas before the conquest many feather artisans worked in royal or elite palaces, now their primary patrons were members of the new religious hierarchy.

Native merchants had even more staying power. Many indigenous products and objects continued in use beyond the Spanish conquest, including foodstuffs such as maize, beans, squash, chiles, tomatoes, and cacao; cloth and clothing; tools; building materials; baskets and ceramics; medicines; salt; brooms; dyes; and on and on. All of these and more were sold and bought in the many marketplaces (*tianquiztli*) that likewise persisted throughout the realm, albeit their five-day schedule adjusted to a seven-day schedule. Local and regional merchants continued to be responsible for moving these goods across the landscape.

Now, in colonial times, they also dealt in wheat as well as maize, wool as well as cotton, machetes as well as obsidian blades, and Spanish-style shirts as well as capes. These new commodities reflected Spanish introductions of agricultural products (such as wheat, sugarcane, and grapes), domesticated animals (cattle, horses, mules, donkeys, domesticated pigs, sheep, goats, and chickens), and metal tools (machetes, knives, hoes, and scissors). New technologies included wheeled objects (e.g., carts, spinning wheels, and potters' wheels), tailored clothing, and distillation. Perhaps the biggest adjustments were shouldered by the wealthy and long-ranging *pochteca* who in Aztec times had largely specialized in trading status-linked luxuries such as shimmering tropical feathers, precious stones, fancy textiles, and other precious goods. These merchants needed to adjust their merchandise to meet new and different demands. Transport was also transformed, with human porters replaced by wheeled vehicles pulled by beasts of burden – this novelty stimulated changes in roads as well.

Farmers were resilient. In Aztec times they had survived frosts, earthquakes, floods, droughts, and bouts of infestations; the farmers were, historically, accustomed to poor yields and even severe famine. They faced some new challenges in colonial times, such as disruptions from the conquest itself, the severe loss of native population (including their own families and neighbors), and appropriation of their lands by Spaniards. Some native farmers were required to learn new skills to produce for the Spanish-dominated world: how to grow wheat or grapes, raise chickens or goats, shear sheep, or manage a team of oxen pulling a steel-tipped plow. Women continued their customary chores almost without interruption – they spun and wove cloth, ground maize and made tortillas, and bore children with the help of a familiar midwife. Their children were given traditional names such as Ten Wind or Three Vulture; but with Christian baptism, these same children were also given Christian names. This arrangement resulted in, for example, the very real name of Pedro Tochtli: Peter Rabbit, who originally may have been named something like Two Rabbit.

The fate of slaves under the new regime is something of a mystery. The preparation of slaves for sacrifice, as well as the capture of warriors also for sacrifice, came to an end. Under the Spanish colonial regime, the native people were not considered slaves. So individuals in that status, who survived the conquest, must have found work and social niches by taking advantage of existing or new opportunities: perhaps putting known skills to work by farming, building, or making paper; perhaps learning a new skill or trade such as making candles, tending livestock, or honing steel. Spanish introductions such as spinning wheels and large treadle looms, both of which tended to employ men in workshop settings, opened up some job opportunities for men, although the working conditions were known to be dreadful. While native slaves moved into other social and economic roles, the status of slave did not disappear under colonial Spanish rule; this niche was filled by introduced slaves, brought unwillingly from Africa.

The Aztecs and their neighbors were not entirely helpless under the new lords of the land. Throughout Mesoamerican history, generation after generation, the native people had found innovative and productive ways to rise above adversities, including repeated conquests. Their elite became proficient in their conquerors' languages, and now many people found it useful to add Spanish to their native Nahuatl, Otomí, or other language. In other examples, feather artisans were clever in transferring their feather mosaic-making skills to Christian motifs; a town of commoners took advantage of Spanish market demands by aggressively producing quantities of cochineal dyes; another community overtly recognized its limitations by hiring a Spaniard to tend their considerable flock of sheep (all the while sternly holding him to high standards of productivity); and people generally meshed their beloved gods with introduced saints. And they learned to take advantage of the Spanish litigious bent. The Aztecs had their own traditional legal and court systems, but after the conquest those were largely replaced by Spanish legal institutions. The natives, individually or communally, were not shy about employing a scribe or going to court. They wrote or arranged for wills and other official documents, and inserted their own domestic, land, and other disputes into the Spanish system. It was a time of cultural transformation, but also a time of cultural resilience.

# Glossary

**Acolhua** peoples of the eastern part of the Basin of Mexico; the Acolhuacan capital city of Texcoco was a partner in the Aztec Triple Alliance

*altepetl* political unit resembling a city-state

*amantecatl* (**pl.** *amanteca*) professional featherworker

*calla amanteca* "house featherworkers"

*calmecac* priestly school attached to a temple

*calpixcan amanteca* mayordomo's featherworkers

*calpolli* district or neighborhood of a city, town, or *altepetl*

*Chichimeca* nomadic hunters-gatherers of the northern deserts

*chinampa* raised bed; cultivated plot of land built up in a lake bed

**Cihuacoatl** "Woman-serpent"; Tenochtitlan's second-in-command

*cihuatlamacazqui* "female giver of things"; priestess

*cihuateteo* "women goddesses"; souls of women who died in childbirth

*comalli* clay griddle

*cuicacalli* "house of song"; school for learning ritual singing and dancing

*ithualli* "those of one yard"; dwellings around a common patio

*macquauitl* obsidian-studded club

**Mesoamerica** culture area ranging from central Mexico into Central America

*metlatl* (*metate*) grinding stone

**Mexica, Culhua-Mexica** group that founded Tenochtitlan and became the dominant partner of the Aztec Triple Alliance

**Mexicano** the Nahuatl language, as spoken by modern-day speakers

*mocihuaquetzque* women who died in childbirth

*momoztli* prominent stone sculpture; central marketplace sculpture

*nahualoztomeca* disguised merchants

**Nahuatl** language of the Aztecs and many of their neighbors

*nixtamal* (*masa*) maize ground into a gruel

*octli* (*pulque*) fermented drink from the maguey plant

**Otomí** ethnic group in northern part of the Basin of Mexico and elsewhere; also a high grade in the Aztec military hierarchy

*patolli* game similar to Pachisi

*petlatl* (*petate*) reed mat

*pochteca* (**sing.** *pochtecatl*) professional merchants

**Quachic** high grade in the Aztec military hierarchy

*quachtli* large white cotton cloths used as one form of money

*tecpan amanteca* palace featherworkers

*tecpancalli* royal or lordly palace

*telpochcalli* military school for commoners, usually at *calpolli* level

*temazcalli* sweat bath

*temixiuitiani* midwife

**Tepaneca** peoples of the western part of the Basin of Mexico; the Tepaneca capital city of Tlacopan was a partner in the Aztec Triple Alliance

*tianquiztli* marketplace

*ticitl* physician, midwife

*tlaaltiltin* bathed slaves, destined for sacrifice

*tlacotli* slave

*tlamacazqui* "giver of things"; offering priest

*tlamacazton* "little priest"; novice priest

*tlamatinime* wise men

*tlatoani* (**pl.** *tlatoque*) ruler, usually of an *altepetl*, or city-state

*tlaxilacalli* like *calpolli*, a local-level political unit

*tlenamacac* "fire seller"; fire priest

*tonalpohualli* "count of days"; 260-day ritual calendar

*tonalpouhque* readers of the book of days

*totocalli* bird house, aviary

*tzompantli* skull rack

*xiuhpohualli* 365-day agricultural calendar

*yaoxochitl* "flower war"

# References

Aguilar-Moreno, Manuel. 2006. *Handbook of Life in the Aztec World.* New York: Facts on File.

Alberti Manzanarez, Pilar. 1994. Mujeres Sacerdotisas Aztecas las *Cihuatlama-cazque* Mencionadas en Dos Manuscritos Ineditos. *Estudios de Cultural Nahuatl* 24: 171–217.

Alva Ixtlilxochitl, Fernando de. 1965. *Obras históricas.* Alfredo Chavero, ed. 2 vols. Mexico City: Editorial Nacional.

Alvarado Tezozomoc, Fernando. 1975. *Crónica mexicana* (Manuel Orozco y Berra, commentary). Mexico City: Editorial Porrúa.

Anderson, Arthur J. O. 1982. The Institution of Slave-Bathing. *Indiana* 7: 81–92.

Anderson, Arthur J. O., and Susan Schroeder. 1997. *Codex Chimalpahin,* vol. 1. Norman: University of Oklahoma Press.

Anderson, Arthur J. O., Frances Berdan, and James Lockhart. 1976. *Beyond the Codices.* Berkeley: University of California Press.

Andrews, J. Richard, and Ross Hassig. 1984. *Treatise on the Heathen Superstitions That Today Live among the Indians Native to This New Spain, 1629, by Hernando Ruiz de Alarcón.* Norman: University of Oklahoma Press.

Avalos, Francisco. 1994. An Overview of the Legal System of the Aztec Empire. *Law Library Journal* 86 (2): 259–276.

Baquedano, Elizabeth. 2014. Tezcatlipoca as a Warrior. In *Tezcatlipoca: Trickster and Supreme Deity* (Elizabeth Baquedano, ed.): 113–133. Boulder: University Press of Colorado.

Berdan, Frances F. 1978. Ports of Trade in Mesoamerica: A Reappraisal. In *Cultural Continuity in Mesoamerica* (D. Browman, ed.): 179–198. The Hague: Mouton.

    1988. Principles of Regional and Long-Distance Trade in the Aztec Empire. In *Smoke and Mist: Mesoamerican Studies in Memory of Thelma D. Sullivan* (J. Kathryn Josserand and Karen Dakin, eds.): 639–656. Oxford: BAR International Series 402.

    1999. Crime and Control in Aztec Society. In *Organised Crime in Antiquity* (Keith Hopwood, ed.): 255–269. London: Duckworth.

    2005. *The Aztecs of Central Mexico: An Imperial Society.* 2nd ed. Belmont, CA: Wadsworth.

2007. Material Dimensions of Aztec Religion and Ritual. In *Mesoamerican Ritual Economy: Archaeological and Ethnological Perspectives* (E. Christian Wells and Karla L. Davis-Salazar, eds.): 245–266. Boulder: University Press of Colorado.

2011. Rebeliones contra Tenochtitlan. *Arqueología Mexicana* 19 (111): 32–36.

2014. *Aztec Archaeology and Ethnohistory.* Cambridge: Cambridge University Press.

2017. The Economics of Mexica Religious Performance. In *Rethinking the Aztec Economy* (Deborah L. Nichols, Frances F. Berdan, and Michael E. Smith, eds.): 130–155. Tucson: University of Arizona Press.

Berdan, Frances F., and Patricia Rieff Anawalt. 1992. *The Codex Mendoza.* 4 vols. Berkeley: University of California Press.

Berdan, Frances F., Richard E. Blanton, Elizabeth H. Boone, Mary G. Hodge, Michael E. Smith, and Emily Umberger. 1996. *Aztec Imperial Strategies.* Washington, DC: Dumbarton Oaks.

Boone, Elizabeth H. 2000. *Stories in Red and Black: Pictorial Histories of the Aztecs and Mixtecs.* Austin: University of Texas Press.

Boyer, Richard. 2000. Catarina María Complains That Juan Teioa Forcibly Deflowered Her. In *Colonial Lives* (Richard Boyer and Geoffrey Spurling, eds.): 155–165. Oxford: Oxford University Press.

Bray, Warwick. 1968. *Everyday Life of the Aztecs.* New York: Dorset Press.

Carrasco, Davíd (with Scott Sessions). 1998. *Daily Life of the Aztecs: People of the Sun and Earth.* Westport: Greenwood Press.

Carrasco, Pedro. 1964. Tres libros del Museo Nacional de México y su importancia para los estudios demográficos. In *35th International Congress of Americanists (Mexico City, 1962)*, vol. 3: 373–378. Mexico City: International Congress of Americanists.

1976. Estratificación social indígena en Morelos durante el siglo XVI. In *Estratificación social en la Mesoamérica Prehispánica* (Pedro Carrasco and Johanna Broda, eds.): 102–117. Mexico City: Instituto Nacional de Antropología e Historia.

Cervantes de Salazar, Francisco. 1953. *Life in the Imperial and Loyal City of Mexico in New Spain and the Royal and Pontifical University of Mexico as Described in the Dialogues for the Study of the Latin Language Prepared by Francisco Cervantes de Salazar for Use in His Classes and Printed in 1554 by Juan Pablos* (Minnie Lee Barrett Shepard, trans.). Austin: University of Texas Press.

The Chronicle of the Anonymous Conqueror. 1963. In *The Conquistadors* (Patricia de Fuentes, ed. and trans.): 165–181. Norman: University of Oklahoma Press.

Cline, S. L. 1993. *The Book of Tributes: Early Sixteenth-Century Nahuatl Censuses from Morelos.* Los Angeles: UCLA Latin American Center.

*Codex Magliabechiano.* 1903. *The Book of the Life of the Ancient Mexicans, Reproduced in Facsimile with Introduction, Translation and Commentary by Zeila Nuttall.* Berkeley: Universitiy of California Press.

*Códice Tudela, José Tudela de la Orden.* 1980. 2 vols. Madrid: Ediciones Cultura Hispánica.

Cortés, Hernando. 1928. *Five Letters of Cortés to the Emperor.* (J. Bayard Morris, trans.) New York: W. W. Norton.

Cruz, Martín de la, and William Gates. 2000. *The Badianus Manuscript (Codex Barberini, Latin 241) Vatican Library: An Aztec Herbal of 1552.* (E. W. Emmert, trans.) New York: Dover Publications.

Davies, Nigel. 1987. *The Aztec Empire.* Norman: University of Oklahoma Press.

Díaz Cadena, Ismael. 1978. *Libro de tributos del Marquesado del Valle: Texto en español y náhuatl.* Cuadernos de la Biblioteca, Investigación, vol. 5. Mexico City: Museo Nacional de Antropología e Historia.

Díaz del Castillo, Bernal. 1963. *The Conquest of New Spain.* Baltimore: Penguin.

Dodds Pennock, Caroline. 2017. Gender and Aztec Life Cycles. In *The Oxford Handbook of the Aztecs* (Deborah L. Nichols and Enrique Rodríguez-Alegría, eds.): 387–398. Oxford: Oxford University Press.

Doolittle, William E. 1990. *Canal Irrigation in Prehistoric Mexico: The Sequence of Technological Change.* Austin: University of Texas Press.

Douglas, Eduardo de J. 2010. *In the Palace of Nezahualcoyotl.* Austin: University of Texas Press.

Durán, Diego. 1971. *Book of the Gods and Rites and the Ancient Calendar* (Fernando Horcasitas and Doris Heyden, eds. and trans.). Norman: University of Oklahoma Press.

    1994. *The History of the Indies of New Spain.* (Doris Heyden, trans.) Norman: University of Oklahoma Press.

Durand-Forest, Jacqueline. 1971. Cambios económicos y moneda entre los Aztecas. *Estudios de Cultura Náhuatl* 9: 105–124.

Dyer, Christopher. 2002. *Making a Living in the Middle Ages: The People of Britain 850–1520.* New Haven: Yale University Press.

Evans, Susan Toby. 1990. The Productivity of Maguey Terrace Agriculture in Central Mexico during the Aztec Period. *Latin American Antiquity* 1: 117–132.

    1991. Architecture and Authority in an Aztec Village: Form and Function of the Tecpan. In *Land and Politics in the Valley of Mexico: A Two Thousand Year Perspective* (Herbert R. Harvey, ed.): 63–92. Albuquerque: University of New Mexico Press.

    2004. Aztec Palaces and Other Elite Residential Architecture. In *Palaces of the Ancient New World* (Susan Toby Evans and Joanne Pillsbury, eds.): 7–58. Washington, DC: Dumbarton Oaks Research Library and Collection.

Filloy Nadal, Laura, and María de Lourdes Navarijo Ornelas. 2015. Currents of Water and Fertile Land: The Feather Disk in the Museo Nacional de Antropología, Mexico. In *Images Take Flight* (Alessandra Russo, Gerhard Wolf, and Diana Fane, eds.): 252–259. Munich: Hirmer Verlag.

Filloy Nadal, Laura, and María Olvido Moreno Guzmán. 2017. Precious Feathers and Fancy Fifteenth-Century Feathered Shields. In *Rethinking the Aztec Economy* (Deborah L. Nichols, Frances F. Berdan, and Michael E. Smith, eds.): 156–194. Tucson: University of Arizona Press.

Gates, William. 2000. *An Aztec Herbal: The Classic Codex of 1552*. New York: Dover Publications.

Gibson, Charles. 1964. *The Aztecs under Spanish Rule*. Stanford: Stanford University Press.

González Torres, Yolotl. 1976. La esclavitud entre los Mexica. In *Estratificación social en la Mesoamérica Prehispánica* (Pedro Carrasco and Johanna Broda, eds.): 78–87.

Haag, Sabine, Alonso de María y Campos, Lilia Rivero Weber, and Christian Feest, coords. 2012. *El Penacho del México Antiguo*. Altenstadt, Germany: ZKF Publishers.

Haskett, Robert. 1991. *Indigenous Rulers*. Albuquerque: University of New Mexico Press.

Hassig, Ross. 1988. *Aztec Warfare*. Norman: University of Oklahoma Press.

Hébert, John R., et al., eds. 1995. *El Códice de Huexotzinco*. Mexico City and Washington, DC: Coca-Cola International División Norte de América Latina, Ediciones Multiarte, and Library of Congress.

Hernández, Francisco. 1959. *Historia natural de Nueva España*. 2 vols. (*Obras completas*, vols. 2 and 3). Mexico City: Universidad Nacional de Mexico.

Hicks, Frederic. 1974. Dependent Labor in Prehispanic Mexico. *Estudios de Cultura Náhuatl* 11: 243–266.

Hinz, Eike, Claudine Hartau, and Marie Heimann-Koenen. 1983. *Aztekischer Zensus: Zur Indianischen Wirtschaft und Gesellschaft im Marquesado um 1540*. Hanover: Verlag fur Ethnologie.

Hirth, Kenneth G. 2009. Craft Production in a Central Mexican Marketplace. *Ancient Mesoamerica* 20, no. 1: 89–102.

2013. The Merchant's World: Commercial Diversity and the Economics of Interregional Exchange in Highland Mesoamerica. In *Merchants, Markets, and Exchange in the Pre-Columbian World* (Kenneth G. Hirth and Joanne Pillsbury, eds.): 85–112. Washington, DC: Dumbarton Oaks Research Library and Collection.

2016. *The Aztec Economic World: Merchants and Markets in Ancient Mesoamerica*. New York: Cambridge University Press.

Johnson, Benjamin D. 2017. *Pueblos within Pueblos: Tlaxilacalli Communities in Acolhuacan, Mexico, ca. 1271–1692*. Boulder: University Press of Colorado.

Katz, Solomon H., M. L. Hediger, and Linda A. Valleroy. 1974. Traditional Maize Processing Techniques in the New World. *Science* 184: 765–773.

Klor de Alva, J. Jorge. 1982. Spiritual Conflict and Accommodation in New Spain: Toward a Typology of Responses to Christianity. In *The Inca and Aztec States, 1400–1800: Anthropology and History* (George A. Collier, Renato I. Rosaldo, and John D. Wirth, eds.): 345–366. New York: Academic Press.

Lee, Jongsoo. 2017. The Europeanization of Prehispanic Tradition: Bernardino de Sahagún's Transformation of Aztec Priests (*tlamacazque*) into Classical Wise Men (*tlamatinime*). *Colonial Latin American Review* 26 (3): 291–312.

León-Portilla, Miguel. 1963. *Aztec Thought and Culture: A Study of the Ancient Nahuatl Mind.* Norman: University of Oklahoma Press.

Lesbre, Patrick. 1998. Manumission d'esclaves dans la Mappe Quinatzin? *Amerindia* 23: 99–119.

Lewis, Oscar. 1951. *Life in a Mexican Village: Tepoztlan Restudied.* Urbana: University of Illinois Press.

Lockhart, James. 1992. *The Nahuas after the Conquest.* Stanford, CA: Stanford University Press.

Lockhart, James, Frances Berdan, and Arthur J. O. Anderson. 1986. *The Tlaxcalan Actas: A Compendium of the Records of the Cabildo of Tlaxcala (1545–1627).* Salt Lake City: University of Utah Press.

López Austin, Alfredo, and Leonardo López Luján. 2017. State Ritual and Religion in the Sacred Precinct of Tenochtitlan. In *The Oxford Handbook of the Aztecs* (Deborah L. Nichols and Enrique Rodríguez-Alegría, eds.): 605–621. Oxford: Oxford University Press.

López de Gómara, Francisco. 1966. *Cortés: The Life of the Conqueror by His Secretary* (Lesley Byrd Simpson, trans. and ed.). Berkeley: University of California Press.

López Luján, Leonardo. 2005. *The Offerings of the Templo Mayor of Tenochtitlan* (Bernard Ortiz de Montellano and Thelma Ortiz de Montellano, trans.). Albuquerque: University of New Mexico Press.

McCafferty, Sharisse D., and Geoffrey G. McCafferty. 2000. Textile Production in Postclassic Cholula, Mexico. *Ancient Mesoamerica* 11: 39–54.

Miller, Mary, and Karl Taube. 1993. *An Illustrated Dictionary of the Gods and Symbols of Ancient Mexico and the Maya.* London: Thames and Hudson.

Molina, Alonso de. 1970. *Vocabulario en Lengua Castellana y Mexicana y Mexicana y Castellana.* Mexico City: Editorial Porrúa.

Morehart, Christopher T. 2016. Chinampa Agriculture, Surplus Production, and Political Change at Xaltocan, Mexico. *Ancient Mesoamerica* 27 (1): 183–196.

Moreno Guzmán, María Olvido, and Melanie Korn. 2012. Construcción y técnicas. In *El Penacho del México Antiguo* (Sabine Haag, Alfonso de María y Campos, Lilia Rivero Weber, and Christian Feest, coords.). Altenstadt, Germany: ZKF Publishers.

Motolinía (Fray Toribio de Benavente). 1971. *Memoriales o libro de las cosas de la Nueva España y de los naturales de ella.* (Edmundo O'Gorman, ed.) Mexico City: Universidad Nacional Autónoma de Mexico, Instituto de Investigaciones Históricas.

Mundy, Barbara E. 2015. *The Death of Aztec Tenochtitlan, the Life of Mexico City.* Austin: University of Texas Press.

Nichols, Deborah L. 2013. Merchants and Merchandise: The Archaeology of Aztec Commerce at Otumba, Mexico. In *Merchants, Markets, and Exchange in the Pre-Columbian World* (Kenneth G. Hirth and Joanne Pillsbury, eds.): 49–83. Washington, DC: Dumbarton Oaks Research Library and Collection.

Nichols, Deborah L., and Enrique Rodríguez-Alegría. 2017. *The Oxford Handbook of the Aztecs.* Oxford: Oxford University Press.

Nowotny, Karl Anton, and Jacqueline de Durand-Forest. 1974. *Codex Borbonicus, Bibliothèque de l'Assemblée nationale, Paris (Y 120): Vollständige Faksimile-Ausgabe des Codex im Originalformat.* Graz: Akadem. Druck- u. Verlagsanst.

Nuttall, Zelia. 1903. *The Book of the Life of the Ancient Mexicans Containing an Account of Their Rites and Superstitions.* Part I: Introduction and Facsimile. Berkeley: University of California Press.

Offner, Jerome A. 1983. *Law and Politics in Aztec Texcoco.* New York: Cambridge University Press.

    2017. The Future of Aztec Law. In *Legal Encounters on the Medieval Globe* (Elizabeth Lambourn, ed.): 1–32. York: Arc Humanities Press.

Olivier, Guilhem. 2003. *Mockeries and Metamorphoses of an Aztec God: Tezcatlipoca, "Lord of the Smoking Mirror."* Boulder: University Press of Colorado.

Olko, Justyna. 2014. *Insignia of Rank in the Nahua World.* Boulder: University Press of Colorado.

Ortiz de Montellano, Bernard R. 1990. *Aztec Medicine, Health, and Nutrition.* New Brunswick: Rutgers University Press.

    2001. Disease, Illness, and Curing. In *Archaeology of Ancient Mexico and Central America* (Susan Toby Evans and David L. Webster, eds.): 215–220. New York: Garland.

Patterson, Orlando. 2001. Slavery: Comparative Aspects. In *International Encyclopedia of the Social and Behavioral Sciences* (Neil J. Smelser and Paul B. Baltes, eds.): 14152–14157. New York: Elsevier.

Phipps, Elena, and Lucy Commoner. 2006. Investigation of a Colonial Latin American Textile. In *Textile Narratives and Conversations*, Textile Society of America, 10th Biennial Symposium, Toronto. Baltimore: Textile Society of America.

Pollard, Helen. 2017. Markets, Tribute, and Class in Tarascan Commodity Consumption: The Lake Pátzcuaro Basin. *Americae* 2: 1–22.

Pomar, Juan Bautista de. 1964. Relación de Juan Bautista de Pomar (Tezcoco, 1582). In *Poesía Nahuatl* (A. M. Garibay, ed.), vol. 1: 149–219. Mexico City: Universidad Nacional Autónoma de Mexico.

Quiñones Keber, Eloise. 1995. *Codex Telleriano-Remensis: Ritual, Divination, and History in a Pictorial Aztec Manuscript.* Austin: University of Texas Press.

Restall, Matthew. 2018. *When Montezuma Met Cortés.* New York: HarperCollins Publishers.

Reyes García, Luis. 1996. El término calpulli en documentos del siglo XVI. In *Documentos nahuas de la Ciudad de México del siglo XVI* (Luis Reyes García, Eustaquio Solís, Armando Valencia Ríos, Constantino Medina Lima, and Gregorio Guerrero Días, eds.): 21–68. Mexico City: CIESAS.

Riedler, Renée. 2015. Materials and Technique of the Feather Shield Preserved in Vienna. In *Images Take Flight* (Alessandra Russo, Gerhard Wolf, and Diana Fane, eds.): 330–341. Munich: Hirmer Verlag.

Rojas, José Luis de. 2012. *Tenochtitlan: Capital of the Aztec Empire.* Gainesville: University Press of Florida.

Román Berrelleza, Juan Alberto. 2008. Health and Disease among the Aztecs. In *The Aztec World* (Elizabeth M. Brumfiel and Gary M. Feinman, eds.): 53–65. New York: Abrams.

Sahagún, Bernardino de. 1905–1907. *Historia de las cosas de la Nueva España, edición parcial en facsimile de los códices matritenses.* 4 vols. Madrid: Hauser y Menet.

⸻ 1950–1982. *Florentine Codex: General History of the Things of New Spain* (Arthur J. O. Anderson and Charles E. Dibble, eds. and trans.). 12 vols. Salt Lake City: University of Utah Press.

Sanders, William T., Jeffrey R. Parsons, and Robert S. Santley. 1979. *The Basin of Mexico: Ecological Processes in the Evolution of a Civilization.* New York: Academic Press.

Sandstrom, Alan R. 1991. *Corn Is Our Blood: Culture and Ethnic Identity in a Contemporary Aztec Indian Village.* Norman: University of Oklahoma Press.

Sandstrom, Alan R., and Pamela Effrein Sandstrom. 2017. The Behavioral Economics of Contemporary Nahua Religion and Ritual. In *Rethinking the Aztec Economy* (Deborah L. Nichols, Frances F. Berdan, and Michael E. Smith, eds.): 105–129. Tucson: University of Arizona Press.

Santamaría, Francisco J. 1978. *Diccionario de Mejicanismos.* 3rd edition. Mexico City: Editorial Porrúa.

Saville, Marshall H. 1920. *The Goldsmith's Art in Ancient Mexico.* New York: Museum of the American Indian, Heye Foundation.

Scheidel, Walter. 2008. The Comparative Economics of Slavery in the Greco-Roman World. In *Slave Systems, Ancient and Modern* (Enrico Del Lago and Constantina Katsari, eds.): 105–126. New York: Cambridge University Press.

Ségota, Dúrdica. 2015. The Radiance of Feathers. In *Images Take Flight* (Alessandra Russo, Gerhard Wolf, and Diana Fane, eds.): 378–385. Munich: Hirmer Verlag.

Shadow, Robert D., and María J. Rodríguez V. 1995. Historical Panorama of Anthropological Perspectives on Aztec Slavery. In *Arqueología del norte y del occidente de México: Homenaje al Doctor J. Charles Kelley* (Barbro Dahlgren de Jordán and María de los Dolores Soto de Arechavaleta, eds.): 299–323. Mexico City: Instituto de Investigaciones Antropológicas, Universidad Nacional Autónoma de México.

Smith, Michael E. 1993. Houses and Settlement Hierarchy in Late Postclassic Morelos: A Comparison of Archaeology and Ethnohistory. In *Prehispanic Domestic Units in Western Mesoamerica: Studies of the Household, Compound, and Residence* (Robert S. Santley and Kenneth G. Hirth, eds.): 191–206. Boca Raton: CRC Press.

⸻ 2008. *Aztec City-State Capitals.* Gainesville: University Press of Florida.

⸻ 2012. *The Aztecs.* 3rd ed. Oxford: Blackwell Publishers.

⸻ 2016. *At Home with the Aztecs: An Archaeologist Uncovers Their Domestic Life.* New York: Routledge.

Smith, Michael E., and Frederic Hicks. 2016. Inequality and Social Class. In *Oxford Handbook of the Aztecs* (Deborah L. Nichols and Enrique Rodríguez-Alegría, eds.): 425–436. New York: Oxford University Press.

Smith, Michael E., and T. Jeffrey Price. 1994. Aztec-Period Agricultural Terraces in Morelos, Mexico: Evidence for Household-Level Agricultural Intensification. *Journal of Field Archaeology* 21: 169–179.

Sousa, Lisa Mary. 1997. Women and Crime in Colonial Oaxaca. In *Indian Women of Early Mexico* (Susan Schroeder, Stephanie Wood, and Robert Haskett, eds.): 199–214. Norman: University of Oklahoma Press.

Soustelle, Jacques. 1970. *Daily Life of the Aztecs on the Eve of the Spanish Conquest.* Stanford: Stanford University Press.

Spores, Ronald. 1984. *The Mixtecs in Ancient and Colonial Times.* Norman: University of Oklahoma Press.

Sullivan, Thelma. 1966. Pregnancy, Childbirth, and the Deification of the Women Who Died in Childbirth. Trans. Thelma D. Sullivan. *Estudios de Cultura Nahuatl* 6: 63–95.

Tapia, Andrés de. 1971. Relación hecha por el Señor Andrés de Tápia sobre la Conquista de Mexico. In *Colección de Documentos para la Historia de Mexico.* (Joaquin García Icazbalceta, ed.) Vol. 2: 554–600.

Tavárez, David. 2011. *The Invisible War: Indigenous Devotions, Discipline, and Dissent in Colonial Mexico.* Stanford: Stanford University Press.

Thomas, Hugh. 1993. *Conquest: Montezuma, Cortés, and the Fall of Old Mexico.* New York: Simon and Schuster.

*Tira de la peregrinación mexicana.* 1944. Mexico City: Libreria Anticuaria G. M. Echaniz.

Torquemada, Juan de. 1969. *Monarquía Indiana.* 3 vols. Mexico City: Editorial Porrúa.

Townsend, Richard F. 1987. Coronation at Tenochtitlan. In *The Aztec Templo Mayor* (Elizabeth Hill Boone, ed.): 371–409. Washington, DC: Dumbarton Oaks Research Library and Collection.

    2009. *The Aztecs.* 3rd edition. London: Thames and Hudson.

Vela, Enrique. 2011. Ahuitzotl "El espinoso del agua" (1486–1502). *Arqueologia Mexicana, edicion especial Los Tlatoanis Mexicas*: 58–65.

Watson, James L. 1980. Slavery as an Institution, Open and Closed Systems. In *Asian and African Systems of Slavery* (James L. Watson, ed.): 1–15. Berkeley: University of California Press.

Wood, Diana. 2002. *Medieval Economic Thought.* Cambridge: Cambridge University Press.

Zorita, Alonso de. 1994. *Life and Labor in Ancient Mexico: The Brief and Summary Relation of the Lords of New Spain* (Benjamin Keen, trans.). Norman: University of Oklahoma Press.

# Index

**Page numbers in italics indicate illustrative material.**